Ontario's Bike Paths
and Rail Trails

Travel better, enjoy more

ULYSSES
Travel Guides

Author John Lynes	*Copy Editing* Eileen Connolly Jacqueline Grekin	*Artistic Director* Patrick Farei (Atoll)
Additional Writing: Anne-Marie Grandtner Jacqueline Grekin	*Cartographers* Patrick Thivierge Yanik Landreville André Duchesne	*Illustrations* Lorette Pierson Valérie Fontaine Myriam Gagné Josée Perreault
Editor André Duchesne	*Computer Graphics* Stéphanie Routhier	*Photography* *Cover Page* Superstock
Publisher Pascale Couture		

OFFICES

Canada: Ulysses Travel Guides, 4176 Saint-Denis, Montréal, Québec, H2W 2M5, ☎(514) 843-9447 or 1-877-542-7247
Fax: (514) 843-9448, info@ulysses.ca, www.ulyssesguides.com

Europe: Les Guides de Voyage Ulysse SARL, BP 159, 75523 Paris Cedex 11, France, ☎01 43 38 89 50, Fax: 01 43 38 89 52
voyage@ulysse.ca, www.ulyssesguides.com

U.S.A.: Ulysses Travel Guides, 305 Madison Avenue, Suite 1166, New York, NY 10165, ☎1-877-542-7247, info@ulysses.ca
www.ulyssesguides.com

DISTRIBUTORS

Canada: Ulysses Books & Maps, 4176 Saint-Denis, Montréal, Québec, H2W 2M5, ☎(514) 843-9882, ext.2232 or ☎800-748-9171
Fax: 514-843-9448, info@ulysses.ca, www.ulyssesguides.com

Great Britain and Ireland: World Leisure Marketing, Unit 11, Newmarket Court, Newmartket Drive, Derby DE24 8NW
☎1 332 57 37 37, Fax: 1 332 57 33 99, office@wlmsales.co.uk

Scandinavia: Scanvik, Esplanaden 8B, 1263 Copenhagen K, DK, ☎(45) 33.12.77.66, Fax: (45) 33.91.28.82

Spain: Altaïr, Balmes 69, E-08007 Barcelona, ☎454 29 66
Fax: 451 25 59, altair@globalcom.es

Switzerland: OLF, P.O. Box 1061, CH-1701 Fribourg
☎(026) 467.51.11, Fax: (026) 467.54.66

U.S.A.: The Globe Pequot Press, 246 Goose Lane, Guilford, CT 06437 - 0480, ☎1-800-243-0495, Fax: 800-820-2329
sales@globe-pequot.com

Other countries, contact Ulysses Books & Maps
4176 Saint-Denis, Montréal, Québec, H2W 2M5
☎(514) 843-9882, ext.2232 or ☎800-748-9171, Fax: 514-843-9448
info@ulysses.ca, www.ulyssesguides.com

Canadian Cataloguing-in-Publication Data (see page 6)
© April 2001, Ulysses Travel Guides.
All rights reserved. Printed in Canada

The use of the bicycle...allows people to create a new relationship between their life-space and their life-time, between their territory and the pulse of their being, without destroying their inherited balance.

Ivan Illich, *Energy and Equity*

Table of Contents

Write to Us

The information contained in this guide was correct at press time. However, mistakes can slip in, omissions are always possible, places can disappear, etc. The authors and publisher hereby disclaim any liability for loss or damage resulting from omissions or errors.

We value your comments, corrections and suggestions, as they allow us to keep each guide up to date. The best contributions will be rewarded with a free book from Ulysses Travel Guides. All you have to do is write us at the following address and indicate which title you would be interested in receiving.

Ulysses Travel Guides
4176 Saint-Denis
Montréal, Québec
Canada H2W 2M5
www.ulyssesguides.com
E-mail: text@ulysses.ca

Acknowledgements

We gratefully acknowledge the cities, towns and organizations who generously assisted us with this project.

We acknowledge the financial support of the Government of Canada through the Book Publishing Industry Development Program (BPIDP) for our publishing activities.

We would also like to thank SODEC (Québec) for its financial support.

Cataloguing

Canadian Cataloguing-in-Publication Data

Lynes, John Allan, 1956-

Ontario's Bike Paths and Rail Trails

(Ulysses Green Escapes)

Inlcudes Index
ISBN 2-89464-263-6

1. Bicycle trails - Ontario- Guidebooks. 2. Trails - Ontario - Guidebooks.
3. Bicycle touring - Ontario- Guidebooks. 4. Ontario-Guidebooks. I. Title.
II. Series.

GV 1046.C32057 2000   796.6409713   C00-940798-7

Map Symbols

⌒ Tourist information (Ontario)	=⊙= Toronto subway
? Tourist information (Québec)	▲ Lock
✈ Airport	CN CP CN and CP railways
🚢 Car ferry	∅ Beach
🚢 Ferry	◐ Park
🚌 Bus station	⛫ Museum
🚆 Train station	⚐ Golf course
P Parking lot	⊼ Picnic area

Legend

Bicycle Paths and Rail Trails

▬▬▬ Paved path

= = = = = Gravel path or rail trail

□·□·□·□ Unsurfaced natural trail

Bicycle Routes

▪▪▪▪▪▪ Paved multi-use roadway

▬▬▬ Paved multi-use with cycling lane

Travel better, enjoy more

ULYSSES

Travel Guides

Table of distances (km)
Via the shortest route

	Chicago (Il.)	Hamilton	Kingston	Kitchener-Waterloo	London	Montréal (Qué.)	New York (N.Y.)	Niagara Falls	Ottawa	Sault Ste. Marie	Sudbury	Toronto	Thunder Bay
Hamilton	788												
Kingston	1100	338											
Kitchener-Waterloo	767	69	369										
London	661	140	451	110									
Montréal (Qué.)	1383	621	299	650	738								
New York (N.Y.)	1294	765	583	838	911	618							
Niagara Falls	896	77	408	156	227	689	690						
Ottawa	1242	480	203	511	600	202	719	544					
Sault Ste. Marie	780	748	894	777	699	1003	1498	814	806				
Sudbury	1079	460	609	490	572	700	1212	529	508	302			
Toronto	855	75	263	123	198	547	829	144	410	696	411		
Thunder Bay	1058	1469	1623	1496	1414	1638	2212	1534	1516	723	1019	1421	
Windsor/Detroit (Mi.)	460	318	626	306	191	912	1018	413	773	584	751	386	1310

Example: The distance between Montréal and Toronto is 547km.

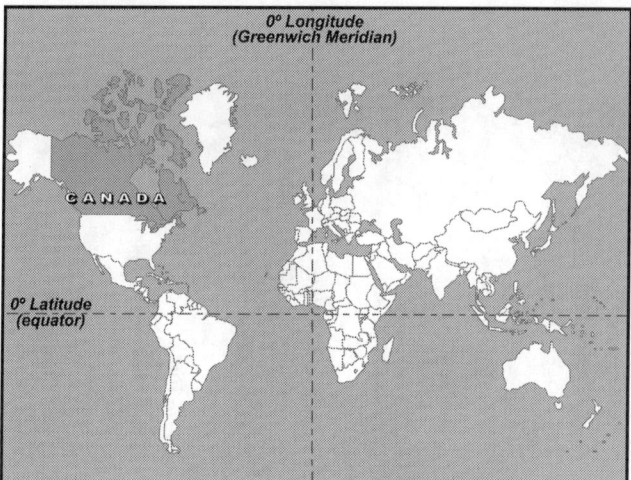

WHERE IS ONTARIO?

Ontario	
Capital:	Toronto
Population:	11,669,300 inhab.
Area:	1,068,630 km²
Currency:	Canadian dollar

© ULYSSES

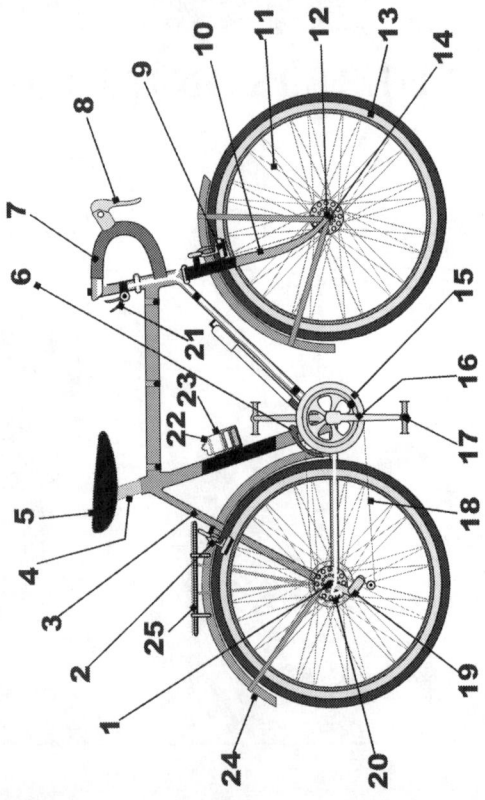

1. Free wheel
2. Rear brakes
3. Rear fork
4. Seat tube
5. Seat
6. Front derailer
7. Handlebars
8. Brake lever
9. Front brakes
10. Front forks
11. Spokes
12. Front hub
13. Rim
14. Front wheel quick release
15. Front plate
16. Crank
17. Pedal
18. Chain
19. Rear derailer
20. Back wheel quick release
21. Gear lever
22. Bottle
23. Bottle holder
24. Fender
25. Rack

Ontario's Bike Paths and Rail Trails

This guide identifies a few of Ontario's most interesting bike paths and rail trails.

Many of these trails follow old railbeds that were once used to connect many of the communities in the province.

Other trails in the guide offer a totally urban experience, providing the cyclist with a safe way to get around in a large city.

In this guide, we devide Ontario into eight regions. Beginning in the west, this guide highlights the most interesting bicycle paths and rail trails in the province. The Waterfront Trail, a 350km trail stretching along Lake Ontario, is presented in the final chapter.

Ontario Regions

A
Southwestern Ontario
B
Niagara Peninsula and Surroundings
C
The Lakelands
D
The Greater Toronto Area
E
Central Ontario
F
Eastern Ontario
G
Ottawa and Surroundings
H
Northern Ontario
I
Waterfront Trail

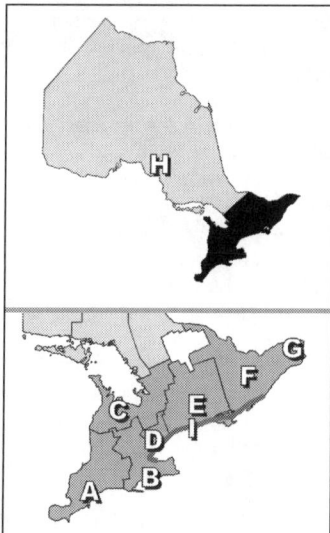

Travelling by Bicycle

Cycling is much like hiking. It allows you to become immersed in the outdoor experience, but at a slightly faster pace. As you explore the different trails in the province, you will find yourself marvelling at the uniqueness and diversity of Ontario's landscape. Bike paths and rail trails also provide safe, environmentally friendly transportation for all kinds of outdoor experiences, including family outings.

Rural rail trails in many ways are repeating the history of railroad development in the late 1800s. They are once again connecting one community with another. They also serve a more environmental purpose in that they provide migration routes for many different species of wildlife.

During the spring, with each pedal stroke you will find yourself enjoying the sweet perfume of rail trail wildflowers. The heat of the summer creates a flurry of activity, and an observant rider will see that life abounds along every kilometre of trail. The cooler temperatures of fall bring forth a colourful canvas of colour. With any luck, you might catch a glimpse of a painted turtle on top of a log catching the last warming rays of sunshine before winter sets in. Even cycling the bicycle paths and rail trails in the winter has it own peculiar rewards and skill testing obstacles.

How to Use this Guide

To make the guide easy to use, the province has been divided into regions. Each region includes many maps highlighting various city bicycle paths and nearby rail trails.

Enjoy the adventure!

General Information

For the purposes of this cycling guide, several definitions have been developed.

Bicycle Path - a path that is separate from the automobile transportation network. These are routes that are always located within a community. Their surfaces are generally comprised of asphalt or crushed limestone. They have two purposes: first, for tourism and secondly, as alternative transportation routes. These paths provide a safe, off-road route for the growing numbers of cyclists, in-line skaters and hikers who have decided to commute to their workplaces using alternative methods.

Bicycle Route – an *on-road* route that makes use of a marked, or signposted, and occasionally, a protected bicycle lane which is part of the local road system.

Rail Trail - a route that follows old, abandoned rail lines and sometimes, closed roads. They generally begin in an urban setting and continue past a community's boundaries into the countryside.

This guide looks at the rail trails that have already been completed. This is a trail that has been resurfaced with a hard-packed, crushed limestone or in some cases, the trail has been paved. Rail trails are sometimes used for commuting, but for the most part they are multi-use recreational corridors. In fact, during the summer months a horse and rider are a just as common a sight as snow-mobiles are in the winter.

Multi-Use Trail - the most popular trails used by cyclists today. They generally follow the above definitions. However, some of these trails are also shared by horseback riders and in winter, snow-mobiles. In some rare cases, the trail will share a roadway with automobiles and motor-cycles

Trans Canada Trail

The Trans Canada Trail is legacy of the Canada 125 Celebration in 1992. A promise was made that interconnected greenways would be built across the country in an effort to unify all its regions. The Trans Canada Trail will be a shared-use recreational trail stretching more than 15,000km from the Atlantic to the Pacific, and north to the Arctic Ocean. When fully completed, it will accommodate hikers, walkers, horseback riders, cyclists, cross-country skiers and where appropriate, snowmobilers.

Trans Canada Trail (Ontario)
Box 462, Station D
Etobicoke, ON M9A 4X4
☎(416) 234-5057

Rails to Trails in Ontario
As rail lines become abandoned in Ontario communities, it has been discovered that these trails blend with the natural environment and fulfil the needs of many people. The surface of these redeveloped railbeds varies depending upon the character and needs of the communities through which the trail passes. Local terrain, the frequency of use, the type of use, and the availability of funds, manpower and local governmental support are all factors which affect the condition and maintenance of the trails. Currently there are just over 241km of designated rail trails in Southern Ontario.

Ontario's Bike Paths and Rail Trails

Ontario Trails

1st Floor
90 Sheppard Ave E.
North York, ON M2N 3A1
☎(416) 314-1092

Ontario Cycling Laws

The following laws must be observed by all cyclists in Ontario:

1. Your bicycle must have a warning device such as a bell or horn that sounds loud and clear.

2. When cycling 30min before sunrise, 30min following sunset or when the light is poor, your bicycle must have a white or amber light on the front and a red light on the rear. Also, reflective material at least 25cm long and 2.5cm wide should be visible (white in the front and red in the back).

3. All riders under the age of 18 must wear a government-approved cycling helmet.

4. Bicycles are prohibited on expressways and freeway-type highways such as the 400 series, the Queen Elizabeth Way and on roads where "no bicycle" signs have been posted.

5. Cyclists are required to obey all traffic laws under the Highway Traffic Act.

Signals and Other Pecular Traffic Rules

Right Turns: In Ontario, a right turn may be made at a traffic light when it is red. The turn can be completed if there is no oncoming traffic and it is safe to make the turn.

Single File Only: Toronto is currently the only city in Ontario that has a bylaw that prohibits riding two abreast.

Cycling Etiquette

It is important to remember when cycling that you are only an observer and should therefore respect all that Mother Nature has provided for us. The old Boy Scout

| Left turn | Right turn | Stop |

adage of "leaving a place visited in a better condition than one found it in" is an excellent way to treat this world and more particularly, the communities that you are cycling through. After all, the impression you make will affect others that follow.

Whether cycling a path in the city or a trail in the country, some cycling courtesies are expected. Direction of travel is similar to cycling on the road. That is, keep to the right-hand side of the path or trail. It is also important to yield the right of way to slow-moving trail users such as pedestrians. Horseback riders and in-line skaters should be approached with caution, as the nature of their transportation can be unpredictable.

Safety and Courtesy

Although cycling is an internationally recognised form of transportation, Canada is still a relatively young country where cycling is concerned. Over the last few years, Ontario has made great strides in public education and drivers are gradually becoming more aware of and considerate towards cyclists. Likewise, cyclists must adopt a respectful attitude towards cars, as well as their fellow cyclists. For example, on the less travelled back roads where traffic is light, it is legal to ride two abreast, but it's common courtesy to get into single file when traffic approaches from the front or rear.

Use your hand signals to let others know your intentions and keep at least one bicycle length between you and the rider in front of you. This is especially true when travelling with children who constantly wander off and on the road. If you do go off the road, ride on the shoulder for a while until you have regained control, then return to the pavement once the way is clear. Be aware of what is going on both in front of and behind you at all times. If you find yourself in an uncomfortable situation, always yield the right of way, take to the shoulder, walk your bike, or stop for a while until the situation improves and you are again comfortable riding your bicycle.

What You'll Need

Types of Bicycles

Hybrid bicycles are an excellent choice because they often serve as an all-purpose adventure bike. These bicycles are essentially a cross between a mountain bike and a road bicycle. They have cantilever-style brakes, triple chain rings, wide-range gearing, and flat handlebars similar to mountain bikes. On the other hand, they have somewhat larger diameter

Ontario's Bike Paths and Rail Trails

wheels and narrower tires. The frames are more like those of road bikes: 72° head tube angles and 73° seat angles are common, as are 43cm or shorter chain stays.

The **mountain bike** is a sturdily built bicycle specially designed for off-road or rough terrain riding. Mountain bikes have flat handlebars, cantilever-style brakes, triple chain rings, wide-range gearing, and knobby tires, approximately 5cm wide. Most mountain bikes now have a 70° to 72° head angle, 3.75cm to 5cm of fork rake, and a seat tube angle of 68° to 74°. On a good road, a mountain bike is about 10% slower than a road bike. When used for touring they offer the rider stability, load carrying ability and long distance comfort. They have a long wheelbase with a generous fork rake and long chain stays. The handlebars are wider than on other bikes, and there are rack-mounting bosses near the front and rear wheels.

Touring bicycles are more robust versions of road bicycles and can be used on most of the bicycle paths and rail trails in this guide. They have heavy-duty components and construction. They offer a wide range of gears and often have triple chain rings for hill climbing. A touring bicycle is designed to carry 18 to 23kg of cargo and is suitable for most city bike paths and completed rail trails.

Accessories

Today anything and everything is available. State-of-the-art nighttime lighting systems, heart rate monitors, computer odometers, myriad colourful fenders to keep you dry on rainy days and sonic horns are just a few of the items that will enhance your cycling experience. Two items that will be indispensable are a rear rack and top bags. These racks and bags are lightweight and are great for carrying a lock, your repair kit and a lunch if you are just out for the day. Riding time will also determine what type of basic sundries you should be taking along on a cycling outing. The items listed below are the bare minimum cycling accessories.

Water Bottle

A water bottle is one item that should always be taken, even if your planned ride is less than an hour. Your body should constantly be kept hydrated. A good rule of thumb for water consumption is to drink one 500ml bottle per hour; for every 5km travelled, at least a quarter of the water in the bottle should be consumed. (Hint: to remove the plastic taste from newer water bottles, fill the bottle with water and allow it to stand open overnight.)

Repair Kit

Even in the city, every cyclist should have a repair kit. However, before packing a complete toolbox into your pannier, here are a few questions that might help you decide which tools to bring:

•What repairs can I make myself (people, not tools, repair mechanical problems)?

•In what condition is my bicycle? Is it maintained regularly?

•Will my ride take me 10,000km from civilization? Will I be able to call a bicycle repair shop?

In any case, here is a short list of basic tools you might want to consider bringing with you.

  •spoke wrench, and the appropriate wrenches and hex keys as required by your bicycle

•two tire levers

•box of patches (with rubber cement, sandpaper and chalk) or a spare bicycle tube

•a rag

•a pump (optional in the city)

The routes suggested in this guide rarely take you far from big urban centres, so you are not likely to be far from a bicycle mechanic. To be safe, always carry some coins to call home with, just in case you encounter a problem you can't fix.

Helmets

Helmets are not expensive. On the other hand, consider how much your brain is worth to you! Proper fit is important for comfort and safety. A helmet must fit snugly and squarely atop your head. It should not be tilted too far forward or back. In order to do the job, your helmet must be light, rigid, feature a ventilated shell and be designed to absorb shock. Also note that in Ontario, children under the age of 18 must wear a helmet.

Ontario's Bike Paths and Rail Trails

Lights and Horns

All cyclists in Ontario fall under the auspices of the Ontario Highway Transportation Act. As indicated on p 14, cyclists are required by law to have a front and rear light activated and working 30min after sunrise and 30min before sunset.

Locks

Whenever your bicycle is unattended, lock it up. It is a good idea to lock your panniers as well. Never leave your wallet, expensive camera equipment or any other valuables unattended with your bicycle. They, like your bike, might prove to be just too tempting. Bicycle theft is significantly on the rise, so it is very important to have an anti-theft device. U-locks, especially those made by Kryptonite®, are the most effective locks on the market

Bungee Cords

These extendible cords with a hook on each end are useful for attaching additional or unexpected baggage that cannot be stored in your bags. Shorter bungee cords are more effective.

Safety Flag

Safety flags help increase safety when transporting a child. Whether you are sharing the road with several other vehicles or riding on a very crowded bike path, passing becomes risky and dangerous; a triangular fluorescent-orange safety flag comes in handy.

Bell or Whistle

An increasing number of cyclists who ride in the city or on bike paths like to announce their presence; futhermore, a bell, horn or whistle is required by law (see p 14). Bicycle bells are a good tool, and whistles transmit sound even faster while letting you keep both hands on the handlebars.

Cyclometer

When you want to know your speed, mileage, daily mileage or average daily speed, a cyclometer is indispensable. It also allows you to keep track of pedal cadence. The number of features available depends on the model.

Seat Pads

Some cyclists recognize that comfort is essential and go so far as to add a seat pad to their saddle. Its only drawback is that it takes a long time to dry.

Comfort

Weather

Glancing at the sky or tuning into weather forecasts before going for a ride will let you take off with peace of mind, since you will know the conditions that await. Each cyclist can decide whether he or she wants to risk riding in wind or rain. Both of these factors can either make your ride miserable or please the senses—it's a matter of personal preference.

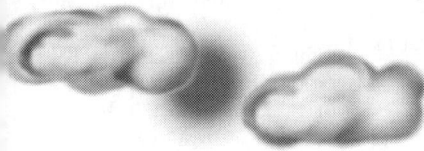

When listening to weather forecasts, remember to pay attention to wind conditions. Winds often shift without warning, sometimes taking on unexpected strength. Wind might have pleasant surprises in store for you at the end of the day, or cut your pace in half and even exhaust you. It is therefore preferable to calculate a reaction time based on forecasted winds for the route you have chosen.

If you still want to go for a ride despite the forecast, you will be able to leave with peace of mind, as you will be prepared for the bad weather.

Cycling Clothing

A good pair of cycling shoes and padded cycling shorts should be mandatory purchases. These two items will help make your ride a more enjoyable experience. However, don't go overboard with cycling-specific clothing. A good rule of thumb is, more than five trips during a cycling season warrant an investment in some additional, specialised clothing.

Gloves

Cycling gloves have many uses. In addition to absorbing sweat from your palms and ensuring a better grip of the handlebars, cycling gloves protect your hands from nicks and scratches suffered in falls (that we wish upon no one). They are also extremely useful for preventing numbness and back pain caused by the pressure of your weight on your arms and hands, which compresses the cubital nerve.

Ontario's Bike Paths and Rail Trails

Shoes

If investing in a pair of cycling shoes seems like a waste of money to you, we recommend that you wear a sports shoe with a stiff sole. This way, the soles of your feet will not suffer from the constant pressure caused by pedalling. Remember that the pedals, handlebars and saddle are the three areas that support your body weight.

Cycling Shorts

Cycling shorts not only make you look like a pro, but also provide the comfort pros enjoy. Lined with a natural or synthetic chamois, which absorbs sweat and protects the skin, cycling shorts ease motion and protect thighs from chaffing. They are worn without underwear and should be washed by hand after each outing. Cycling shorts also help keep your precious muscles warm. Nylon shorts with a chamois lining are increasingly available on the market.

T-shirt

Short-sleeved T-shirts provide an opportunity to show your colours. Clothing made from lycra, ranging from T-shirts to women's sports bras, draws moisture away from the skin. This too is a matter of budget and personal taste.

Windbreaker

Wind is a very important factor to consider when cycling. Since it protects you from wind as much as from rain, a windbreaker can be one of the most useful articles of clothing to bring along, regardless of the weather.

Even on a hot summer day, an unexpected gust of wind can make your warm, sweaty body shiver from cold. Descending a hill at top speed after a strenuous climb can, paradoxically, be rather uncomfortable and bring on a sudden chill. When it is raining, wind can definitely be unpleasant, to the extent that you may want to turn around and head back, especially if you are sweating.

Having an additional article of clothing on hand ensures comfort. Your choice will depend on the other accessories you have chosen to bring with you. If you are prepared to invest in a high-quality windbreaker, you might want to consider those specially designed for cyclists. They have a longer back panel featuring a tail that provides increased protection to your gluteus and saddle during showers.

Eyewear

Sunglasses help protect your eyes from ultraviolet rays. Remember to check the degree of protection your sunglasses provide. Before deciding not to wear sunglasses, remind yourself that they also protect your eyes from wind, dust and...flies, mosquitoes and other identifiable flying objects! Clear lenses are extremely beneficial on overcast days.

Some Safety Considerations

Experienced cyclists like to think they know the highway safety code like the back of their hands. Being familiar with the highway safety code is as important as any of the technical skills needed to ride a bicycle. It is also essential that both you and your bike be outfitted with safety considerations in mind. As memories sometimes fade and become selective over time, here are some reminders:

Reflectors

Reflectors are usually part of the standard equipment included with each bicycle sold on the market. Additional reflectors on panniers or clothing are useful, especially if you plan to ride in the evening.

The Cyclist's Visibility

The basic rule is to wear colourful clothing on sunny days and very bright clothing when riding at night.

Preparation

Although most of the rail trails and bicycle paths in this

First-Aid Kit

Common sense and the vigilant respect of highway safety code regulations can prevent serious accidents. More and more cycling paths are patrolled and the routes suggested in this guide are located near population centres, and therefore within reach of emergency services. However, here is a short list of first-aid supplies to bring along on your ride, especially if you are planning a day trip:

adhesive tape
antiseptic cream
bandage
scissors
safety pins
compress

To this list, we add two indispensable items: some money (especially quarters) and a phone card to reach emergency services.

book can be cycled by almost everyone, before embarking on a long tour, some physical and mental preparation should be undertaken.

The most important consideration for any trip is to know your equipment, meaning your bicycle and your body.

Make Yourself Comfortable

You must make sure you are comfortable on your bicycle. After all, you will be spending many hours in the saddle. Your bicycle seat and handlebar position affects your knees, your back, your neck and your wrists. If they are not in the correct position, your trip will be more difficult and uncomfortable. Try adjusting your riding position so that you are as upright as possible; about 75% of your weight should be on the seat and you should be able to grip the handlebars from the top. Take some time to determine your correct riding position. If unsure, consult your local bicycle shop.

Know Your Bike

Learn how to complete some simple mechanical repairs. Don't rely on someone in your group coming to your rescue because problems inevitably seem to occur

Adjusting Your Saddle

The saddle should be parallel with the ground. Saddle manufacturers recognize that no two cyclists are built alike and certain models on the market are specially designed for men or women. Remember that your centre of gravity is located where your body weight rests; there is no compromise when seeking saddle, handlebar or pedal comfort

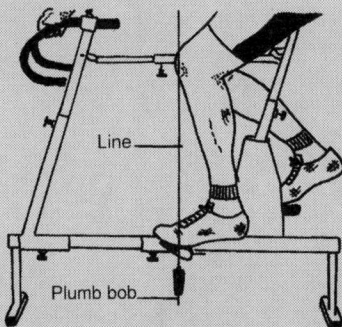

Line

Plumb bob

To adjust saddle to handlebar distance (i.e. closer or farther), keep the cranks horizontal and use a plumb bob line to move the saddle backwards or forwards until your kneecap and the pedal axle line up with the plumb bob line. Secure the saddle's position.

when you become separated for one reason or another. Again, if you are unsure, turn to your local bicycle shop for advice or refer to one of the many repair manuals available.

Physical Training

A little physical training is recommended before embarking on any bicycle trip, but don't go to extremes. The more often you ride your bicycle, the more comfortable your cycling experience will be. This will not only help you become more familiar with your bicycle, but will enable you to build some rear end stamina!

The most effective training to prepare for cycling is... cycling.

In wintertime, if the prospect of logging kilometres only to go nowhere on a stationary bike at the gym is not appealing, there are other options. Cross-country skiing, skating, running or even swimming are complementary sports that work the same muscle groups used in cycling and also develop aerobic capacity.

If you are among those who still want to take advantage of winter to train at the gym, it is preferable to increase your cardiovascular capacity gradually according to your personal fitness level. Focus weight training on quadri-ceps, glutes, as well as back and shoulder muscles to improve your cycling form.

As soon as the weather improves, you should resume cycling gradually on a regular basis, steadily increasing the distance and intensity of your rides. This is the time to practice spinning as much as possible to ensure good flexibility and improve technique. The main goal: to increase pleasure and reduce discomfort.

Stretching

Stretching before and after your rides will ensure better conditioning. Even if you cycle regularly, spending a few minutes stretching will help keep you flexible, increase your muscles' capacity to recover, and reduce discomfort and the risk of injury.

Stretching techniques remain the same regardless of the type of physical activity. Hold a stretch (without bouncing) for at least 30 seconds. You should not feel sharp pain as you stretch; pain does not equal gain. In fact, you may even injure yourself by wanting to do too much. Instead, start with a lighter stretch, as it will intensify as you breathe in deeply. You will feel your stretch deepen on its own.

It is especially important that cyclists stretch their neck, shoulders, glutes, quadriceps and knees.

Pain caused by exerting a muscle beyond its limit will be felt 24 to 48hrs after exercising and will peak between 48 to 72hrs after the activity. Should you develop cramps over the course of your bike ride, stop exercising. If possible, massage the area of the heart, and drink and eat a little to recharge the depleted muscle. Good training, proper stretching and a healthy diet will help prevent such nasty surprises.

Diet and Nutrition

Numerous books have been written on this subject. Fresh fruit is a must and can be complimented by granola bars, as these items will help to keep your energy level up throughout the day.

Most important is water! Good health demands that you keep your body saturated with fluids. Just remember, dehydration is a cyclist's greatest concern. Drink plenty of water throughout the day.

Equipment Check

Before leaving, do a complete circle-check of your bicycle and equipment. Look at your tires, spokes, rack bolts and brakes. An early morning start is always recommended. The sun is low in the sky, the temperatures are cooler and thus more comfortable for riding. An early morning departure is even more important if you are camping, as it always seems to take more time than expected to break camp, repack your gear and get going. Review the maps before setting out; never try to read a map while riding. Here are some basics to cover before heading off for the day:

Oil or Grease?

Lubricants are often used to ensure the proper functioning of mechanical parts. But which to use—oil or grease?

Oil: transmission cables, front derailleur mechanism, brake mechanism

Grease: freewheel, bottom bracket, pedal axle, head tube, hubs

Additional lubrication can be applied after you have cleaned your bicycle with water and mild soap, rinsed it off gently and sponged it off well.

Tires

Tire pressure should be checked before every ride. An air-pressure gauge will indicate (in kg/cmΔ) whether tires are inflated to the correct pressure. Checking tires for small cracks (resembling old paper) and wear near the brakes is also a good idea.

Brakes

Brakes are without a doubt among the most important parts of your bicycle, after the pedals, of course! Before every ride, make sure your brakes do not squeak. You should also ensure that brake pads are parallel to and at equal distance from the rim. This is also a good opportunity to check whether your wheels are properly aligned and secured to the frame.

Brake cables should be loose in the cable housing. A few drops of lubricant at the cable housing's opening and a few repeated applications can prevent brakes from sticking. Rusted brake cables should be replaced immediately.

Derailleurs

Riding slowly over a short distance will enable you to check whether your derailleurs are working properly. You chain should not skip and gear shifting should be smooth. Using an Allen key, tighten the freewheel, which should bring sprockets together as close as possible. Cable tension should also be checked.

Ontario's Bike Paths and Rail Trails

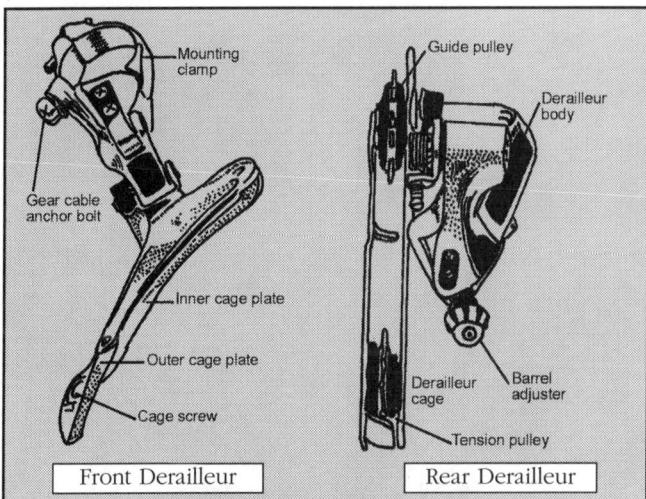

Mounting clamp

Gear cable anchor bolt

Inner cage plate

Outer cage plate

Cage screw

Guide pulley

Derailleur body

Derailleur cage

Barrel adjuster

Tension pulley

Front Derailleur   Rear Derailleur

Increasing Your Efficiency

Pedaling

Your pedal stroke will be more efficient if you place the sole of your foot on the pedal with the big toe slightly overlapping the pedal axle and keep your knees parallel to the frame. Toeclips further increase pedaling efficiency.

Even though toeclips may require some time getting used to, they quickly become indispensable as they stabilize your feet, especially when pedaling standing up. The double action of pushing down with one foot as you pull up with the other allows for a more efficient, fluid motion, enabling you to maximize each pedal stroke by using half the energy. Proper use of toeclips is very important when climbing.

Spinning

Mastering the art of spinning will move your pedalling efficiency up a notch. Spinning consists of a smooth, continuous cadence between 65 and 85 revolutions per minute (rpm), and enables you to attain cruising speed and minimize muscular effort. Coupled with essential toeclips, spinning continuously helps prevent discomfort and knee pain.

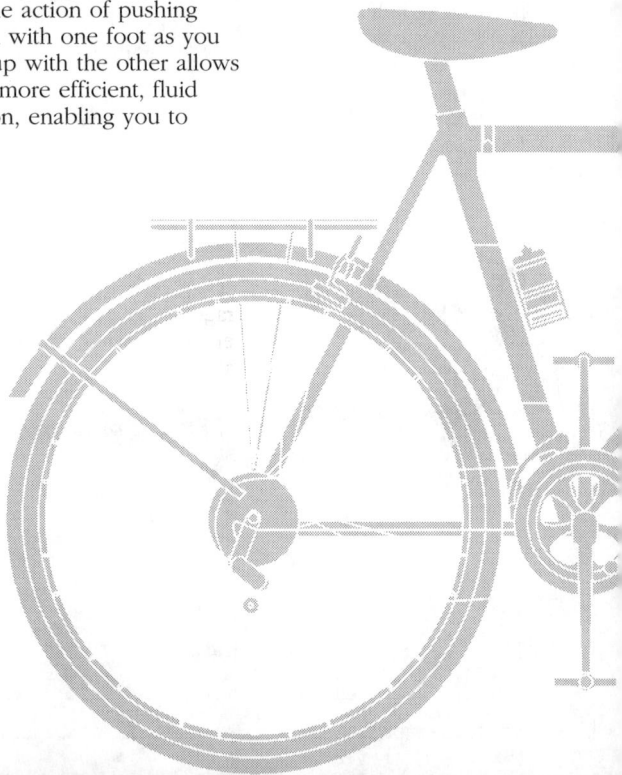

Cycling with Children

Cycling with children of any age can be a very rewarding experience. Listed below are some suggestions that will help make any ride even more enjoyable.

1. Make sure they know the rules of the road and traffic signs.

2. Make sure they are familiar with their bicycle.

3. Make sure the bike is equipped with a working front light, rear light and bell (an odometer is optional, but can be helpful when setting targets).

4. Make sure they keep at least one bicycle length between them and the rider in front—young eyes tend to wander when experiencing new sights and sounds.

5. Set time goals for stops—this will keep them pedalling in anticipation of an upcoming stop.

6. Provide them with a set of panniers (large or small, no matter) so that they will feel that they are contributing to the cycling adventure by carrying their own gear.

7. Provide a disposable camera so they can create their own memories of the cycling trip.

8. Allow them time to play; pack a card game, a frisbee and a small toy.

9. Involve them in pre-trip preparations and map reading. Ask them from time to time what direction they are travelling when on route.

10. Relay any local information you have gathered—it will help to entertain them, keep their minds off the chore at hand and may lead to questions that together you can find the answers to.

Lastly, when choosing a tour for children, take into consideration that they will require more breaks and the average speed will be lower. When doing your pre-tour calculations on the length of your day, remember to add at least one to 2hrs.

Ontario's Bike Paths and Rail Trails

Further Information

Southwestern Ontario

Erieau
Rondeau Provincial Park
District Manager
Ministry of Natural Resources
Chatham District
P.O. Box 1168
1023 Richmond St.
Chatham, ON
N7M 5L6
☎ (519) 354-7340
www.mnr.gov.on.ca/MNR/parks/rond.html

Rondeau Provincial Park
RR 1
Morpeth, ON
N0P 1X0
☎ (519) 674-1750
Park Office
☎ (519) 674-5405

Chatham
City Tour of Chatham
Municipality of Chatham – Kent
Customer Service
P.O. 640
P.O. Box 315 King St. W.
Chatham, ON N7M 5K8
☎ (519) 360-1998\

Goderich
Auburn Rail Trail and Tiger Dunlop Heritage Trail
County of Huron
Planning and Development Department
Court House Square,
Goderich, ON

N7A 1M2
☎ (519) 524-2188

Grand Bend - Grand Bend Bicycle Path and Pinery Cycling Trails
Grand Bend District Chamber of Commerce
P.O. Box 248
1-81 Crescent St.
Grand Bend, ON
N0M 1T0
☎ (519) 238-2001
www.grandbend.com

Pinery Provincial Park
RR 2
Grand Bend, ON
N0M 1T0
☎ (519) 243-2220
www.pinerypark.on.ca.

Hanover - Hanover Recreational Trail
Hanover Parks & Recreation Department
269 seventh Ave.
Hanover, ON
N4N 2H5
☎ (519) 364-2310
www.town/hanover/on/ca

Walkerton - Severn River Walk
Municipality of Walkerton
Parks and Recreation Department
P.O. Box 850
Walkerton, ON
N0G 2V0
☎ (519) 881-0625
www.town.walkerton/on/ca

Leamington - Point Pelee National Park
Point Pelee National Park
RR 1
Leamington, ON
N8H 3V4
☎(519) 322-5700 Visitor Centre
☎(519) 322-2365
www.parkscanada.pch.gc.ca/pelee

London - Bicycle Paths
City of London Parks and Recreation
P.O. Box 5035
London, ON N6A 4L9
☎(519) 661-2356
(519) 661-2362

Tourism London
300 Dufferin Ave.
London, ON
N6B 1Z2
☎(519) 661-6336
☎1-800-265-2602
www.city.london.on.ca

Sarnia - Howard Watson Nature Trail & Point Edward Waterfront Trail
Convention and Visitors Bureau of Sarnia
Lambton Visitor and Convention Bureau
556 North Christina St.
Sarnia, ON
☎1-800-265-0316
☎(519)-336-3232
www.city.sarnia.on.ca

Simcoe - Lynn Valley Trail
Lynn Valley Trail Association
137 Decou Rd.
Simcoe, ON
N3Y 4K2
☎(519) 428-3292

☎(519) 426-3715
www.kwic.com/~chamber/simcoe.html
www.kwic.com/~kwic/lynntrail

St. Marys - Grand Trunk Trail and Wildwood Conservation Area
Grand Trunk Trail Committee
P.O. Box 998
St. Marys, ON
N4X 1B6
☎(519) 284-3556 (Museum)
www.stonetown.com/gttsm

St. Marys and Area Parks and Recreation
P.O. Box 218,
St. Marys, ON
N4X 1B1
☎(519) 284-4763
www.stonetown.com

Wildwood Conservation Area
Upper Thames River Conservation Authority
RR 2
St. Marys, ON
N4X 1C5
☎(519) 284-2292

Tillsonburg - Liscar Lake and Port Burwell Rail Trail
Town of Tillsonburg
200 Broadway St. 2nd Floor
Tillsonburg, ON
N4G 5A7
☎(519) 842-6428
www.town.tillsonburg.on.ca

Ontario's Bike Paths and Rail Trails

Woodstock - Hickson Trail and Credit Valley Rail Trail

The Corporation of the City of Woodstock
P.O. Box 40
Woodstock, ON
N4S 7W5
☎ (519) 539-1291
www.city.woodstock.on.ca

Windsor - City Bicycle Paths - Essex County Greenway

City of Windsor
P.O. Box 1607
Windsor, ON
N9A 6S1
www.city.windsor.on.ca
☎ (519) 253-2300
☎ (519) 255-6500

Essex Region Conservation Authority

360 Fairview Ave. W.
Essex, ON
N8M 1Y6
☎ (519) 776-5209
www.city.windsor.on.ca/home/visitors

Niagara Peninsula and Surroundings

Hamilton - Brantford - Cambridge Rail Trail

City of Brantford Parks and Recreation
& Tourism
1 Sherwood Dr.
Brantford, ON N3T 1N3
☎ 1-800-265-6299
☎ (519) 751-9900
www.city.brantford.on.ca

Grand River Conservation Authority

P.O. Box 729, 400 Clyde Rd.
Cambridge, ON
N1R 5W6
☎ (519) 621-2761
www.grandriver.on.ca

The Corporation of the City of Cambridge

73 Water St. N. (2nd Floor)
Cambridge, ON N1R 5W8
☎ (519) 623-1340
www.city.cambridge.on.ca
www.cambridge.galgonov.net

Elora to Cataract Rail Trail

Grand River Conservation Authority

P.O. Box 729, 400 Clyde Rd.
Cambridge, ON
N1R 5W6
☎ (519) 621-2761
www.grandriver.on.ca

Elora Cataract Trailway Association

P.O. Box 99
Fergus, ON
N1M 2W7
☎ (519) 843-3650
www.eic.elora.on.ca/index.html

Guelph Royal Recreation Trails

City Hall
Parks and Recreation Department
59 Carden St.
Guelph, ON
N1H 3A1
☎ (519) 837-5618
www.city.guelph.on.ca

**Hamilton Bicycle and
Recreational Trails**

Grand River Conservation Authority
P.O. Box 729, 400 Clyde Rd.
Cambridge, ON
N1R 5W6
☎(519) 621-2761
www.grandriver.on.ca

**The Regional Municipality of
Hamilton – Wentworth and the
City of Hamilton**

77 James St. N.
Suite 320
Hamilton, ON L8R 2K3
☎(905) 546-2453
www.city.hamilton.on.ca

**Halton Region Conservation
Authority**

838 Mineral Springs Rd., P.O. Box 7099
Ancaster, ON L9G 3L3
☎(905) 648-4427

**Kitchener - Bicycle Routes
Regional Municipality of
Waterloo**

150 Frederick St., 7th Floor
Kitchener, ON N2G 4J3
☎(519) 575-4515
www.city.kitchener.on.ca

**Niagara Falls and
St. Catharines Bicycle Routes**

The Regional Municipality of Niagara
2201 St. David's Rd.
P.O. Box 1042
Thorold, ON
L2V 4T7
☎(905) 984-3630
☎(905) 984-3376
www.npiec.on.ca/~info3012

Tourism of Welland Niagara

Seaway Mall
800 Niagara St. N.
Welland ON
L3C 5Z4
☎(905) 735-8696

**St. Catharines Recreation and
Community Services**

P.O. Box 3012
St. Catharines, ON
L2R 7C2
☎(905) 937-7210
www.stcatharines.com/trails.html

The Lakelands

**Barrie - North Simcoe Rail
Trail/ Floss Corridor and
Kempenfelt Bay Bicycle Route**

City of Barrie
Parks & Recreation
P.O. Box 400
Barrie, ON
L4M 4T5
☎(705) 726-4242 ext 4507
www.city.barrie.on.ca

**Bracebridge - Strawberry Bay
Lookout Trail and South Monk
Trail**

The Town of Bracebridge
Public Works
23 Dominion St.
Bracebridge, ON
P1L 1R6
☎(705) 645-5264
www.town.bracebridge.on.ca/

Ontario's Bike Paths and Rail Trails

**Collingwood - Georgian Trail
Georgian Triangle Tourist
Association**
601 First St.
Collingwood, ON
L9Y 4L2
☎ (705) 445-7722
www.georgiantriangle.org

**Orillia - Orillia to Coldwater
Rail Trail including the Utoff
and Lightfoot Trail**
The City of Orillia
Parks and Recreation
50 Andrew St. S.
L3V 7T5
☎ (705) 325-1311
www.city.orillia.on.ca/

**Port Elgin - Saugeen Rail Trail
The Saugeen Railtrail
Association**
P.O. Box 2313
Port Elgin, ON
N0H 2C0
☎ (519)-832-6443
www.wcl.on.ca/~rotary/projects.htm#A

The Greater Toronto Area

Toronto

Toronto Bicycling Network
131 Bloor St. W.
Suite 200, Box 279,
Toronto, ON
M5S 1R8
☎ (416) 760-4191
www.tbn.on.cg

Metro Parks & Culture
24th Floor, Metro Hall, 55 John St.
Toronto, ON
M5V 3C6
☎ (416) 392-8186
www.metrotor.on.ca

City of Mississauga
300 City Centre Dr.
Mississauga, ON
L5B 3C1
☎ (905) 896-5342
www.city.mississauga.on.ca
Mississauga Cycling Advisory Committee
☎ (905) 896-5471

Caledon - Caledon Trailway
Town of Caledon
Parks and Recreation
6311 Old Church Rd.
P.O. Box 1000
Caledon E., ON
L0N 1E0
☎ (905) 584-2272

Central Ontario

**Haliburton - Lindsay to
Haliburton to Kinamount Rail
Trail**
The Haliburton Highlands Chamber of
Commerce
P.O. Box 147,
Minden, ON
K0M 2K0
☎ (705) 286-1760
☎ 1-800-461-7677

Haliburton Cycling Club
P.O. Box 475
Haliburton, ON
K0M 1S0

☎(705) 457- 9785

Victoria County
26 Francis St.
Box 9000
Lindsay, ON
K9V 5R8

Peterborough
Greater Peterborough Chamber of Commerce
175 George St. N.
Peterborough, ON
K9J 3G6
(705) 748-9771
www.city.peterborough,on.ca

Eastern Ontario

Bancroft - Hastings Heritage Trail
County Hastings County Administration Office
☎(613) 966-1319

East ON Trails Alliance
RR 2
Tweed ON K0K 3J0
☎(613) 478-5262
☎(613) 478-1444 — office
www.thetrail.on.ca

Barryvale - K&P Trail
Mississippi Valley Conservation
Box 268,
Lanark, ON
K0G 1K0
☎(613) 259-2421

The Township of Central Frontenac
P.O Box 89,
Sharbot Lake, ON
K0H 2P0

☎(613) 279-2935
www.335net.com/cfront.htm
☎(613) 279-2935 ext. 222

St Lawrence Recreational Trail (2 parts of the Waterfront Trail)
The City of Cornwall
Parks & Recreation
100 Water St. Box 877
Cornwall, ON
K6H 6G4
☎(613) 938-9400
www.city.cornwall.on.ca/

City of Brockville
1 King St.W.
Brockville, K6V 7A5
☎(613) 342-8772
www.brockville.com/

City of Brockville - Tourism
1 King St. W., Box 5000
Community Services
Brockville, ON K6V 7A5
☎(613) 342-8772 ext. 430
☎1-888-251-7676

Trenton
City of Quinte West
P.O. Box 490
Trenton, ON
K8V 5R6
☎(613) 392-2841

Ontario's Bike Paths and Rail Trails

Ottawa and Surroundings

Ottawa
NCC - National Capital Commission
40 Elgin St.
Ottawa, ON
KIP 1C7
☎ (613)-239-5000
☎ (613)-239-5450
☎ 1-800-465-1867
www.capcan.ca

Ottawa Tourism and Convention Authority
130 Albert St.
Suite 1800
Ottawa, ON
KIP 5G4
☎ (613) 237-5150
www.tourottawa.org

Kingston - City Bicycle Routes
Greater Kingston Tourist Association
209 Welling St.
Kingston, ON
K7K 2Y6
☎ (613) 548-4453
☎ 1-888-855-4555

City of Kingston
Parks and Recreation
Kingston, ON
K7L 2Z3
☎ (613) 546-4291 ext. 1297

Northern Ontario

Algonquin Park
Ministry of Natural Resources Information Centre
MacDonald Block, Room M1-73
900 Bay St., Toronto, ON
M7A 2C1
☎ (416) 314-1717
☎ (705) 633-5572
☎ (613)-637-2780 ext. 210

Parry Sound - Seguin Trail
Ministry of Natural Resources
7 Bay St.
Parry Sound, ON
P2A 1S4
☎ (705) 746-4201

Town of Parry Sound
Parry Sound Area Chamber of Commerce
☎ 1-800-461-4261
Community and Business Development Centre
Park to Park Trail
Economic Development
17 Bay St.
Unit C
Parry Sound, ON
P2A 1S4
☎ (705) 746-4455
☎ 1-888-746-4455

Sault Ste. Marie
City of Sault Ste. Marie
Box 580
99 Foster Dr.
Sault Ste. Marie, ON
P6A 5N1
☎ 1-800-461-6020

Civic Centre – Parks and Recreation
☎ (705) 759-2500

Sudbury - Rice Lake Bicycle Route
Rainbow Country Travel Association
2726 Whipporwill Ave.
Sudbury, ON
P3G IE9
☎ (705) 522-0104
www.city.sudbury.on.ca

City of Sudbury
P.O. Box 5000
Station A
Sudbury, ON
P3A 5P3
☎ (705) 674-3141

Thunder Bay
City of Thunder Bay
500 E. Donald St.
Thunder Bay, ON
P7E 5V3
☎ (807) 625-2313
www.city.thunder-bay.on.ca

Waterfront Trail

Waterfront Trail Association
Waterfront Trail Regeneration Trust
207 Queen's Quay W., Suite 580
Toronto, ON
M5J 1A2
☎ (416) 314-9490

Ontario's Bike Paths and Rail Trails

Southwestern Ontario

Bike Paths and Rail Trails

City/Area	Total Length (km)	Page
Windsor	65	40
Windsor (Downtown)	-	41
Downtown Windsor (Enlargement)	-	42
Chrysler Canada Greenway	44	43
Point Pelee National Park	10	44
Rondeau Park	20	45
Chatham	25	46-47
Sarnia	67	48
Sarnia (Point Edward Waterfront Trail)	-	49
Grand Bend	24	50
St. Marys	2.5	51
Goderich to Auburn Rail Trail (GART)	12	52
The Tiger Dunlop Heritage Trail	7	53
London	185	54-55
London (downtown)	-	56-57
Tillsonburg	1.5	58
Tillsonburg to Port Burwell	35	59
Woodstock - Hickson Trail	14	60
Simcoe (Lynn Valley Trail)	8	61
Stratford	38	62-63
Hanover	-	64
Walkerton - Saugeen River Walk	6	65

Southwestern Ontario

Southwestern Ontario stretches eastward from Windsor to Woodstock, the "dairy capital" of Canada and from the shipping port of Goderich in the north to the city of Leamington, in the south.

Situated between Lake Erie and Lake Huron, southwestern Ontario is a wonderful place to enjoy the scenery of vast expanses of fresh water.

The sparkling blue waves that delight beach-loving vacationers today were equally attractive in the past to the Aboriginal people who settled and prospered in this area.

Fascinating tourist attractions, most notably around London, trace the history of these First Nations. However, this fertile region is also near the navigation routes that were vital to the early colonists and they, too, wanted to settle here.

The colonists founded little villages that eventually became lovely cities, such as London and St. Marys. Some of these towns are outstanding for the exceptional cultural initiatives they have undertaken.

Stratford is one of these, with its famous Shakespeare festival that attracts huge crowds every summer.

First St. Andrew's United Church , London

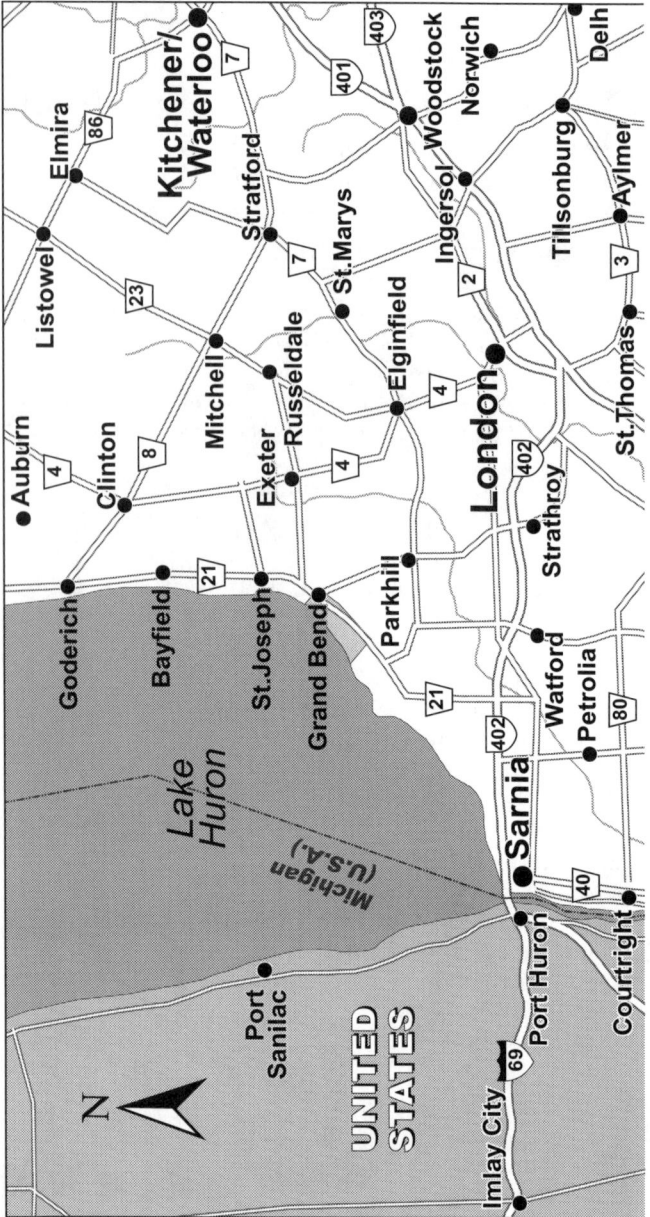

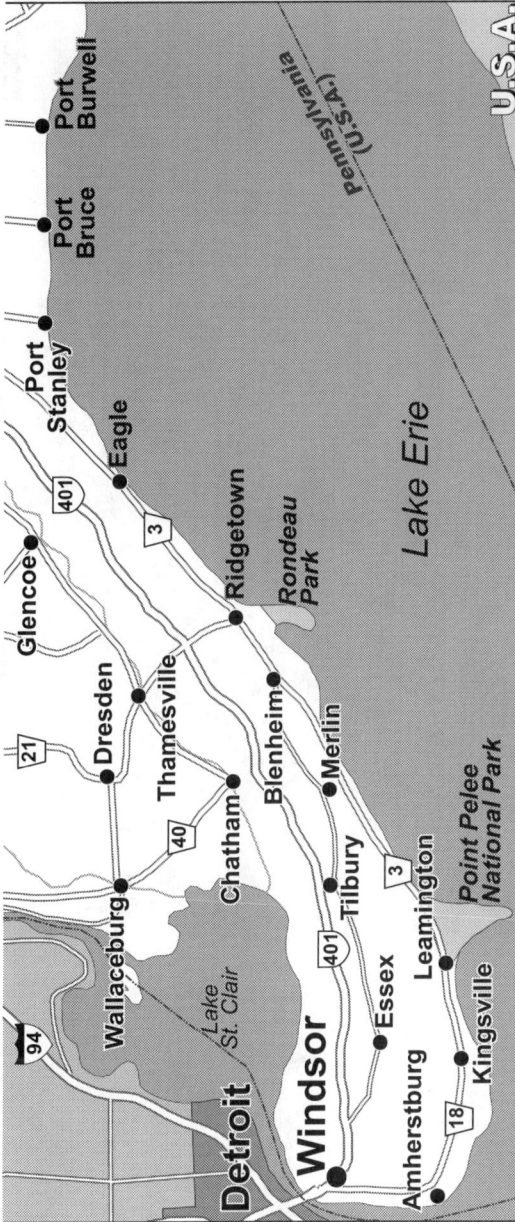

Southwestern Ontario

© ULYSSES

0   100   200km

Detroit

Windsor

Lake St. Clair

Lake Erie

Pennsylvania (U.S.A.)

U.S.A.

Port Burwell

Port Bruce

Port Stanley

Eagle

Glencoe

Dresden

Thamesville

Ridgetown

Rondeau Park

Blenheim

Merlin

Wallaceburg

Chatham

Tilbury

Leamington

Point Pelee National Park

Essex

Amherstburg

Kingsville

401

3

21

40

94

18

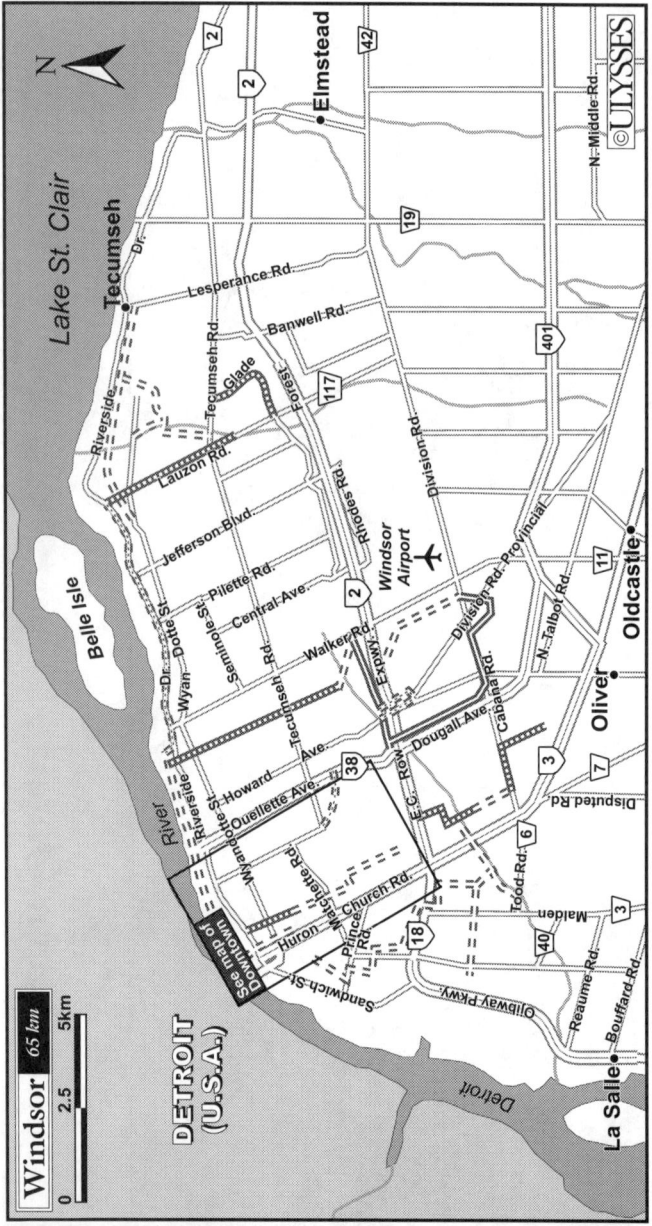

Windsor   65 km

0   2.5   5km

DETROIT (U.S.A.)

Lake St. Clair

Belle Isle

Detroit

River

See map of Downtown

N

Tecumseh

Elmstead

2

42

2

19

401

11

Oldcastle

Oliver

7

3

6

40

3

Malden

18

38

117

La Salle

Riverside Dr.

Lesperance Rd.

Tecumseh Rd.

Banwell Rd.

Glade

Forest

Rhodes Rd.

Lauzon Rd.

Jefferson Blvd.

Pilette Rd.

Central Ave.

Seminole St.

Dotte St.

Wyan...

Dr.

Howard Ave.

Tecumseh Ave.

Walker Rd.

Windsor Airport

Division Rd.

Division Rd.

Provincial

N. Talbot Rd.

Cabana Rd.

Dougall Ave.

E.C. Row

E.C. Row Expwy.

Riverside Dr.

Wyandotte St.

Ouellette Ave.

Huron Church Rd.

Manchester Rd.

Prince Rd.

Sandwich St.

Ojibway Pkwy.

Todd Rd.

Reaume Rd.

Bouffard Rd.

Disputed Rd.

© ULYSSES

N. Middle Rd.

© ULYSSES

Detroit River

Centennial   Park

Riverside Drive West

N

University Ave. West

McKay Ave.
Curry Ave.
Cameron Ave.
Caron Ave.
Janette Ave.
Bruce Ave.
Church St.
Dougall Ave.

University of Windsor

California Ave.
Sunset Ave.
Patricia Rd.
Randolph Ave.
Rankin Ave.
Josephine Ave.
Martindale St.
McEwan Ave.
McKay Ave.
Wellington Ave.
Elm Ave.
Oak Ave.
Crawford Ave.

Wyandotte St. West

Elliott St.

Rodney St.

Union St.

College Ave.

Erie St. West

Pine St.

University of Windsor

Huron Church Rd.
Dot Ave.
Askin Ave.
Merritt Ave.
Rankin
California Ave.
Girardot St.
Tilston Dr.
Rankin Ave.
Josephine Ave.
Campbell Ave.
McEwan Ave.
Curry Ave.
McKay Ave.
Elm Ave.
Oak Ave.

Grove Ave.
Giles Blvd. W.

Grove Ave.

Mitchell Park

Pelletier St.

Clinton St.
Ellis St.
Wahketa St. W.
Shepherd St. W.

University Mall

Tecumseh   Road West

Partington
Roxborough
Campbell Ave.

Hanna St. W.

③

Algonquin St.

Redwood Rd.
Northway Ave.
Betts Ave.
California Ave.
Askin Ave.
St. Patrick's Dr.
Partington Ave.
Rankin Ave.
Mark Ave.
Everts Ave.

Totten St.

Superior Park

Rosemont Ave.

Québec St.

Ambassador Dr.
Huron Church Rd.
Daytona Ave.
St. Claire Ave.
Randolph Ave.
Dominion Blvd.
Longfellow Ave.

0   1   2km

Windsor
Downtown

Southwestern Ontario

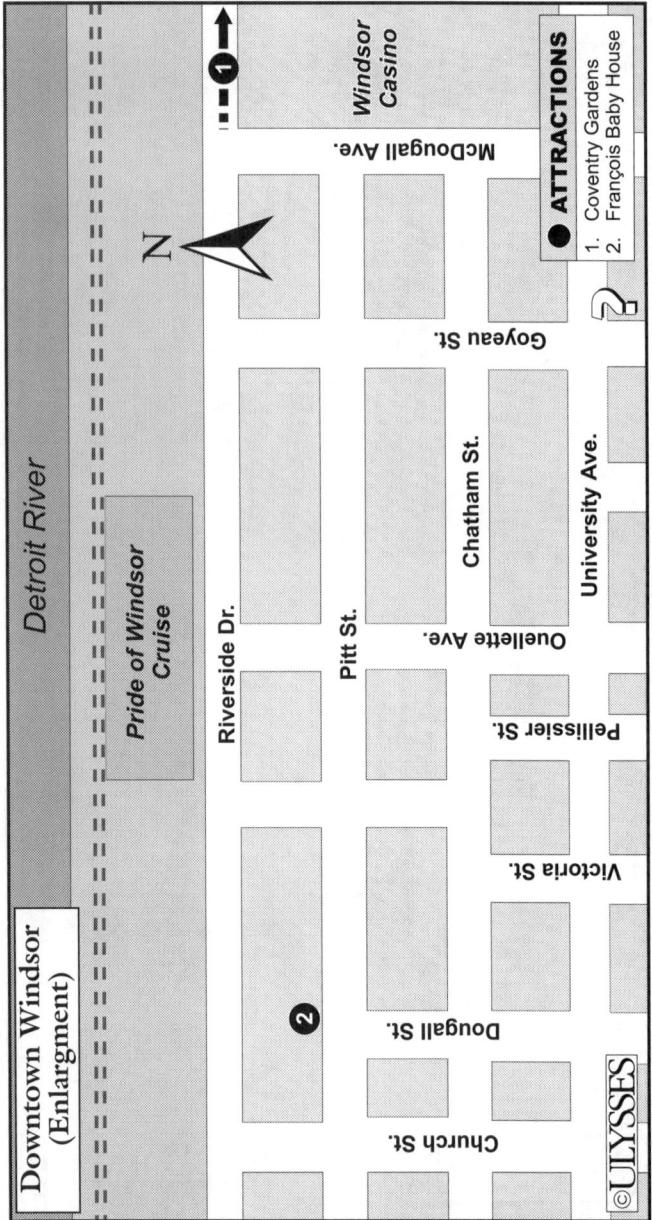

Downtown Windsor (Enlargment)

Detroit River

Pride of Windsor Cruise

Riverside Dr.

Pitt St.

Chatham St.

Ouellette Ave.

University Ave.

Pellissier St.

Victoria St.

Dougall St.

Church St.

Goyeau St.

McDougall Ave.

Windsor Casino

N

● ATTRACTIONS

1. Coventry Gardens
2. François Baby House

© ULYSSES

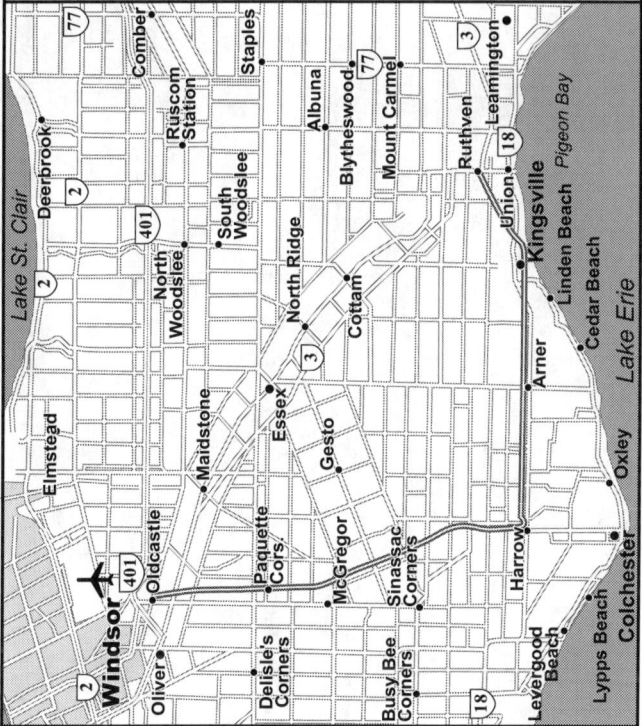

Southwestern Ontario

© ULYSSES

Chrysler Canada
Greenway **44 km**

0   6   12km

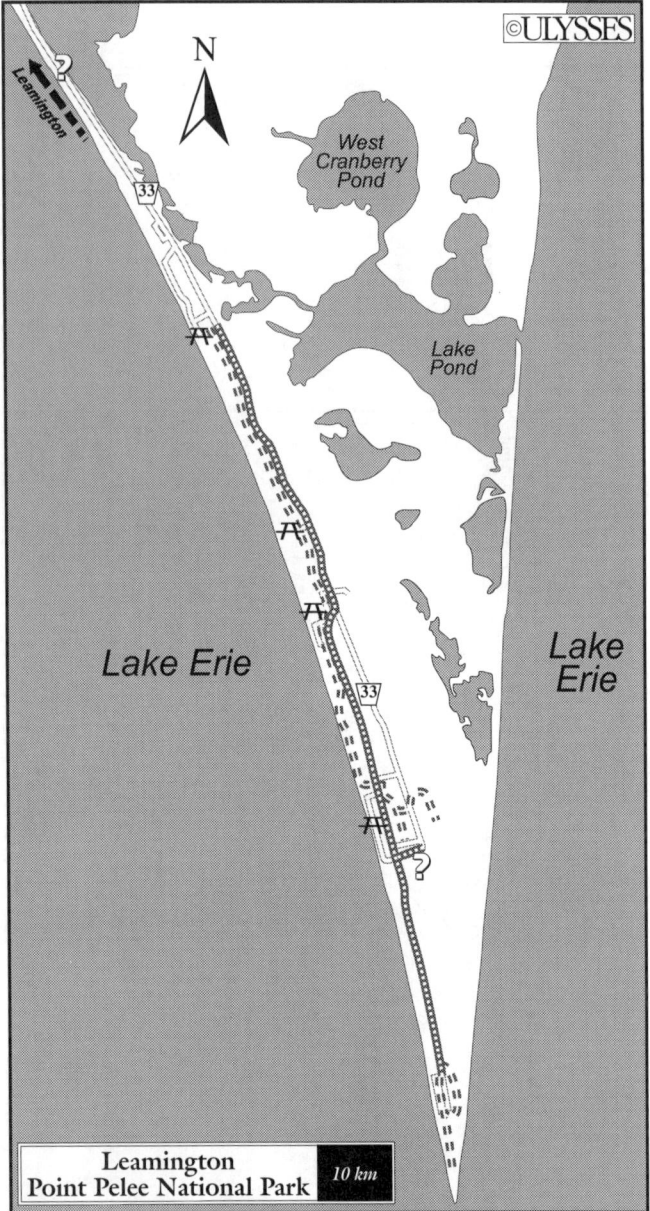

©ULYSSES

N

West
Cranberry
Pond

Lake
Pond

33

Lake Erie

Lake
Erie

33

Leamington
Point Pelee National Park   10 km

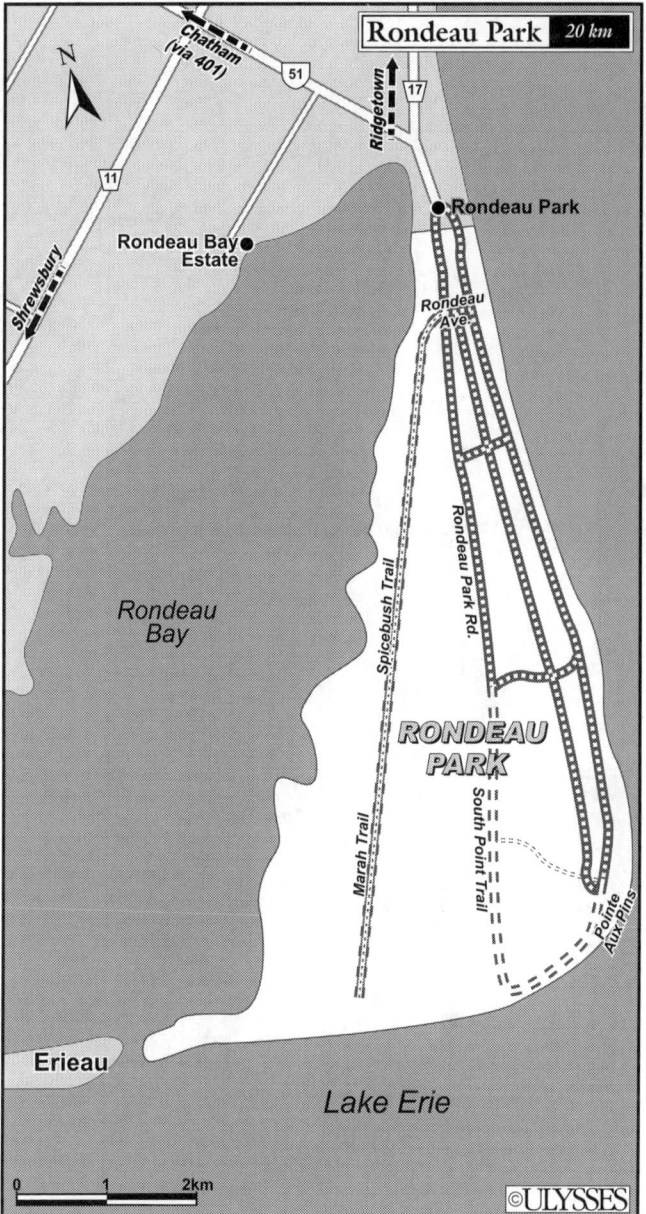

Rondeau Park *20 km*

N

Chatham
(via 401)

51

Ridgetown

17

● Rondeau Park

11

Rondeau Bay
Estate ●

Shrewsbury

Rondeau
Ave.

*Rondeau
Bay*

Spicebush Trail

Rondeau Park Rd.

*RONDEAU
PARK*

Marah Trail

South Point Trail

Pointe
Aux Pins

Erieau

Lake Erie

0   1   2km

©ULYSSES

Southwestern Ontario

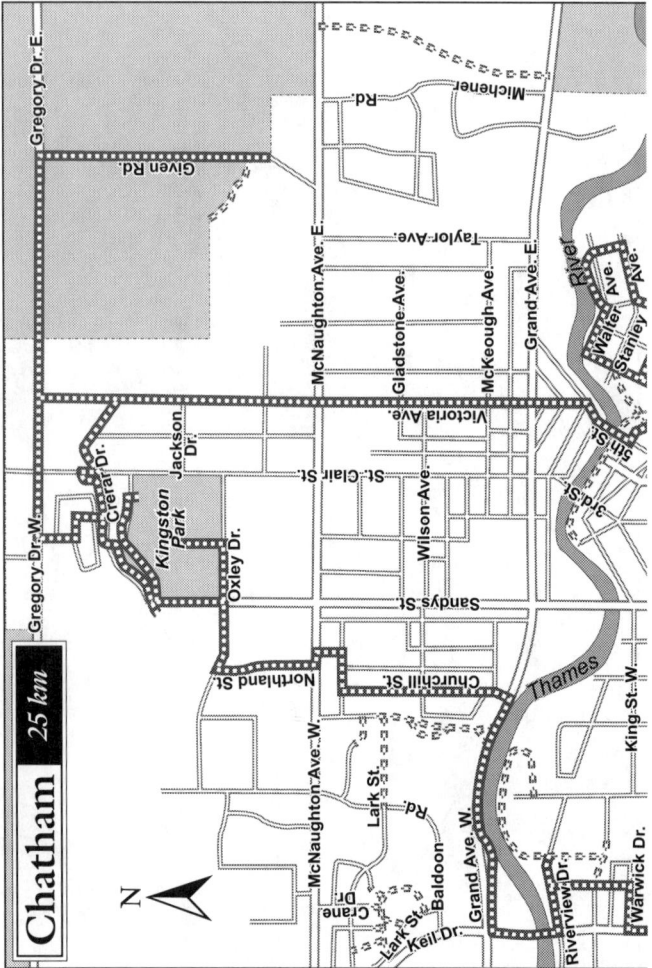

Chatham

25 km

N

Gregory Dr. E.

Given Rd.

Michener Rd.

Taylor Ave.

McNaughton Ave. E.

Gladstone Ave.

McKeough Ave.

Grand Ave. E.

River

Walter Ave.

Stanley Ave.

Victoria Ave.

5th St.

3rd St.

Crerar Dr.

Jackson Dr.

Kingston Park

St. Clair St.

Wilson Ave.

Gregory Dr. W.

Oxley Dr.

Sandys St.

Northland St.

Churchill St.

Thames

McNaughton Ave. W.

Lark St.

Baldoon Rd.

Crane Dr.

Lark St.

Keil Dr.

Grand Ave. W.

Riverview Dr.

King St. W.

Warwick Dr.

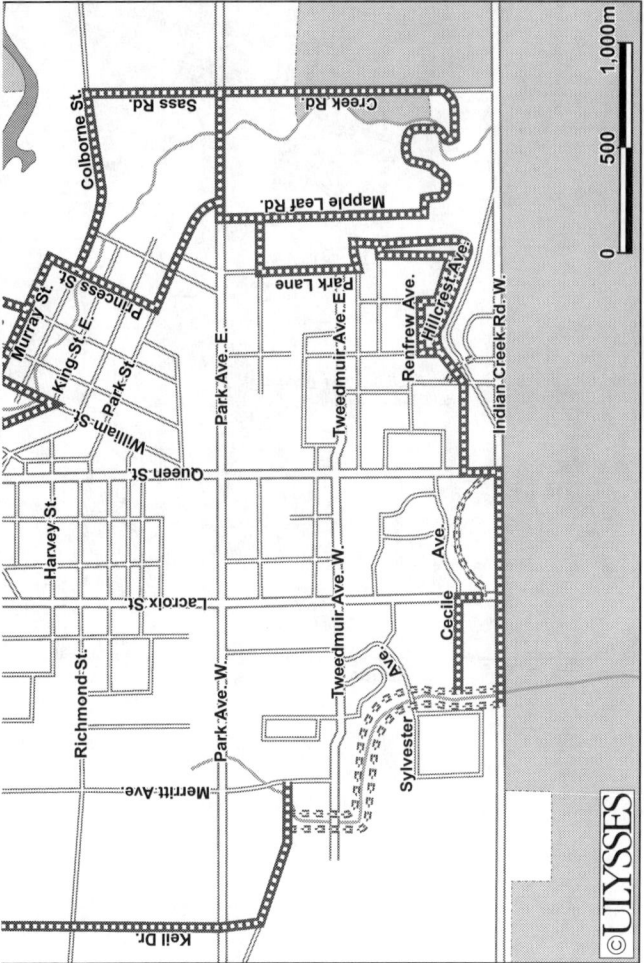

Southwestern Ontario

Streets labeled on map:
- Colborne St.
- Sass Rd.
- Creek Rd.
- Maple Leaf Rd.
- Murray St.
- Princess St.
- King St. E.
- Park St.
- William St.
- Queen St.
- Park Ave. E.
- Park Lane
- Tweedmuir Ave. E.
- Renfrew Ave.
- Hillcrest Ave.
- Indian Creek Rd. W.
- Harvey St.
- Lacroix St.
- Ave.
- Cecile
- Richmond St.
- Merritt Ave.
- Park Ave. W.
- Tweedmuir Ave. W.
- Sylvester Ave.
- Keil Dr.

Scale: 0   500   1,000m

© ULYSSES

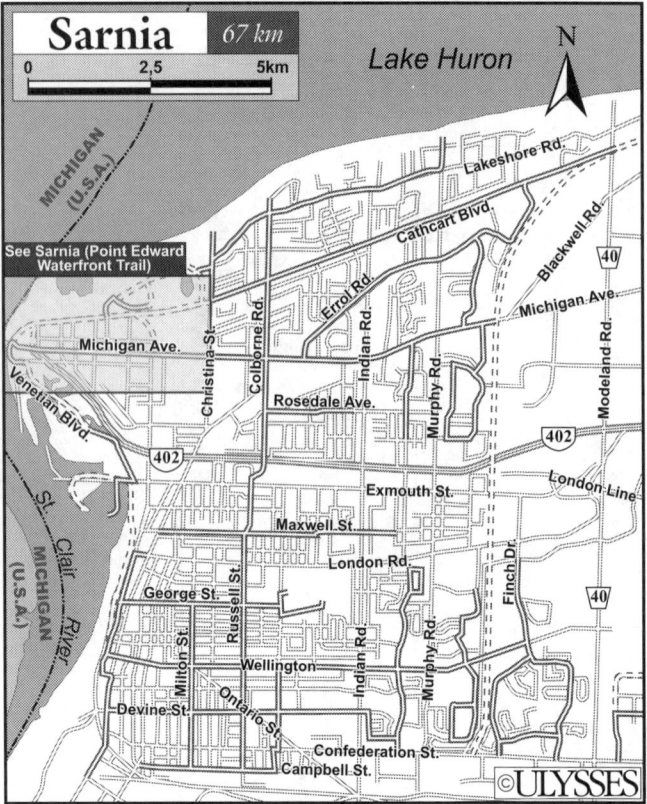

Sarnia 67 km

0   2,5   5km

Lake Huron

N

MICHIGAN (U.S.A.)

See Sarnia (Point Edward Waterfront Trail)

Lakeshore Rd.

Cathcart Blvd.

Blackwell Rd.

40

Michigan Ave.

Michigan Ave.

Christina St.

Colborne Rd.

Errol Rd.

Indian Rd.

Murphy Rd.

Modeland Rd.

Venetian Blvd.

Rosedale Ave.

402

402

London Line

St. Clair River MICHIGAN (U.S.A.)

Exmouth St.

Maxwell St.

London Rd.

Finch Dr.

40

George St.

Russell St.

Indian Rd.

Murphy Rd.

Milton St.

Wellington

Ontario St.

Devine St.

Confederation St.

Campbell St.

©ULYSSES

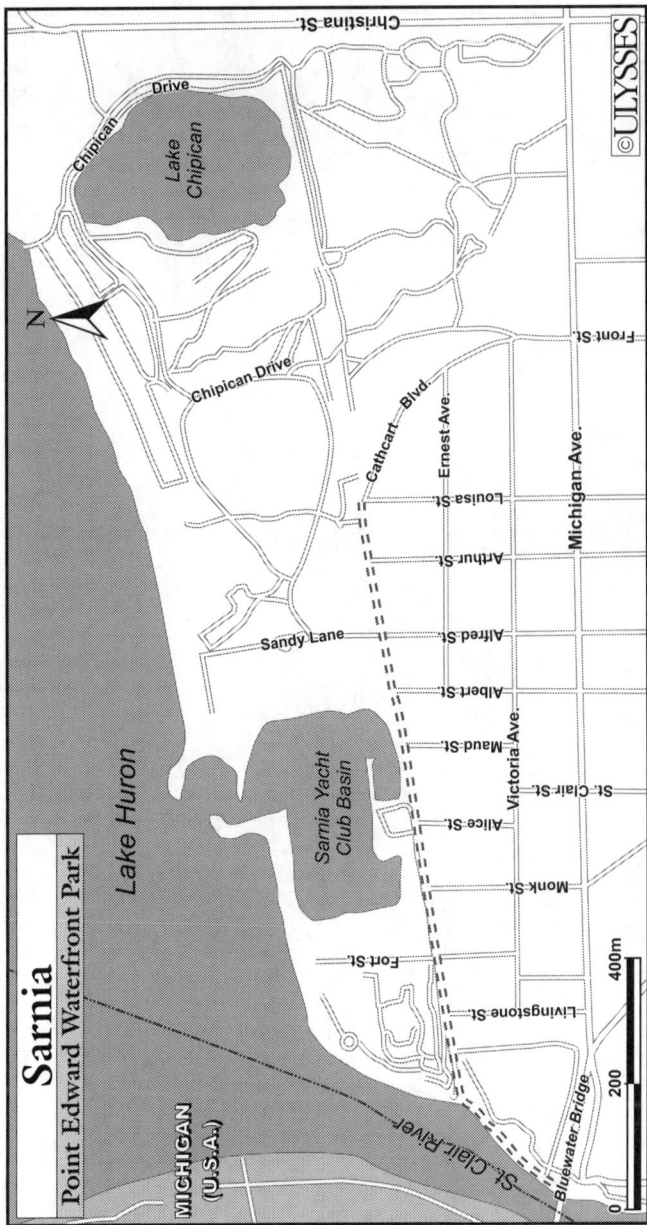

Sarnia
Point Edward Waterfront Park

MICHIGAN (U.S.A.)

Lake Huron

St. Clair River

Bluewater Bridge

Lake Chipican

Chipican Drive

Chipican Drive

Christina St.

N

Sarnia Yacht Club Basin

Sandy Lane

Cathcart Blvd.

Front St.

Ernest Ave.

Louisa St.

Arthur St.

Alfred St.

Albert St.

Maud St.

Alice St.

Monk St.

Fort St.

Livingstone St.

Victoria Ave.

St. Clair St.

Michigan Ave.

0   200   400m

© ULYSSES

Southwestern Ontario

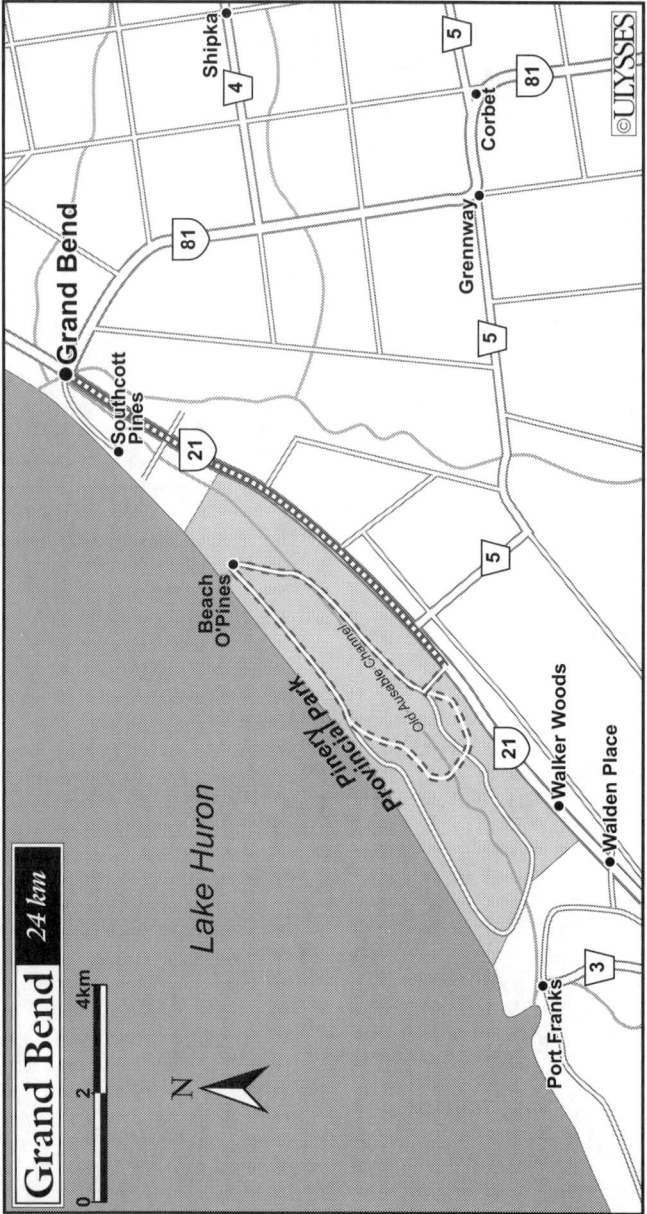

Grand Bend

24 km

0   2   4km

N

Lake Huron

Grand Bend

Southcott Pines

Shipka

Grennway

Corbet

Beach O'Pines

Pinery Provincial Park

Old Ausable Channel

Walker Woods

Walden Place

Port Franks

© ULYSSES

Southwestern Ontario

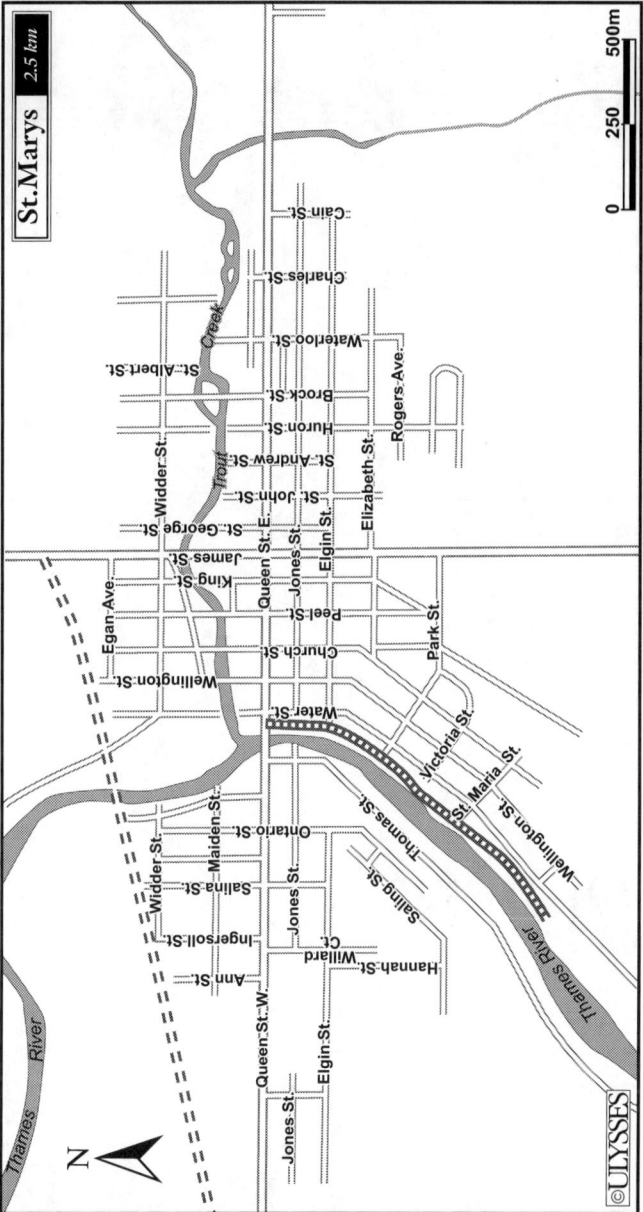

St.Marys 2.5 km

N

500m
250
0

Thames River

Thames River

Trout Creek

St.Albert St.
Cain St.
Charles St.
Waterloo St.
Brock St.
Huron St.
Rogers Ave.
St. Andrew St.
St. John St.
Elizabeth St.
St. George St.
Widder St.
Egan Ave.
James St.
King St.
Queen St. E.
Jones St.
Elgin St.
Peel St.
Church St.
Wellington St.
Park St.
Water St.
Victoria St.
St. Maria St.
Wellington St.
Ontario St.
Thomas St.
Saling St.
Maiden St.
Salina St.
Ingersoll St.
Jones St.
Willard Ct.
Hannah St.
Ann St.
Widder St.
Queen St. W.
Elgin St.
Jones St.

© ULYSSES

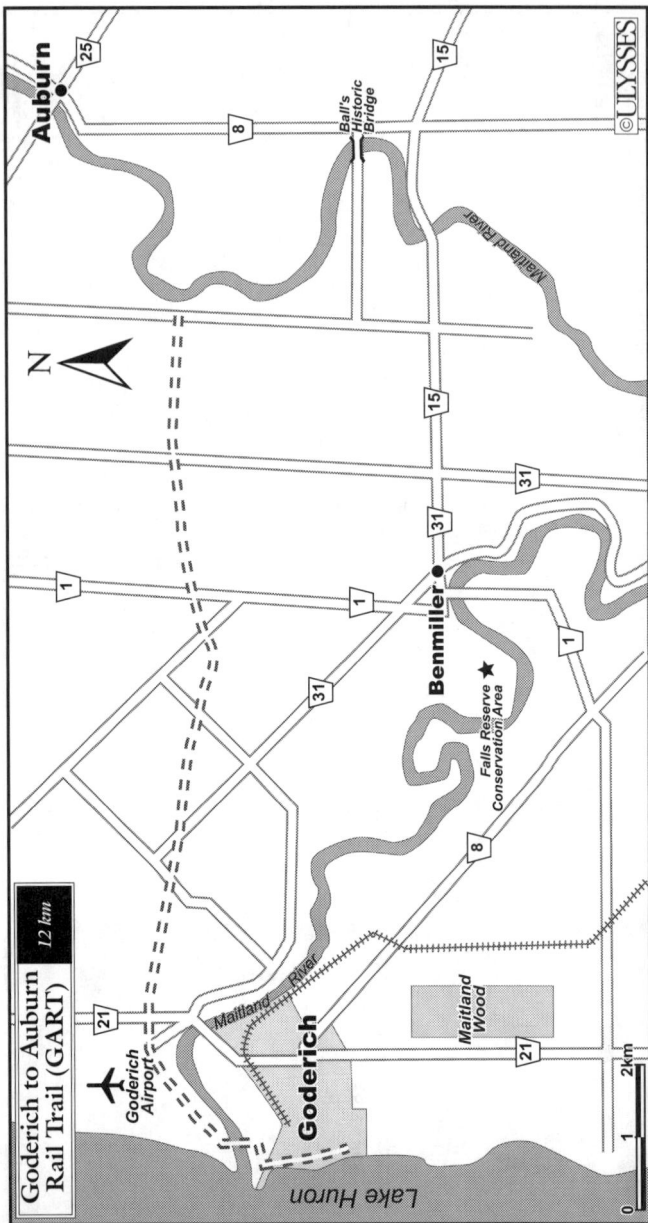

Goderich to Auburn
Rail Trail (GART)

12 km

Lake Huron

Goderich

Goderich Airport

Maitland River

Maitland Wood

Falls Reserve
Conservation Area

Benmiller

Ball's
Historic
Bridge

Auburn

Maitland River

© ULYSSES

0 1 2km

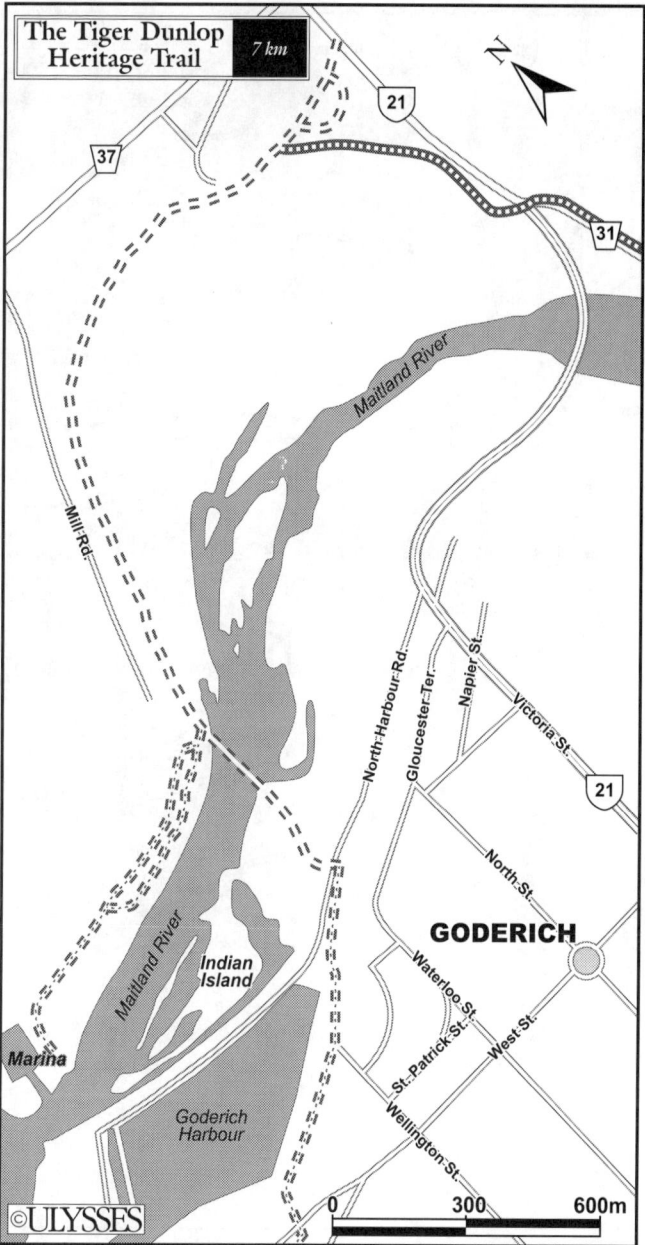

The Tiger Dunlop
Heritage Trail   7 km

21

37

31

Maitland River

Mill Rd.

Maitland River

North Harbour Rd.

Gloucester Ter.

Napier St.

Victoria St.

21

North St.

GODERICH

Indian
Island

Waterloo St.

St. Patrick St.

West St.

Marina

Goderich
Harbour

Wellington St.

©ULYSSES

0   300   600m

Southwestern Ontario

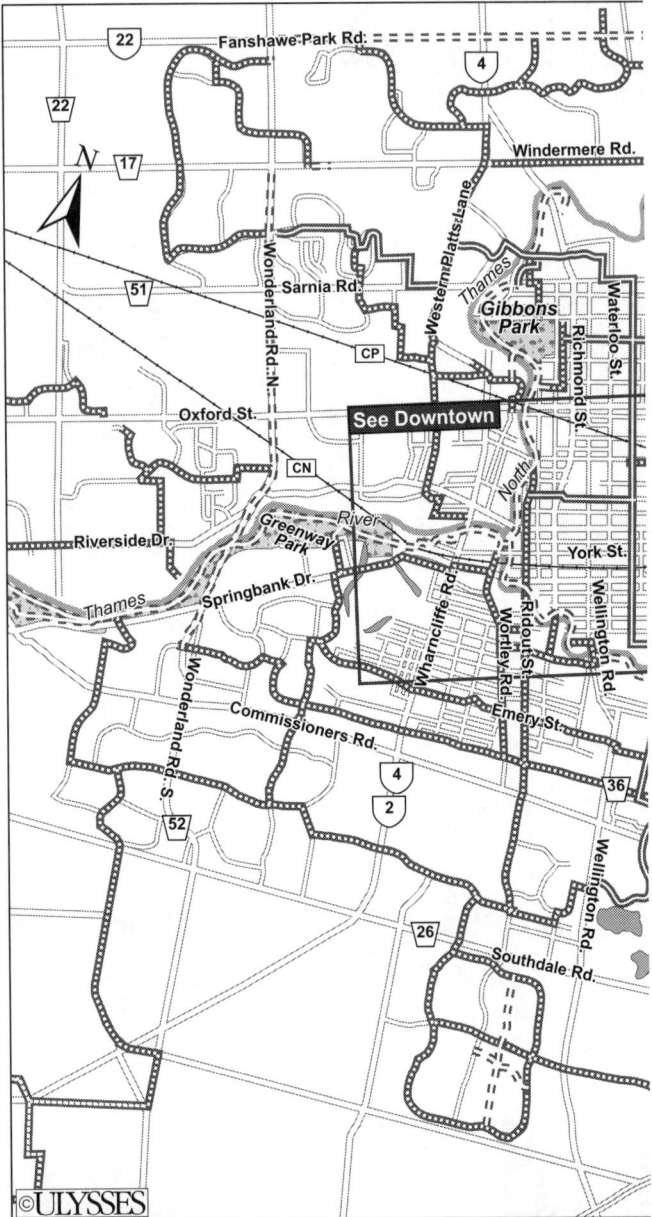

22

22

17

N

51

Fanshawe Park Rd.

4

Windermere Rd.

Wonderland Rd. N.

Sarnia Rd.

Western Platts Lane

Thames

Gibbons Park

Waterloo St.

Richmond St.

CP

Oxford St.

See Downtown

CN

North

Riverside Dr.

Greenway Park

River

Thames

Springbank Dr.

York St.

Wellington Rd.

Wharncliffe Rd.

Ridout St.

Wortley Rd.

Commissioners Rd.

Wonderland Rd. S.

4

2

Emery St.

36

52

26

Wellington Rd.

Southdale Rd.

©ULYSSES

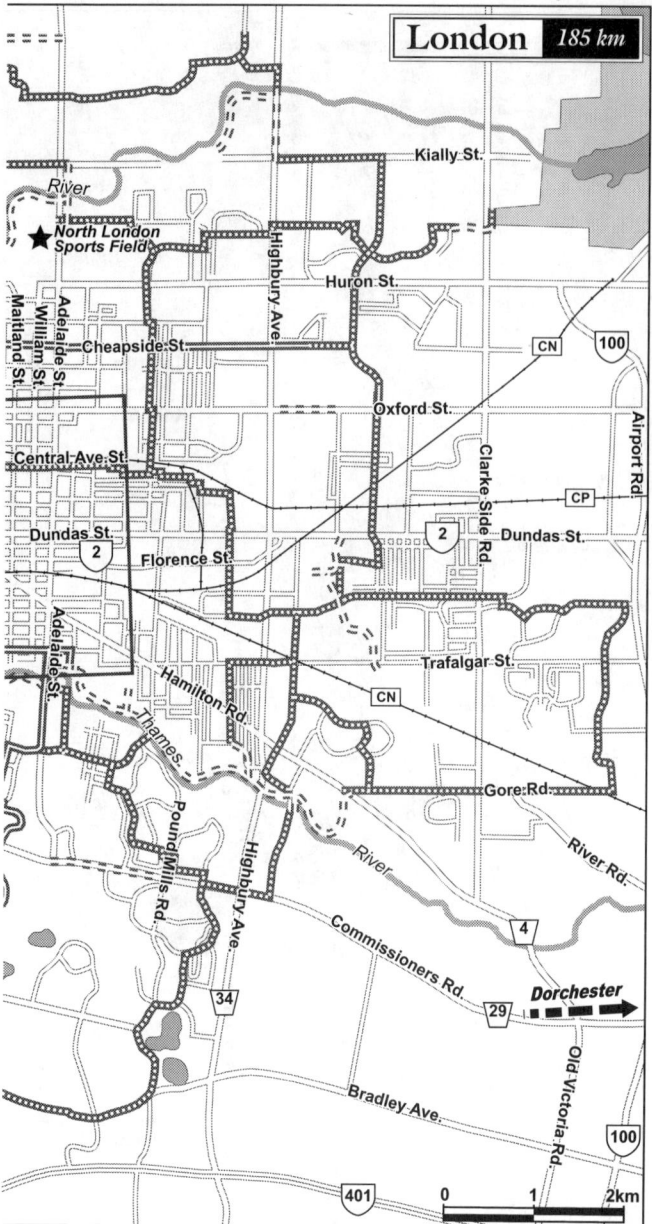

London 185 km

Kially St.

River

★ **North London Sports Field**

Huron St.

Highbury Ave.

Cheapside St.

CN 100

Adelaide St.
William St.
Maitland St.

Oxford St.

Central Ave. St.

Clarke Side Rd.

Airport Rd.

CP

Dundas St.
2

Florence St.

2 Dundas St.

Adelaide St.

Hamilton Rd.

Trafalgar St.

Thames

CN

Pound Mills Rd.

Gore Rd.

Highbury Ave.

River

River Rd.

Commissioners Rd.

4

34

29 **Dorchester** ➡

Old Victoria Rd.

Bradley Ave.

100

401

0   1   2km

Southwestern Ontario

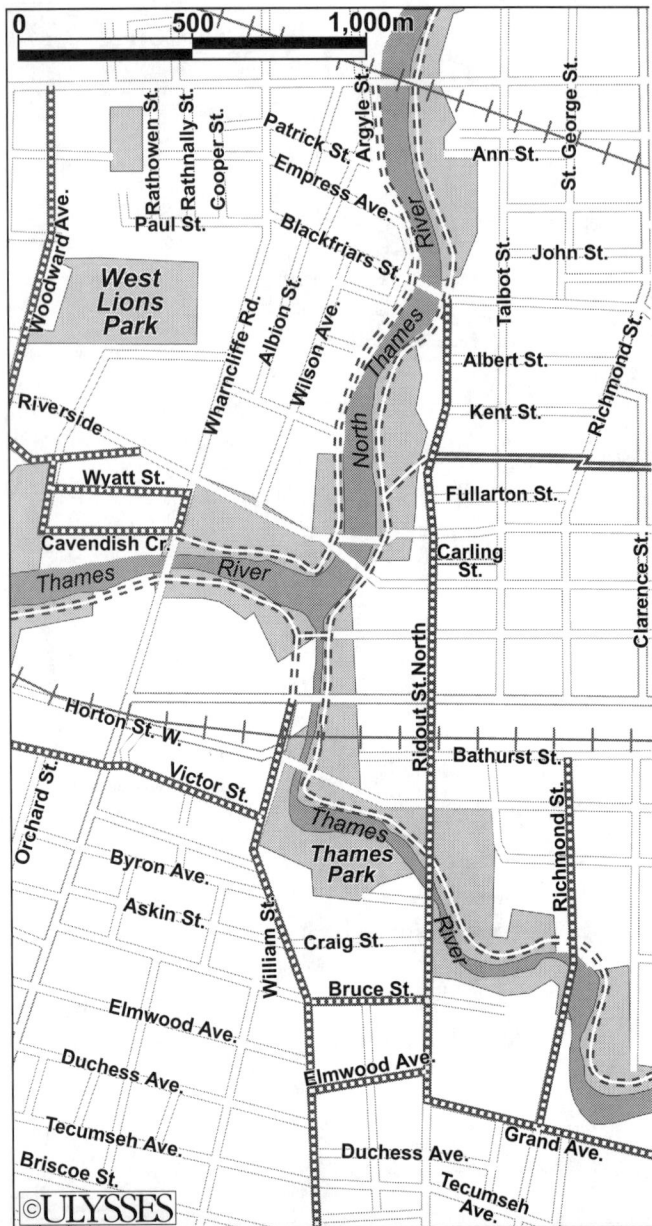

0   500   1,000m

Rathowen St.
Rathnally St.
Cooper St.
Patrick St.
Argyle St.
Ann St.
St. George St.
Empress Ave.
River
Talbot St.
John St.
Paul St.
Blackfriars St.
Woodward Ave.
West Lions Park
Wharncliffe Rd.
Albion St.
Wilson Ave.
North
Thames
Albert St.
Kent St.
Richmond St.
Riverside
Wyatt St.
Fullarton St.
Cavendish Cr.
Thames
River
Carling St.
Clarence St.
Horton St. W.
Victor St.
Ridout St. North
Bathurst St.
Orchard St.
Byron Ave.
Thames
Thames Park
Richmond St.
Askin St.
William St.
Craig St.
River
Elmwood Ave.
Bruce St.
Duchess Ave.
Elmwood Ave.
Tecumseh Ave.
Grand Ave.
Briscoe St.
Duchess Ave.
Tecumseh Ave.

©ULYSSES

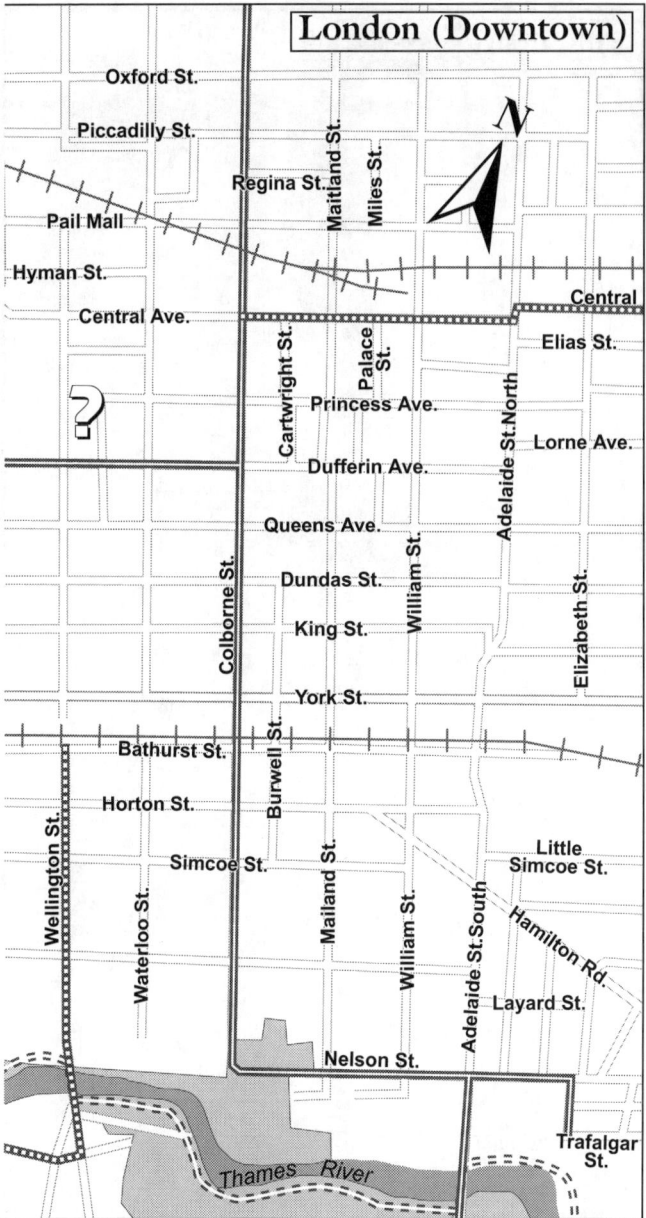

London (Downtown)

Oxford St.

Piccadilly St.

Regina St.

Maitland St.

Miles St.

N

Pall Mall

Hyman St.

Central Ave.

Central

Cartwright St.

Palace St.

Elias St.

Princess Ave.

Adelaide St.North

Lorne Ave.

Dufferin Ave.

Queens Ave.

William St.

Dundas St.

Colborne St.

Elizabeth St.

King St.

York St.

Bathurst St.

Burwell St.

Horton St.

Simcoe St.

Wellington St.

Little Simcoe St.

Mailand St.

Waterloo St.

William St.

Hamilton Rd.

Adelaide St.South

Layard St.

Nelson St.

Trafalgar St.

Thames River

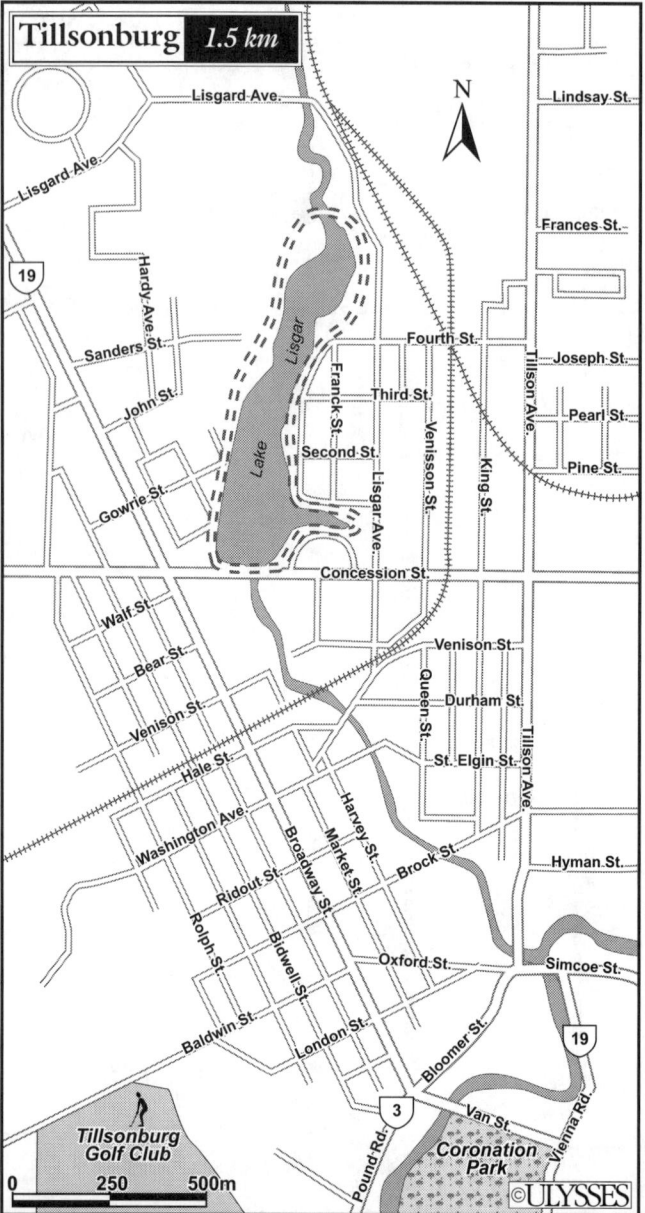

Tillsonburg *1.5 km*

Lisgard Ave.

Lindsay St.

Lisgard Ave.

19

Frances St.

Hardy Ave.

Sanders St.

Fourth St.

Joseph St.

Lake Lisgar

Franck St.

Third St.

Tilson Ave.

Pearl St.

John St.

Second St.

Pine St.

Venisson St.

Gowrie St.

Lisgar Ave.

King St.

Concession St.

Walf St.

Venison St.

Bear St.

Durham St.

Queen St.

Venison St.

St. Elgin St.

Hale St.

Washington Ave.

Harvey St.

Market St.

Brock St.

Hyman St.

Broadway St.

Ridout St.

Rolph St.

Bidwell St.

Oxford St.

Simcoe St.

Baldwin St.

London St.

Bloomer St.

3

19

Van St.

Tillsonburg Golf Club

Pound Rd.

Coronation Park

Vienna Rd.

0   250   500m

©ULYSSES

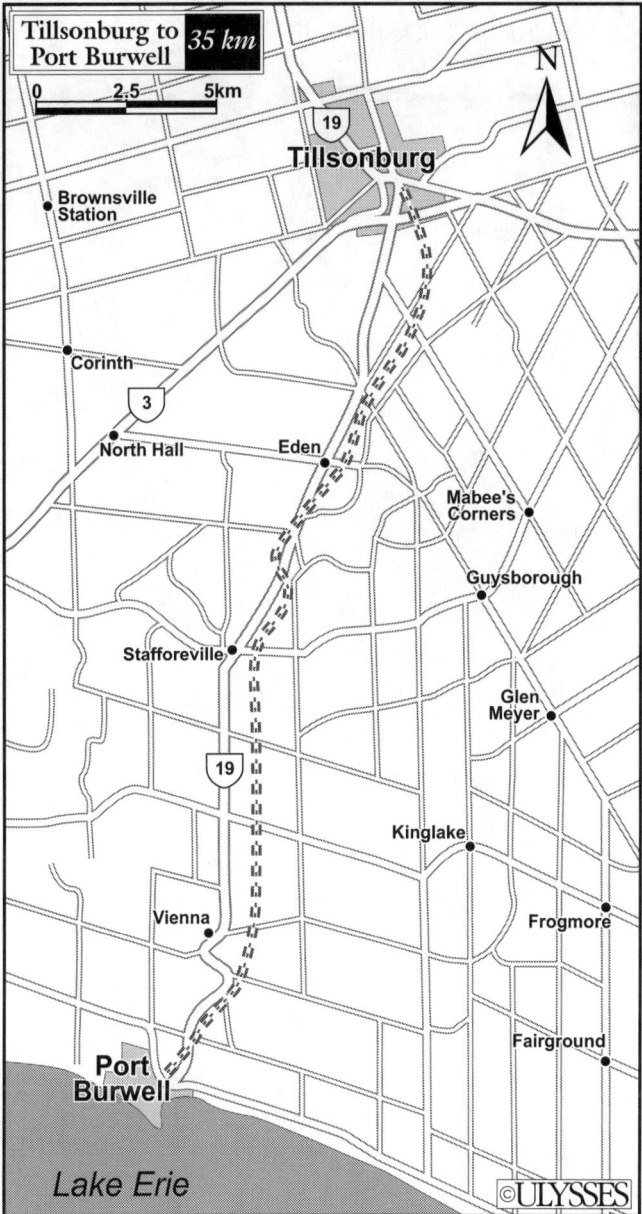

Tillsonburg to Port Burwell 35 km

0   2.5   5km

N

19 Tillsonburg

Brownsville Station

Corinth

3

North Hall

Eden

Mabee's Corners

Guysborough

Stafforeville

Glen Meyer

19

Kinglake

Frogmore

Vienna

Fairground

Port Burwell

Lake Erie

©ULYSSES

Southwestern Ontario

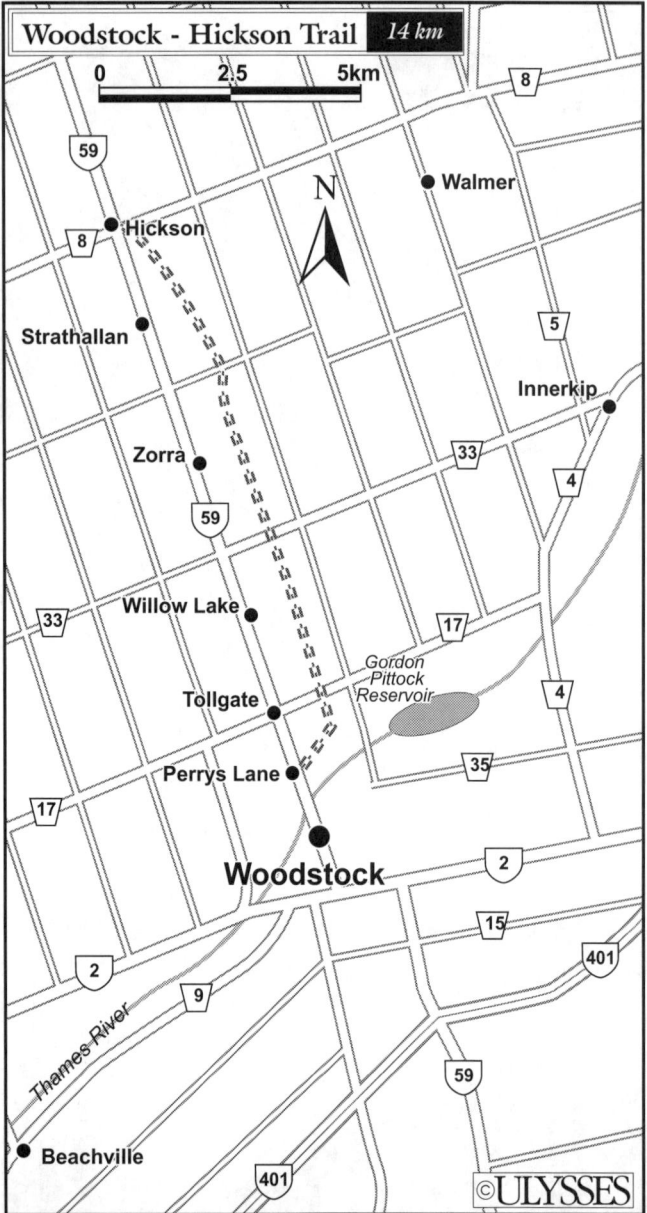

Woodstock - Hickson Trail 14 km

0   2.5   5km

N

8

59

8 Hickson

Walmer

Strathallan

5

Innerkip

Zorra

33

59

4

33 Willow Lake

17

Gordon
Pittock
Reservoir

4

Tollgate

35

Perrys Lane

17

Woodstock

2

2

15

9

401

59

Thames River

Beachville

401

©ULYSSES

Southwestern Ontario

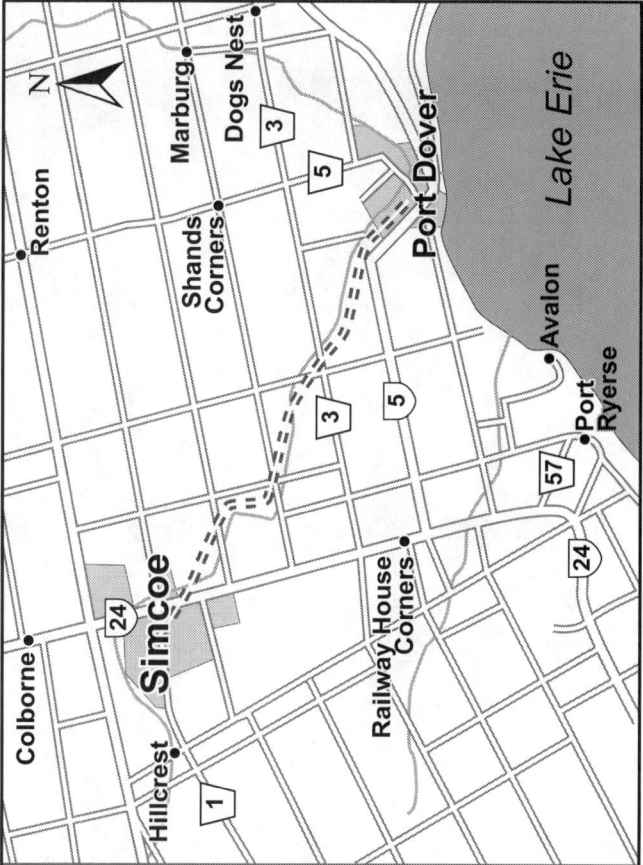

Simcoe
Lynn Valley Trail
8 km

N

Renton

Marburg

Dogs Nest

3

5

Colborne

Shands Corners

Port Dover

Lake Erie

Hillcrest

24

Simcoe

3

5

Avalon

1

Port Ryerse

57

Railway House Corners

24

0   2.5   5km

© ULYSSES

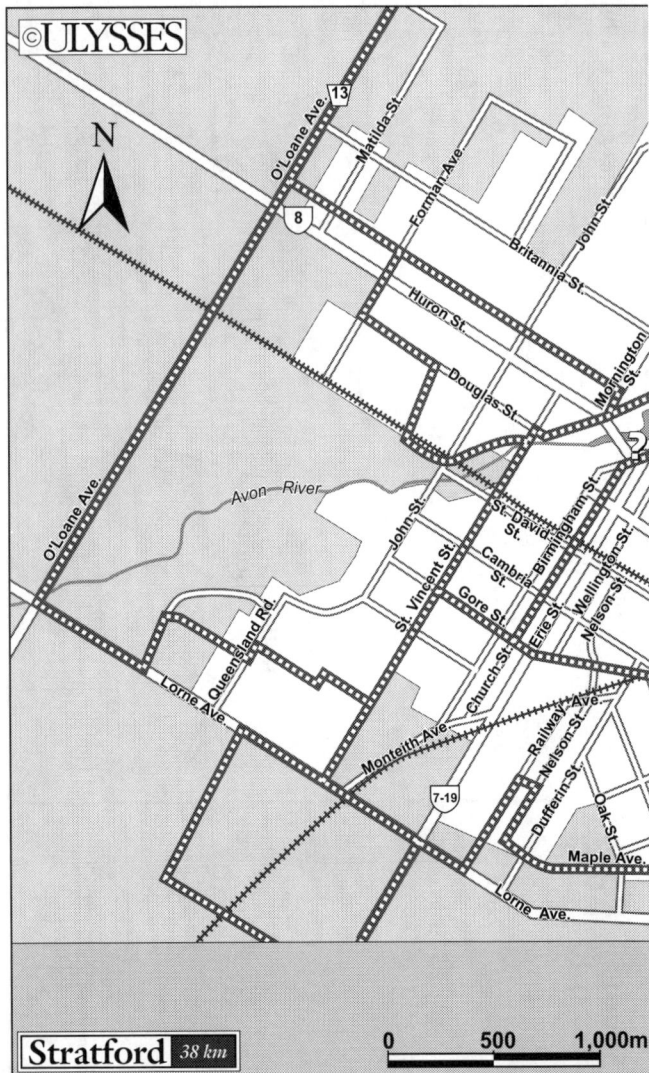

© ULYSSES

N

Stratford 38 km

0   500   1,000m

O'Loane Ave.
13
Matilda St.
Forman Ave.
Britannia St.
John St.
8
Huron St.
Douglas St.
Mornington St.
Avon River
John St.
St. David St.
Cambria St.
St. Vincent St.
Gore St.
Birmingham St.
Wellington St.
Nelson St.
Erie St.
Church St.
O'Loane Ave.
Queensland Rd.
Lorne Ave.
Monteith Ave.
Railway Ave.
Nelson St.
7-19
Dufferin St.
Oak St.
Maple Ave.
Lorne Ave.

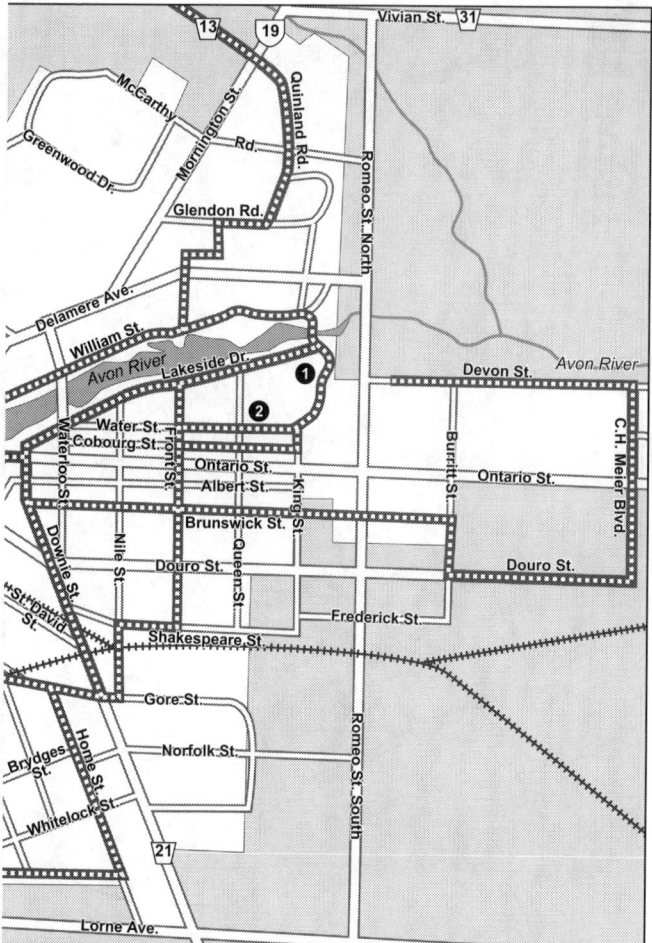

Southwestern Ontario

Vivian St. 31
13 19
McCarthy
Mornington St.
Greenwood Dr.
Quinland Rd.
Romeo St. North
Glendon Rd.
Delamere Ave.
William St.
Avon River Lakeside Dr.
Devon St. Avon River
❶
❷
Water St. C.H. Meier Blvd.
Cobourg St.
Waterloo St. Front St.
Ontario St. Burritt St. Ontario St.
Albert St.
Downie St. King St.
Brunswick St.
Nile St. Douro St. Queen St. Douro St.
St. David St. Frederick St.
Shakespeare St.
Gore St.
Brydges St. Home St. Norfolk St. Romeo St. South
Whitelock St.
21
Lorne Ave.

● **ATTRACTIONS**

1. Festival Theatre
2. Queen's Park

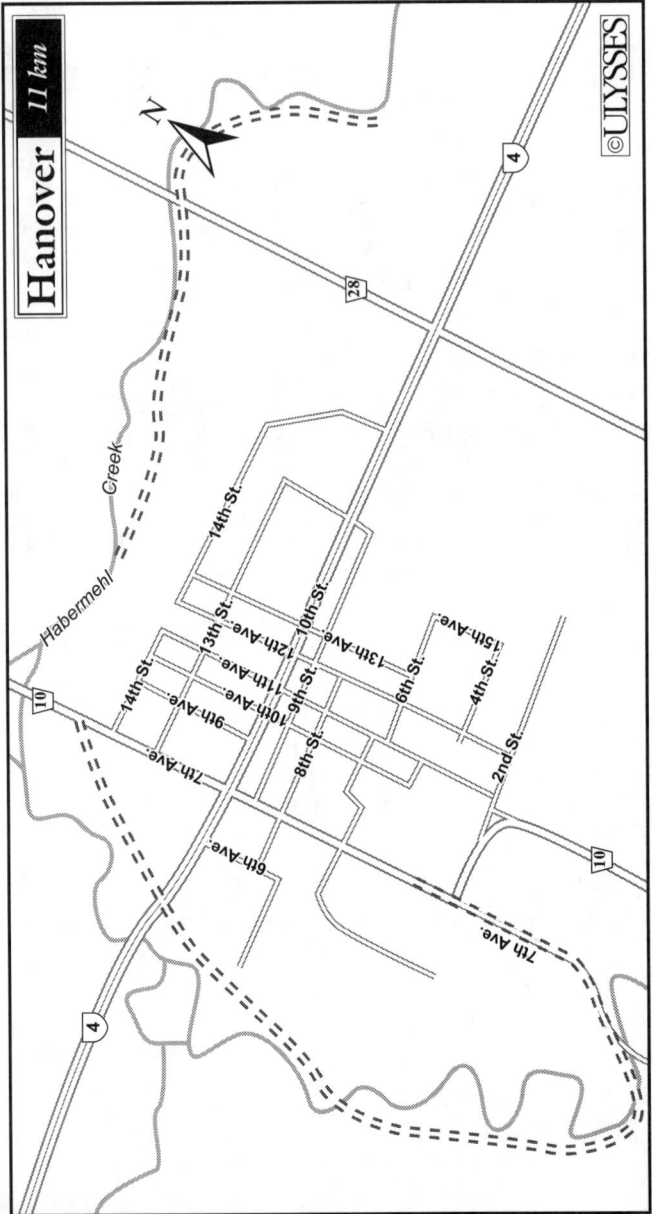

Hanover

11 km

© ULYSSES

Habermehl Creek

N

14th St.
13th St.
12th Ave.
10th St.
9th Ave.
11th Ave.
10th Ave.
13th Ave.
15th Ave.
6th St.
4th St.
2nd St.
8th St.
14th St.
7th Ave.
6th Ave.
7th Ave.

4
28
10
10

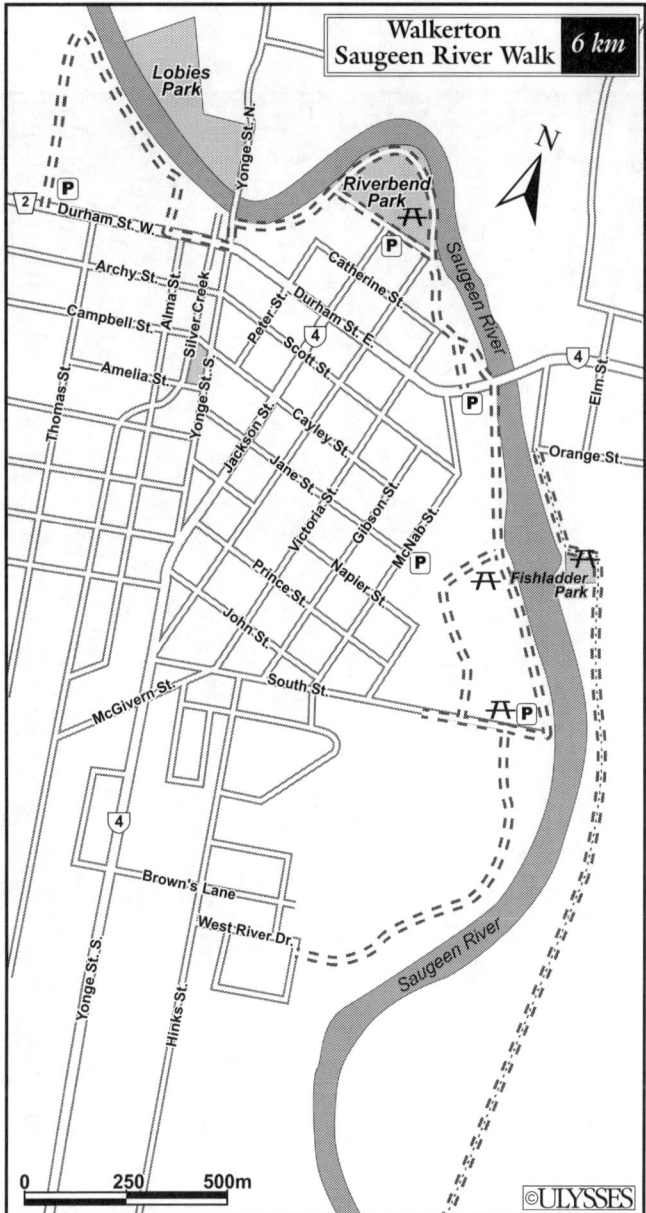

Walkerton Saugeen River Walk — 6 km

Lobies Park

Yonge St. N.

2

P

Durham St. W.

Archy St.

Alma St.

Silver Creek

Campbell St.

Amelia St.

Thomas St.

Yonge St. S.

Jackson St.

Peter St.

Scott St.

Catherine St.

Durham St. E.

P

Riverbend Park

Saugeen River

4

P

4

Elm St.

Orange St.

Cayley St.

Jane St. S.

Victoria St.

Gibson St.

McNab St.

Napier St.

Prince St.

John St.

South St.

McGivern St.

P

Fishladder Park

P

4

Yonge St. S.

Hinks St.

Brown's Lane

West River Dr.

Saugeen River

0   250   500m

©ULYSSES

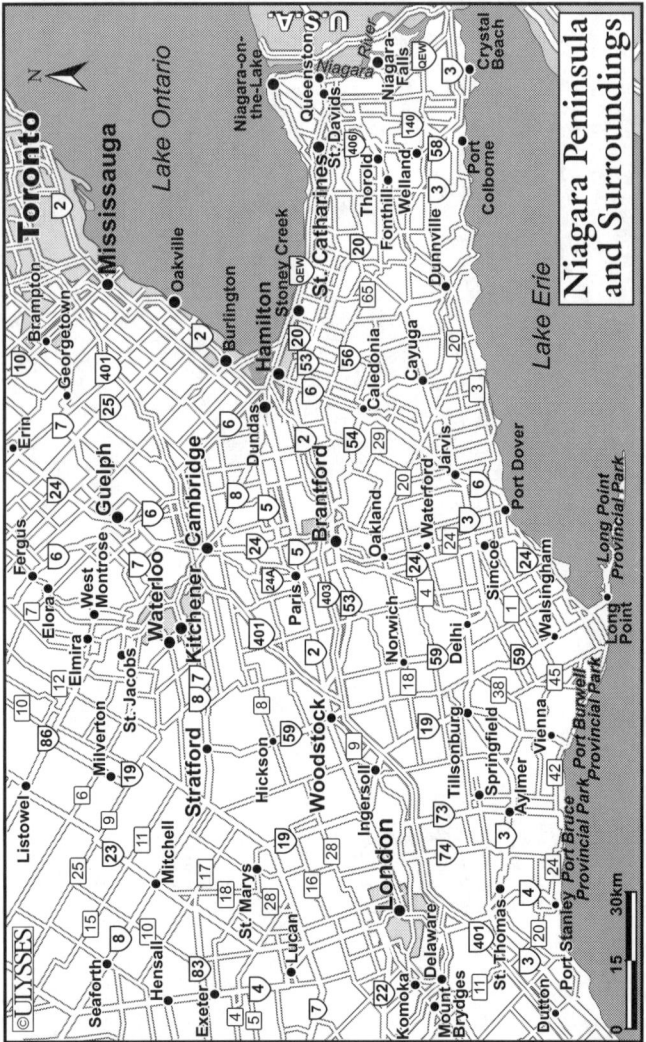

Niagara Peninsula and Surroundings

Niagara Peninsula and Surroundings

Festival Country meanders along the north shore of Lake Erie from Port Rowan to Fort Erie, passing through the fruit and wine producing region of Niagara, and finally reaching Ontario's Mennonite community, with its time-honoured traditions.

Whitehern House, Hamilton

One urban area leads into the next at the eastern end of Lake Ontario. The city of Toronto dominates the landscape for many kilometres in all directions.

And, just as you think you have finally left Toronto city traffic behind, you enter one of the large towns that surround the metropolis.

Among these are the very pleasant towns of Oakville, Burlington, and above all, Hamilton, which is tucked away at the end of the lake. There are some interesting places to visit along this route, but the real treasures in this part of Ontario are found on the south shore of the lake.

Little by little, urban areas give way to vast, furrowed fields and vineyards that grow some very good wine. Finally, you reach the area's most splendid natural attraction, Niagara Falls, which has impressed visitors from all over the world for more than a hundred years.

Our Lady of Immaculate Conception, Guelph

Niagara Peninsula and Surroundings

Bike Paths and Rail Trails

City/Area	Total Length (km)	Page
Cambridge to Hamilton Rail Trail	75	69
Paris to Cambridge Rail Trail	19	70
Cambridge	20	71
Cambridge - Downtown	-	72
Elora to Cataract Rail Trail	47	73
Guelph	18	74-75
Hamilton	358	76
Hamilton - West	-	77
Hamilton - East	-	78
Hamilton - Centre	-	79
Hamilton - Downtown	-	80
Fonthill (Steve Bauer Trail)	6	81
Kitchener-Waterloo	40	82-83
Kitchener-Waterloo (Kitchener Area)	-	84
Kitchener-Waterloo (Waterloo Area)	-	85
Niagara Falls Area	58	86
St. Catharines	34.7	87

Dundurn Castle, Hamilton

Cambridge to Hamilton Rail Trail
75km

Niagara Peninsula and Surroundings

See Paris to Cambridge Rail Trail

© ULYSSES

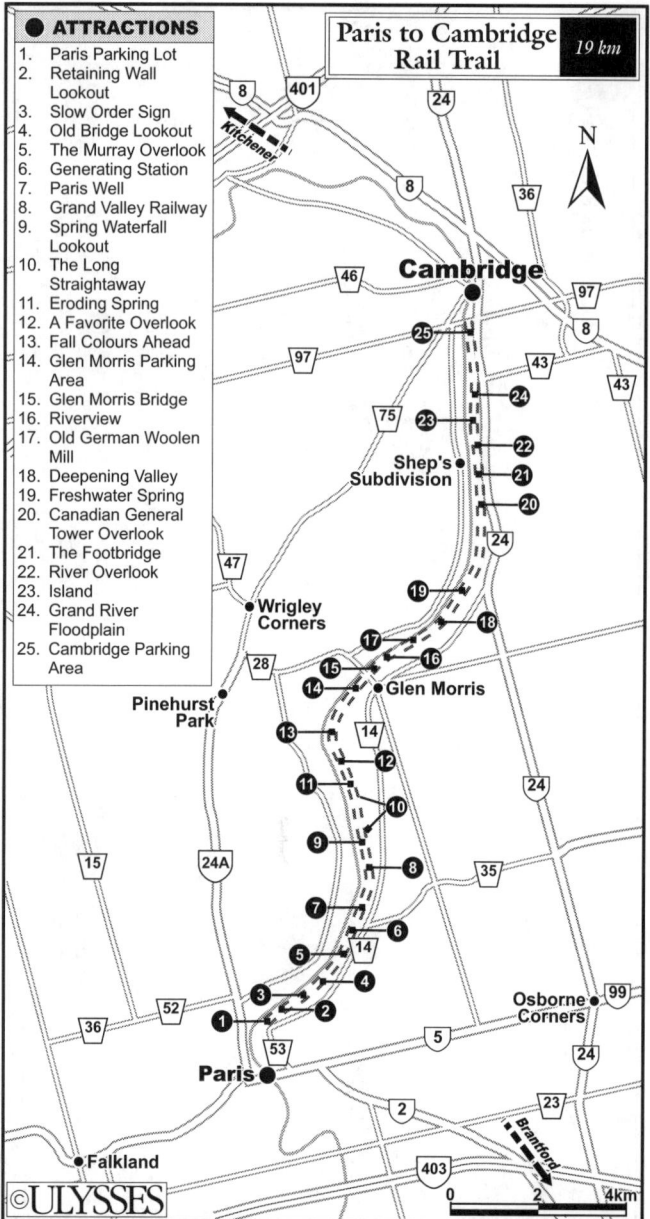

● ATTRACTIONS

1. Paris Parking Lot
2. Retaining Wall Lookout
3. Slow Order Sign
4. Old Bridge Lookout
5. The Murray Overlook
6. Generating Station
7. Paris Well
8. Grand Valley Railway
9. Spring Waterfall Lookout
10. The Long Straightaway
11. Eroding Spring
12. A Favorite Overlook
13. Fall Colours Ahead
14. Glen Morris Parking Area
15. Glen Morris Bridge
16. Riverview
17. Old German Woolen Mill
18. Deepening Valley
19. Freshwater Spring
20. Canadian General Tower Overlook
21. The Footbridge
22. River Overlook
23. Island
24. Grand River Floodplain
25. Cambridge Parking Area

Paris to Cambridge Rail Trail 19 km

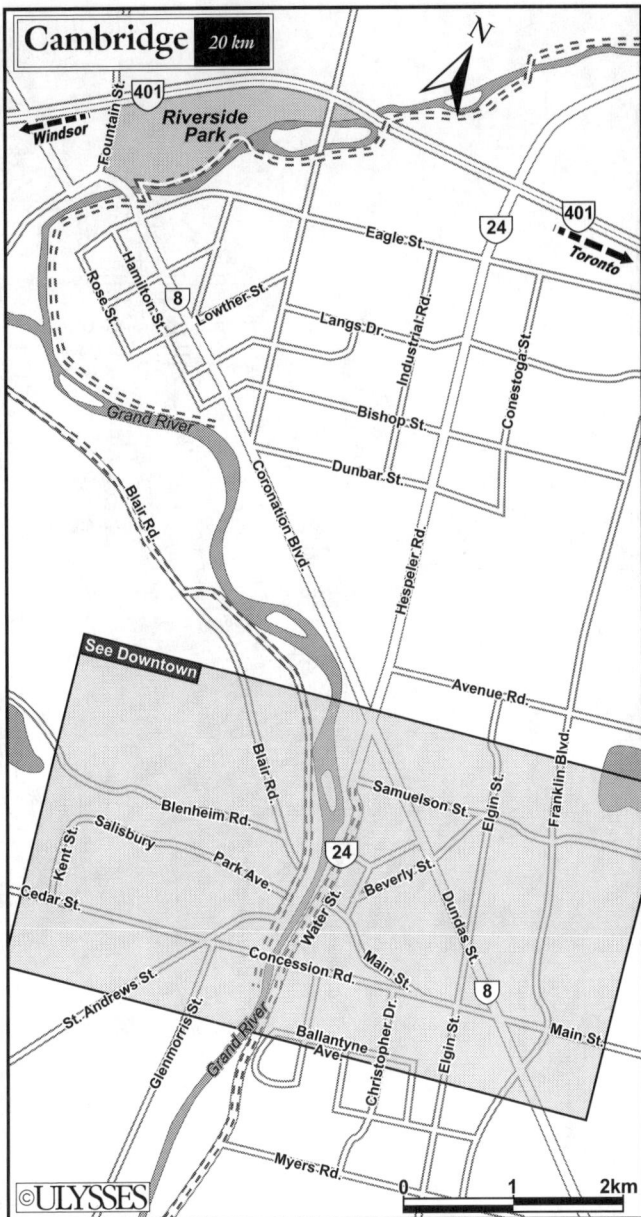

Cambridge 20 km

401 Windsor

Riverside Park

N

401 Toronto

Eagle St.

24

Fountain St.

Hamilton St.

Rose St.

8

Lowther St.

Langs Dr.

Industrial Rd.

Conestoga St.

Grand River

Bishop St.

Dunbar St.

Blair Rd.

Coronation Blvd.

Hespeler Rd.

Avenue Rd.

See Downtown

Blair Rd.

Blenheim Rd.

Samuelson St.

Elgin St.

Franklin Blvd.

Kent St.

Salisbury

Park Ave.

24

Beverly St.

Cedar St.

Water St.

Dundas St.

Concession Rd.

Main St.

St. Andrews St.

8

Glenmorris St.

Ballantyne Ave.

Christopher Dr.

Elgin St.

Main St.

Grand River

Myers Rd.

0   1   2km

©ULYSSES

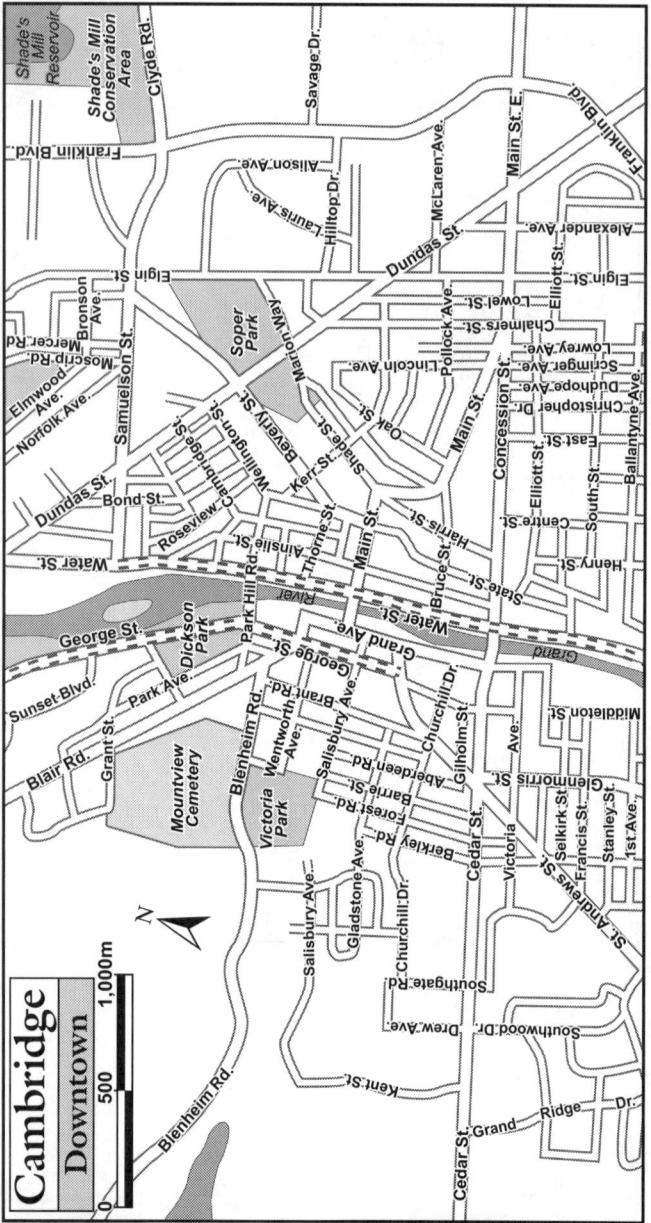

Cambridge
Downtown

0   500   1,000m

N

Shade's Mill Reservoir
Shade's Mill Conservation Area
Clyde Rd.
Savage Dr.
Franklin Blvd.
Main St. E.
Alison Ave.
Hilltop Dr.
Lauris Ave.
Elgin St.
Dundas St.
McLaren Ave.
Alexander Ave.
Elgin St.
Elliott St.
Lowel St.
Chalmers St.
Pollock Ave.
Lowrey Ave.
Scrimger Ave.
Duphope Ave.
Christopher Dr.
Lincoln Ave.
Soper Park
Marion Way
Concession St.
East St.
Ballantyne Ave.
Bronson Ave.
Mercer Rd.
Moscrip Rd.
Elmwood Ave.
Norfolk Ave.
Samuelson St.
Cambridge St.
Wellington St.
Beverly St.
Shade St.
Kerr St.
Oak St.
Main St.
Elliott St.
Centre St.
South St.
Dundas St.
Bond St.
Roseview C.
Ainslie St.
Thorne St.
Harris St.
Henry St.
Water St.
Park Hill Rd.
Main St.
Bruce St.
State St.
River
George St.
Dickson Park
Grand Ave.
Water St.
Grand
Sunset Blvd.
Park Ave.
George St.
George St.
Brant Rd.
Churchill Dr.
Middleton St.
Blair Rd.
Grant St.
Blenheim Rd.
Wentworth Ave.
Salisbury Ave.
Gilholm St.
Mountview Cemetery
Victoria Park
Barrie St.
Aberdeen St.
Glenmorris St.
Selkirk St.
Francis St.
Stanley St.
1st Ave.
Forest Rd.
Berkley Rd.
Cedar St.
Victoria
St. Andrews St.
Salisbury Ave.
Gladstone Ave.
Churchill Dr.
Southgate Rd.
Drew Ave.
Southwood Dr.
Kent St.
Cedar St.
Grand
Ridge Dr.
Blenheim Rd.

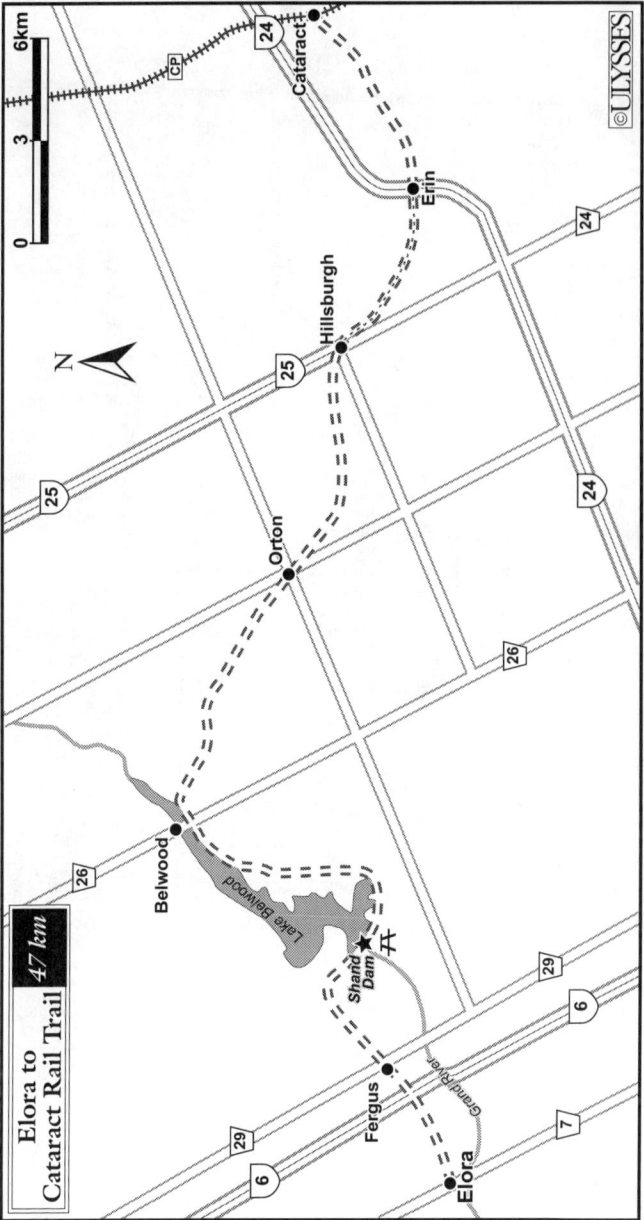

Niagara Peninsula and Surroundings

Elora to
Cataract Rail Trail
47 km

Cataract

Erin

Hillsburgh

Orton

Belwood

Lake Belwood

Shand
Dam

Fergus

Grand River

Elora

© ULYSSES

0   3   6km

N

CP

24

25

26

29

6

7

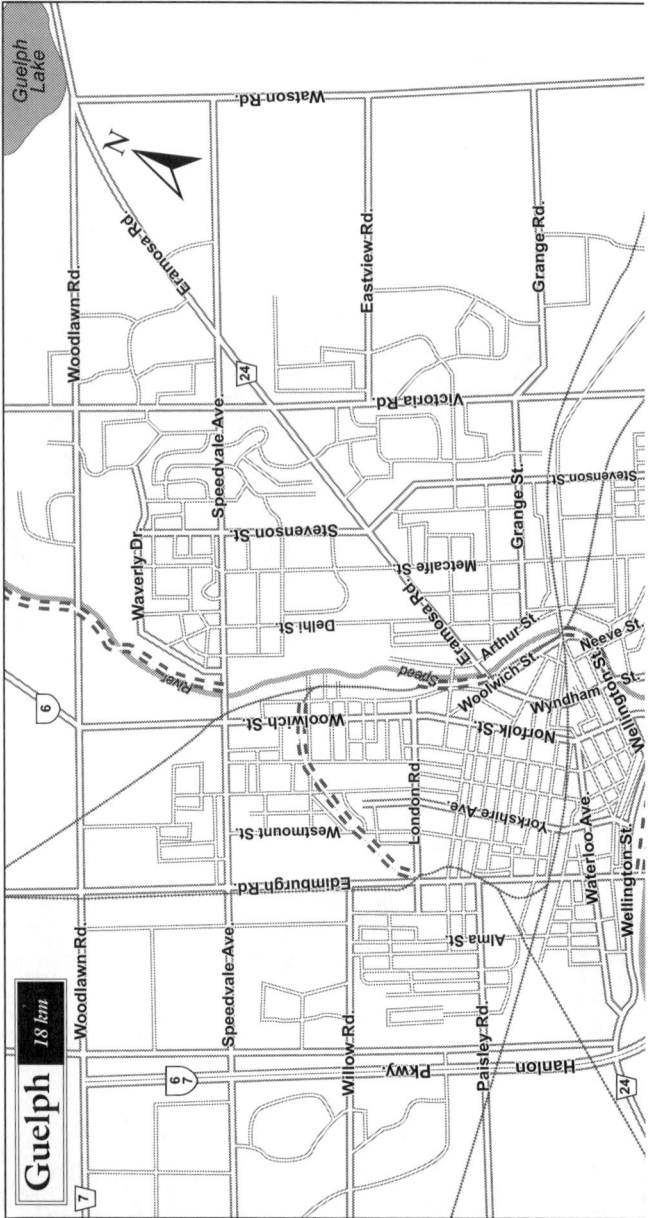

Guelph

18 km

Guelph Lake

N

Watson Rd.
Woodlawn Rd.
Eramosa Rd.
24
Eastview Rd.
Grange Rd.
Victoria Rd.
Speedvale Ave.
Stevenson St.
Grange St.
Stevenson St.
Waverly Dr.
Stevenson St.
Metcalfe St.
Delhi St.
Eramosa Rd.
Arthur St.
River
6
Speed
Woolwich St.
Neeve St.
Woolwich St.
Woolwich St.
Wyndham
Norfolk St.
Wellington St.
London Rd.
Yorkshire Ave.
Westmount St.
Waterloo Ave.
Edinburgh Rd.
Wellington St.
Alma St.
Woodlawn Rd.
Speedvale Ave.
Willow Rd.
Paisley Rd.
Hanlon
24
6
7
Pkwy
7

© ULYSSES

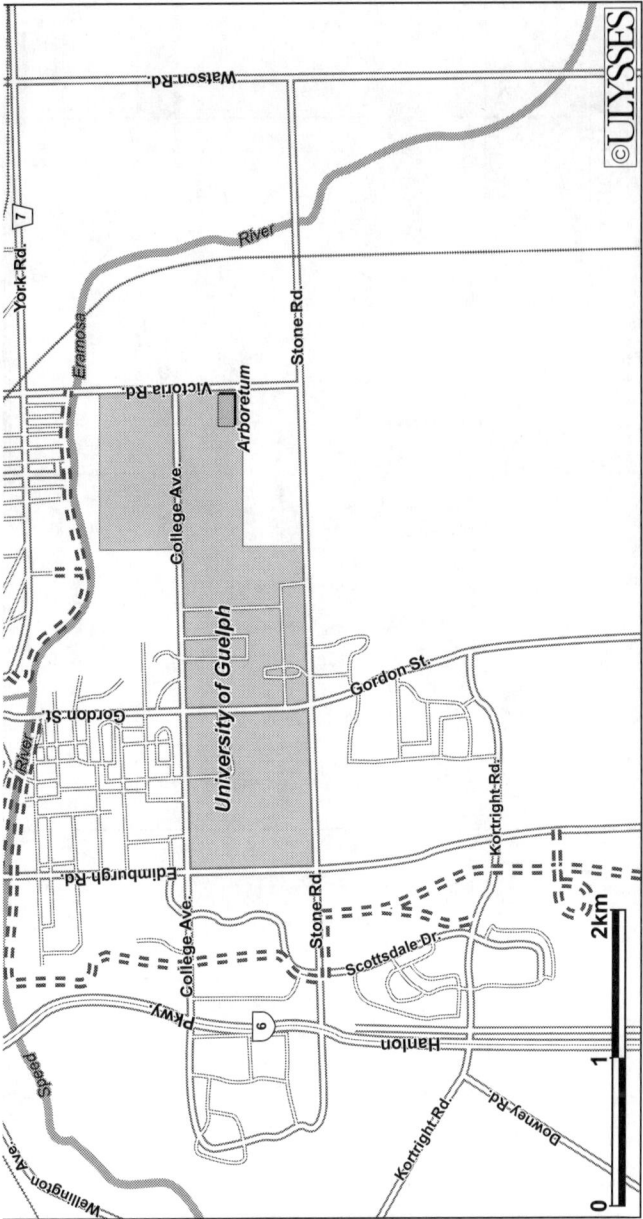

Niagara Peninsula and Surroundings

Watson Rd.

York Rd.

7

Eramosa

River

Stone Rd.

Victoria Rd.

Arboretum

College Ave.

University of Guelph

River

Gordon St.

Gordon St.

Edinburgh Rd.

College Ave.

Stone Rd.

Kortright Rd. E.

Scottsdale Dr.

Prkwy.

Hanlon

6

Kortright Rd.

Downey Rd.

Wellington Ave.

Speeds

0   1   2km

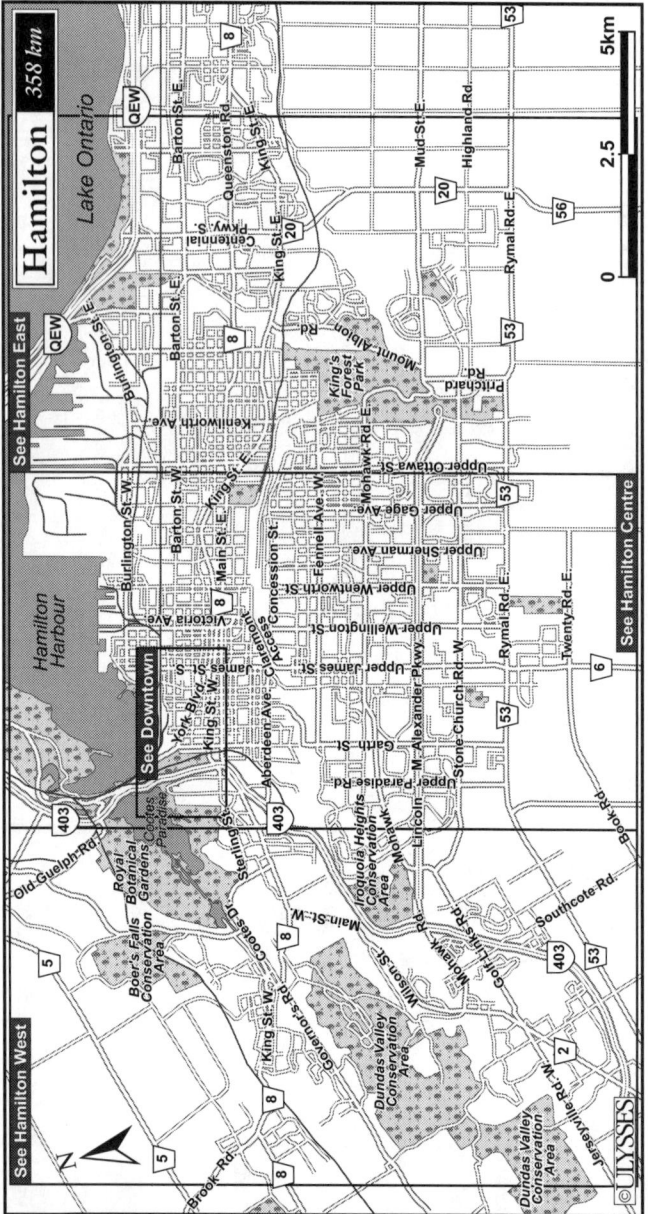

Hamilton

358 km

Lake Ontario

QEW

See Hamilton East

See Hamilton West

See Hamilton Centre

See Downtown

Hamilton Harbour

N

0   2.5   5km

QEW

Barton St. E.
Queenston Rd.
King St. E.
Centennial Pkwy. S.
King St. E.
Barton St. E.
Burlington St. E.
Kenilworth Ave.
King's Forest Park
Mount Albion Rd.
Pritchard Rd.
Upper Ottawa St.
Upper Gage Ave.
Upper Sherman Ave.
Mohawk Rd. E.
Fennell Ave. E.
Upper Wentworth St.
Upper Wellington St.
Upper James St.
Rymal Rd. E.
Twenty Rd. E.
Mud St. E.
Highland Rd.
Rymal Rd. E.
Burlington St. W.
Barton St. W.
King St. W.
Main St. E.
Cannon St.
Catharine St.
Victoria Ave.
Concession St.
Aberdeen Ave.
Garth St.
Upper Paradise Rd.
M. Alexander Pkwy.
Stone Church Rd. W.
Lincoln M. Alexander Pkwy.
York Blvd.
James St. S.
King St. W.
Sterling St.
Royal Botanical Gardens
Old Guelph Rd.
Boer's Falls Conservation Area
Coote's Paradise
Iroquois Heights Conservation Area
Mohawk Rd.
Southcote Rd.
Mohawk St.
Wilson St.
Main St. W.
Cootes Dr.
King St. W.
Governor's Rd.
Brock Rd.
Dundas Valley Conservation Area
Jerseyville Rd. W.
Golf Links Rd.
Dundas Valley Conservation Area

© ULYSSES

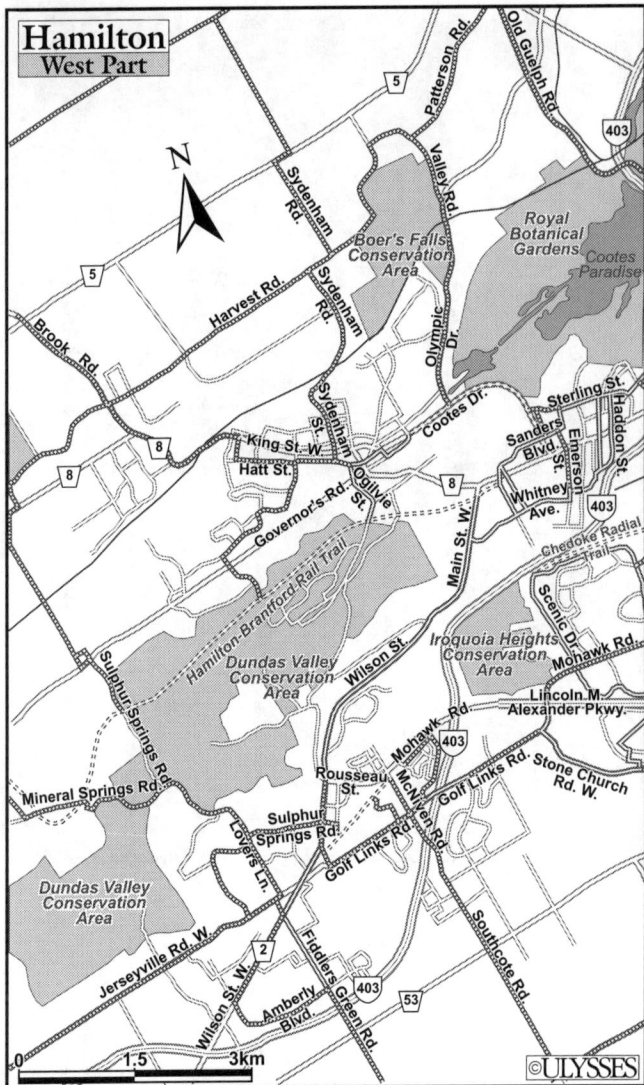

Hamilton
West Part

N

Patterson Rd.

Old Guelph Rd.

5

403

Sydenham Rd.

Valley Rd.

Boer's Falls Conservation Area

Royal Botanical Gardens

Cootes Paradise

5

Harvest Rd.

Sydenham Rd.

Brook Rd.

Olympic Dr.

Sterling St.

Haddon St.

Cootes Dr.

Sanders Blvd.

Emerson St.

8

King St. W.

Sydenham St.

Ogilvie St.

8

Whitney Ave.

403

Hatt St.

Governor's Rd.

Main St. W.

Chedoke Radial Trail

Hamilton-Brantford Rail Trail

Scenic Dr.

Dundas Valley Conservation Area

Wilson St.

Iroquoia Heights Conservation Area

Mohawk Rd.

Sulphur Springs Rd.

Mohawk Rd.

403

Lincoln M. Alexander Pkwy.

Rousseau St.

McNiven Rd.

Golf Links Rd.

Stone Church Rd. W.

Mineral Springs Rd.

Lovers Ln.

Sulphur Springs Rd.

Golf Links Rd.

Dundas Valley Conservation Area

Jerseyville Rd. W.

Wilson St. W.

2

Fiddler's Green Rd.

Amberly Blvd.

403

53

Southcote Rd.

0   1,5   3km

©ULYSSES

Niagara Peninsula and Surroundings

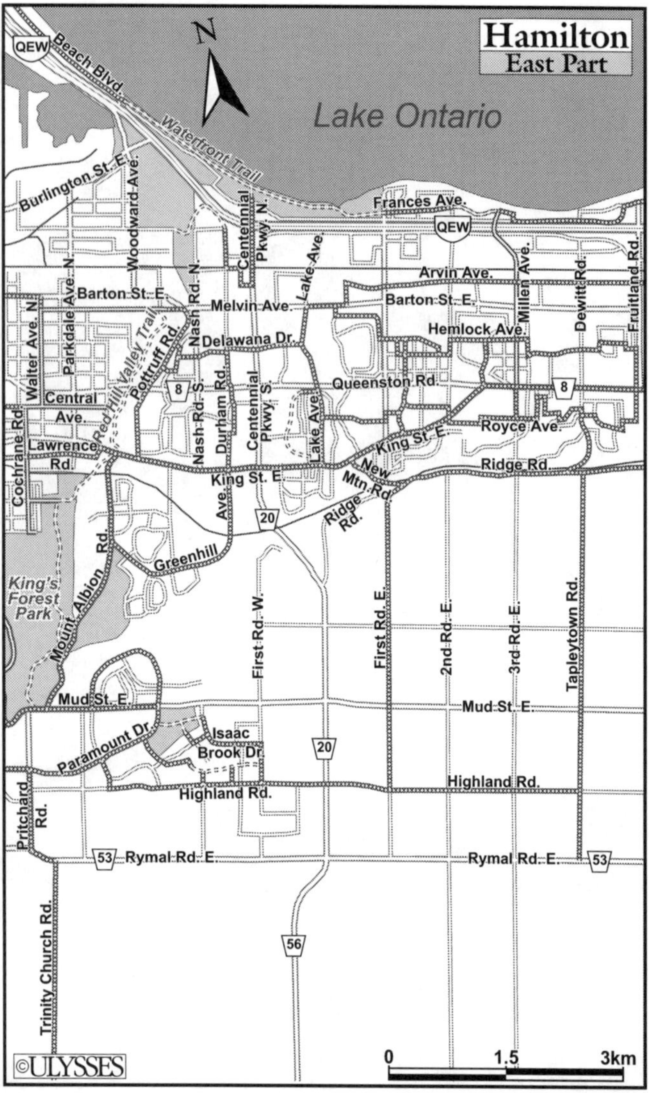

Hamilton
East Part
N
Lake Ontario
QEW
Beach Blvd.
Waterfront Trail
Burlington St. E.
Woodward Ave.
Centennial Pkwy. N.
Frances Ave.
Lake Ave.
Arvin Ave.
Millen Ave.
Dewitt Rd.
Fruitland Rd.
Barton St. E.
Parkdale Ave. N.
Nash Rd. N.
Melvin Ave.
Walter Ave. N.
Red Hill Valley Trail
Pottruff Rd.
Delawana Dr.
Hemlock Ave.
8
Queenston Rd.
Central Ave.
Nash Rd. S.
Durham Rd.
Centennial Pkwy. S.
Royce Ave.
Cochrane Rd.
Lawrence Rd.
King St. E.
Ridge Rd.
New Mtn. Rd.
Ave.
20
Ridge Rd.
Mount Albion Rd.
Greenhill
King's Forest Park
First Rd. W.
First Rd. E.
2nd Rd. E.
3rd Rd. E.
Tapleytown Rd.
Mud St. E.
Paramount Dr.
Isaac Brook Dr.
Highland Rd.
Pritchard Rd.
53
Rymal Rd. E.
Trinity Church Rd.
56
©ULYSSES
0
1.5
3km

Hamilton
Central Part

N

Hamilton
Harbour

403
Plains Rd. W.
Spring Gardens Rd.

Longwood Rd. N.
403

Burlington St. W.
Industrial Dr.
Burlington St. E.

See Downtown

Barton St. W.
James St. N.
Mary St.
Wellington St.
Victoria Ave.
Barton St. E.
Sherman Ave.
Kenilworth

York Blvd.
Dundurn St. S.
King St. W.
Main St. W.
8
Main St. E.
Gage Ave. S.
King St. E.
Ottawa St.
8

Charlton Ave.
Cumberland
Central Ave.
Lawrence Rd.

Aberdeen Ave.
Claremont Access
Ave.
Park Ave.

Chedoke Radial Trail
Beckett Dr.
Concession St.
Queensdale Ave. E.
Brucedale Ave. E.

Fennell Ave. W.
Fennell Ave. E.
Mtn. Brow Blvd.

W. 5th St.
Upper James St.
S. Bend Rd.
Upper Wentworth St.
E. 25th St.
Macassa Ave.
45th St.
Palmer Rd.
Broker Dr.
Upper Ottawa St.

Bendamere Ave.

Upper Paradise Rd.
Garth St.
Mohawk Rd.
Manning Ave.
Mohawk Rd. E.
King's Forest Park

6
Limeridge Rd. W.
Upper Wellington St.
Upper Sherman Ave.
Upper Gage Ave.
Limeridge Rd. E.

Lincoln M. Alexander Pkwy.

Stone Church Rd. W.
Stone Church Rd. E.

W. 5th St.
Eleanor Ave.

53
Malton Dr.
Rymal Rd. E.
Miles Rd.
53

Aldercrest Ave.
Twenty Rd. E.

Book Rd.
6

©ULYSSES
0   1.5   3km

Niagara Peninsula and Surroundings

Downtown Hamilton

● ATTRACTIONS

1. Hess Village
2. Art Gallery of Hamilton
3. Canadian Football Hall of Fame and Museum
4. Whitehern House
5. McMaster University
6. Dundurn Castle
7. Hamilton Military Museum
8. Royal Botanical Gardens

Hamilton Harbour

Bayfront Park

Cootes Paradise

Jackson Square

Hamilton Place

© ULYSSES

0   400   800m

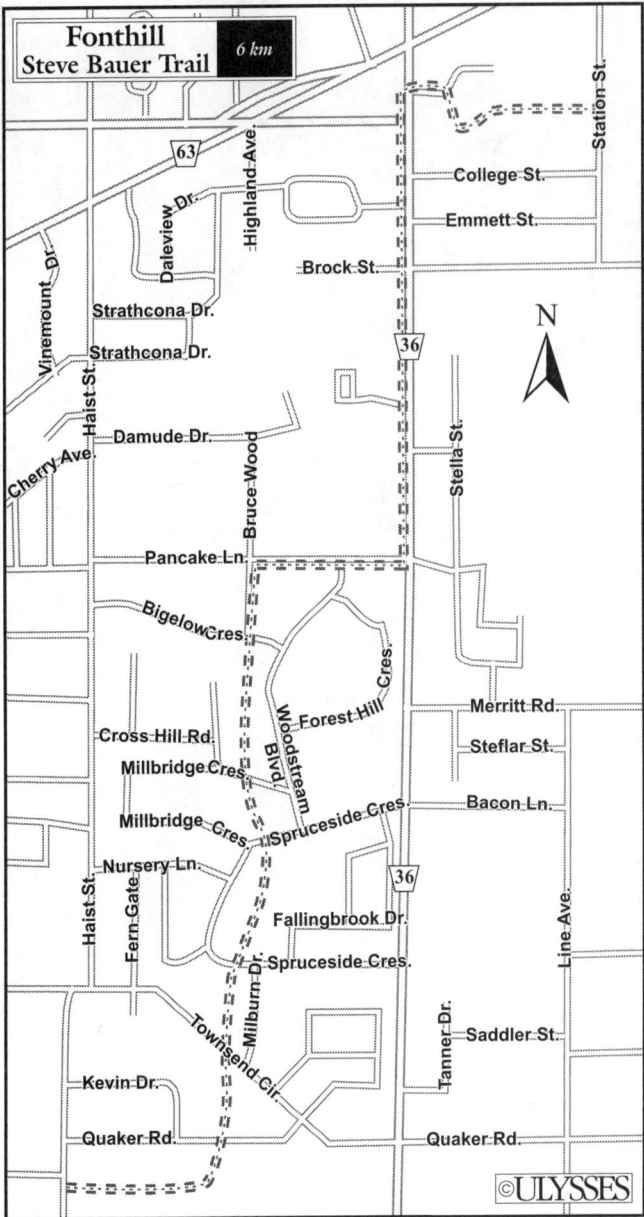

Fonthill
Steve Bauer Trail 6 km

63

College St.

Emmett St.

Station St.

Highland Ave.

Daleview Dr.

Brock St.

N

Vinemount Dr.

Strathcona Dr.

Strathcona Dr.

36

Haist St.

Damude Dr.

Stella St.

Cherry Ave.

Bruce-Wood

Pancake Ln.

Bigelow Cres.

Forest Hill Cres.

Woodstream Blvd.

Merritt Rd.

Cross Hill Rd.

Steflar St.

Millbridge Cres.

Millbridge Cres.

Spruceside Cres.

Bacon Ln.

Nursery Ln.

36

Haist St.

Fern Gate

Fallingbrook Dr.

Spruceside Cres.

Milburn Dr.

Line Ave.

Tanner Dr.

Saddler St.

Townsend Cir.

Kevin Dr.

Quaker Rd.

Quaker Rd.

©ULYSSES

Niagara Peninsula and Surroundings

Kitchener - Waterloo

40 km

N

Woolwich Rd.

Bingeman Park

Thompson

Bloomingdale Rd.

Bridge St. E.

Waterloo Kitchener

Grand River

Grand River

Thompson Park

86

Victoria St. N.

Bridge St.

Bechtel Park

Lancaster St. W.

Lexington Rd.

Hillside Park

University Ave. E.

Breithaupt Park

Columbia St.

86

Bridgeport Rd.

Webster St. S.

Queen St. N.

King St. N.

Webster St. N.

Webster St. N.

Waterloo Kitchener

Erb St. E.

King St. S.

See Waterloo Area

Waterloo Park

King St. S.

Victoria St. S.

Laurel Creek Conservation Area

Columbia St. W.

Westmount Rd. N.

Westmount Rd. N.

Columbia Lake

Westmount Rd. W.

University Ave. W.

Glasgow St.

Bearinger Rd.

Fischer-Hallman Rd. N.

Erb St. W.

Fischer-Hallman Rd. S.

Waterloo Kitchener

Erbsville Rd.

© ULYSSES

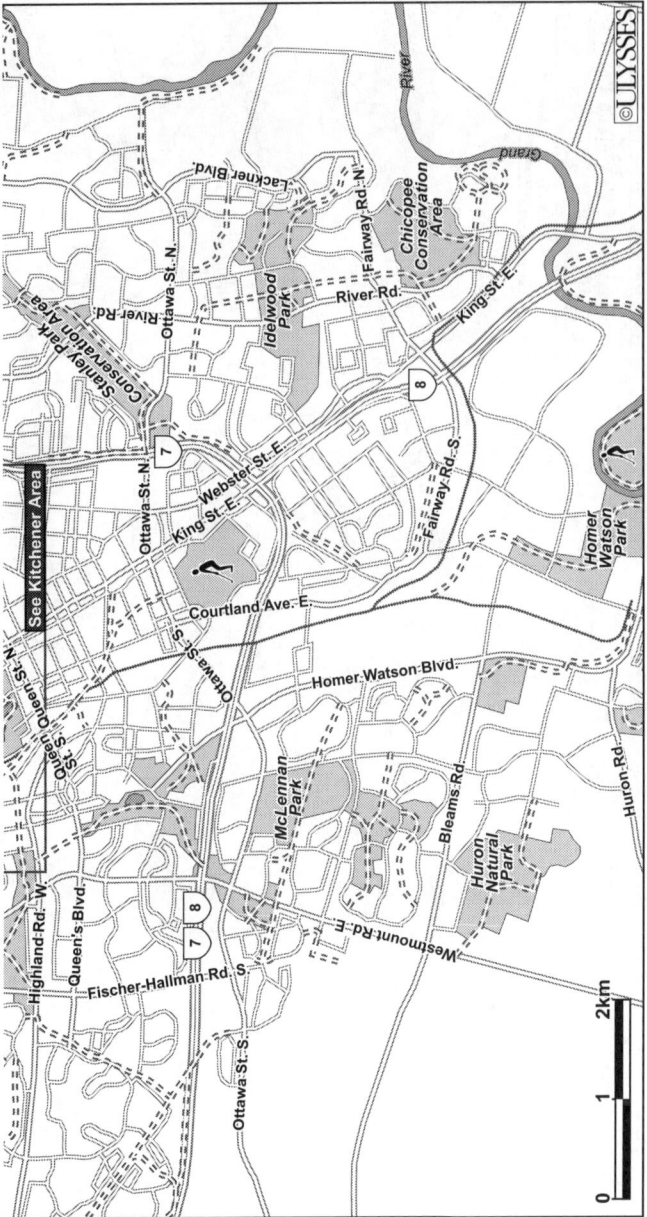

Niagara Peninsula and Surroundings

Grand River

Chicopee Conservation Area

Lacker Blvd.

Fairway Rd. N.

Idelwood Park

River Rd.

Ottawa St. N.

River Rd.

King St. E.

8

Stanley Park Conservation Area

River Rd.

See Kitchener Area

7

Ottawa St. N.

Webster St. E.

King St. E.

Fairway Rd. S.

Homer Watson Park

Courtland Ave. E.

Ottawa St. S.

Queen St. N.

Homer Watson Blvd.

Queen St. S.

McLennan Park

Bleams Rd.

Huron Rd.

Huron Natural Park

Highland Rd. W.

Queen's Blvd.

8

7

Westmount Rd. E.

Fischer-Hallman Rd. S.

Ottawa St. S.

0   1   2km

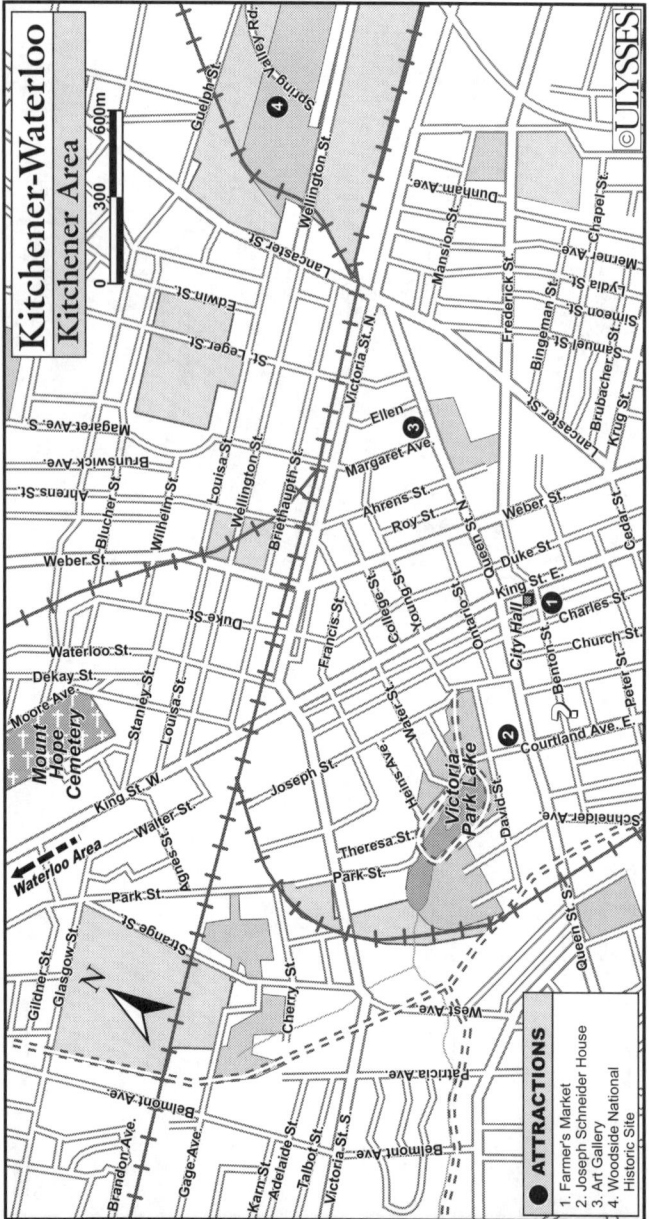

Kitchener-Waterloo

Kitchener Area

© ULYSSES

0   300   600m

Spring Valley Rd.
Guelph St.
Wellington St.
Lancaster St.
Edwin St.
St. Leger St.
Victoria St. N.

Dunham Ave.
Mansion St.
Merner Ave.
Chapel St.
Lydia St.
Frederick St.
Simeon St.
Samuel St.
Bingeman St.
Brubacher St.
Krug St.
Cedar St.

Margaret Ave. S.
Brunswick Ave.
Ahrens St.
Louisa St.
Wellington St.
Breithaupt St.
Ellen
Margaret Ave.
Ahrens St.
Roy St.
Weber St.
Lancaster St.
Blucher St.
Wilhelm St.
Weber St.
Duke St.
Francis St.
College St.
Young St.
Queen St. N.
Ontario St.
Duke St.
King St. E.
Charles St.
Church St.
City Hall
Benton St.
Peter St.

Waterloo St.
Dekay St.
Moore Ave.
Stanley St.
Louisa St.
Mount Hope Cemetery

King St. W.
Walter St.
Agnes St.
Joseph St.
Theresa St.
Park St.
Courtland Ave. E.
Schneider Ave.
Victoria Park Lake
Heins Ave.
Water St.
David St.
Queen St. S.

Waterloo Area

Park St.
Strange St.
Gildner St.
Glasgow St.
Cherry St.
West Ave.
Patricia Ave.
Belmont Ave.
Brandon Ave.
Gage Ave.
Karn St.
Adelaide St.
Talbot St.
Victoria St. S.
Belmont Ave.

N

ATTRACTIONS

1. Farmer's Market
2. Joseph Schneider House
3. Art Gallery
4. Woodside National Historic Site

Kitchener-Waterloo
Waterloo Area

ATTRACTIONS

1. Canadian Clay and Glass Gallery

0   300   600m

Niagara Peninsula and Surroundings

Bechtel Park

86

Bluevale St.

Harvard Rd.

Mayfield Ave.

Christopher Dr.

Lillian Dr.

Meaford Dr.

86

Mayfield Ave.

Margaret Ave.

Bluevale St.

Nelson Ave.

Breithaupt Park

Washington Ave.

Vernon Ave.

Lincoln Rd.

Ellis Cres.

Margaret Ave.

Bellehaven Pl.

Dixie Ct.

Carter Ave.

Allen St. E.

Cornwall St.

Bristol St.

Alvin St.

Weber St. East

University Ave.

Weber St.

Lodge St.

Marshall St.

Brighton St.

Bridgeport Rd.

Devitt Ave.

Dover St.

Rodney St.

Union St.

Kitchener Area

Elgin Cr.

Noecker St.

Pepper St.

Tweed St.

Moore Ave.

Waterloo St.

Bricker Ave.

Ezra Ave.

Central St.

King Street

Bridgeport Rd.

Princess St.

Regina St.

Willow St.

John St.

Herbert St.

Mount Hope Cemetery

Wilfrid Laurier University

Albert St.

Dorset St.

King St.

Union St.

Waterloo Park

Caroline St.

Erb St.

William St.

Park St.

York St.

Allen St. E.

Centennial Park

Euclid Ave.

Euclid Ave.

Belmont Ave.

Norman Ave.

Avondale Ave.

Erb St.

Dunbar Rd.

Dawson St.

Alexandra Ave.

Beverley St.

Roslin Ave.

John St.

©ULYSSES

Niagara Falls Area   58 km

Lake Ontario

Niagara-on-the-Lake

Fort George National Historic Park

87
100
85

McNab

Virgil

55

St. Catharines

QEW

89

405

Queenston

Niagara Parks Botanical Gardens

18

N

93

104

NEW YORK (U.S.A.)

31

429

Power Glen

406

58

St. Johns

Effingham

20

Ridgeville

Pelham Corners

58

Welland

58

58a

58

140

Niagara Falls

420

Victoria Park

Thorold

Cook Mills

Marineland

Chippawa

White Pigeon

Black Creek

Douglastown

Netherby

Snyder

190

Niagara Falls

American Falls

Canadian Falls

Tonawanda   384

Grand Island

290

QEW

190   384

425

Fort Erie

Port Colborne

Gasline

3   Ridgewood

Oak Hill

3

Lorraine

Pine Crest Point

Elco Beach

Cedar Bay

Sherkston Beaches

Thunder Bay

Bay Beach

Crystal Beach

Point Abino

1

Erie Beach

Crescent Park

Wavecrest

Fort Erie Beach

33

Waverly Beach

Buffalo

Lake Erie

CANADA
UNITED STATES

0   5   10km

©ULYSSES

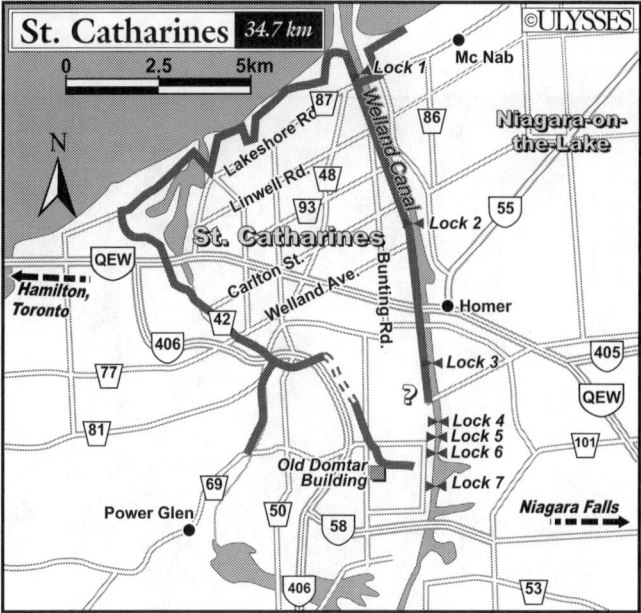

St. Catharines *34.7 km*

0   2.5   5km

©ULYSSES

N

Lock 1   Mc Nab

87   86   Niagara-on-the-Lake

Lakeshore Rd.

Linwell Rd.   48

93   Lock 2   55

St. Catharines

QEW   Carlton st.   Welland Ave.   Lock 3   405

Hamilton, Toronto   42   Homer   QEW

406   Bunting Rd.

77   ?   101

81   Lock 4
Lock 5
Lock 6

Old Domtar Building   Lock 7

69   50   *Niagara Falls*

Power Glen   58   53

406

Welland Canal

McFarland House, Niagara-on-the-Lake

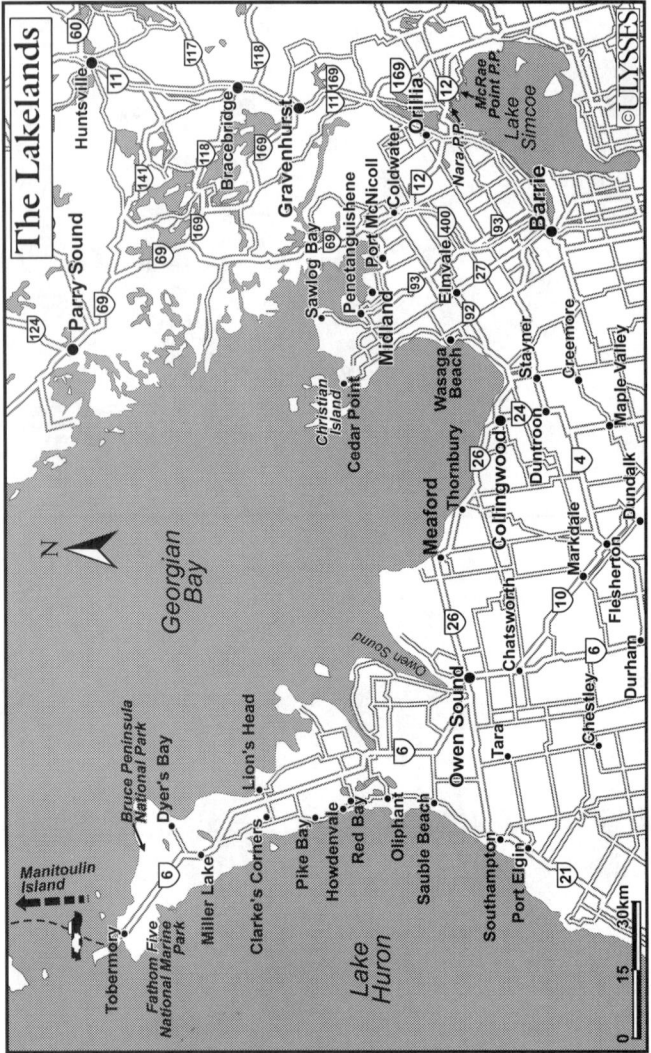

The Lakelands

© ULYSSES

Huntsville
Parry Sound
Bracebridge
Gravenhurst
Orillia
McRae
Point P.P.
Lake
Simcoe
Barrie
Nara P.P.
Coldwater
Port McNicoll
Penetanguishene
Midland
Sawlog Bay
Elmvale
Stayner
Creemore
Christian
Island
Cedar Point
Wasaga
Beach
Maple Valley
Thornbury
Duntroon
Meaford
Collingwood
Markdale
Flesherton
Dundalk
Georgian
Bay
Chatsworth
Durham
Owen Sound
Tara
Chesley
Lion's Head
Dyer's Bay
Bruce Peninsula
National Park
Miller Lake
Clarke's Corners
Pike Bay
Howdenvale
Red Bay
Oliphant
Sauble Beach
Southampton
Port Elgin
Manitoulin
Island
Tobermory
Fathom Five
National Marine
Park
Lake
Huron

N

0   15   30km

The Lakelands

The Lakelands embrace the maple-lined streets of Port Elgin, the inviting waters of Lake Huron and the majestic limestone cliffs of Georgian Bay.

*Longhouse,
Sainte-Marie Among the Hurons*

this territory, each with its own extraordinary scenery. The first region, the Muskoka Lakes, is closest to Toronto and offers high quality tourist facilities that blend into the landscape. Luxurious residences, marinas for pleasure boats and charming villages are the main attractions in this area, cottage country for wealthy Torontonians.

Cycling this area of the province can take your breath away in more ways than one. Enjoy spectacular scenery, awe-inspiring wildlife and some great single-track. All roads in this part of the province follow the Bruce Trail to Tobermory's famous Fathom Five National Marine Park.

For many years, the area north of Toronto, called the "Lakelands," has been popular with visitors seeking a respite from the fast pace of city life in beautiful natural surroundings. There are three distinct regions in

The region further north borders on magnificent Georgian Bay. This area attracts visitors all year long because, in addition to its lovely beaches, it has the only downhill ski centre for many kilometres. It is also well known as the heart of the territory that was once occupied by the Huron Nation. Historical restorations help explain what this Aboriginal people's social structure, customs and traditions were like before the arrival of the first Europeans.

Beaver

The third region, the eastern shore of Lake Huron, has some pleasant little towns. However, its main attractions are the magnificent beaches at the edge of the enormous lake that stretches as far as the eye can see.

The Lakelands

Bike Paths and Rail Trails

City/Area	Total Length (km)	Page
North Simcoe Rail Trail	14.5	91
Barrie	4	92
Bracebridge (Strawberry Bay Lookout Trail)	5	93
Georgian Trail (Meaford to Collingwood)	32	94
Georgian Trail (Meaford)	-	95
Georgian Trail (Collingwood)	-	96
Midland	-	97
Orillia	4	98
Orillia to Coldwater Trail	14	99
Port Elgin - Southampton (Saugeen Railtrail)	7	100
Owen Sound (Bruce Trail)	12	101
Wasaga Beach	7	102

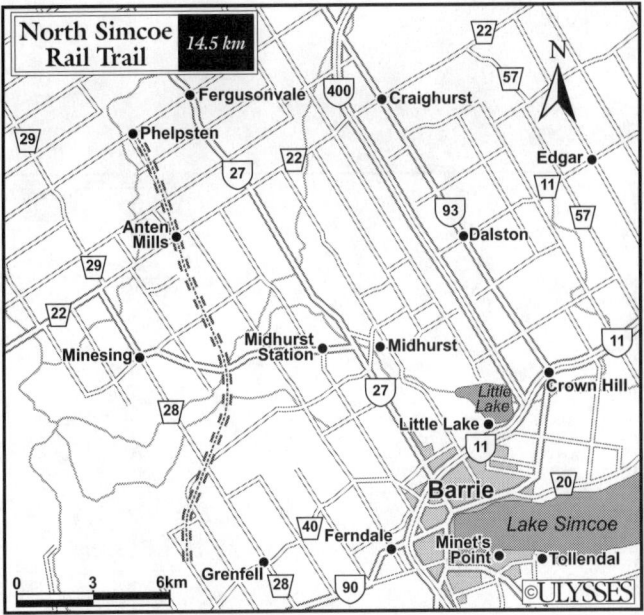

North Simcoe Rail Trail — 14.5 km

- Fergusonvale
- Phelpsten
- Craighurst
- Edgar
- Anten Mills
- Dalston
- Midhurst Station
- Midhurst
- Minesing
- Crown Hill
- *Little Lake*
- Little Lake
- Barrie
- Lake Simcoe
- Ferndale
- Minet's Point
- Tollendal
- Grenfell

0 3 6km

©ULYSSES

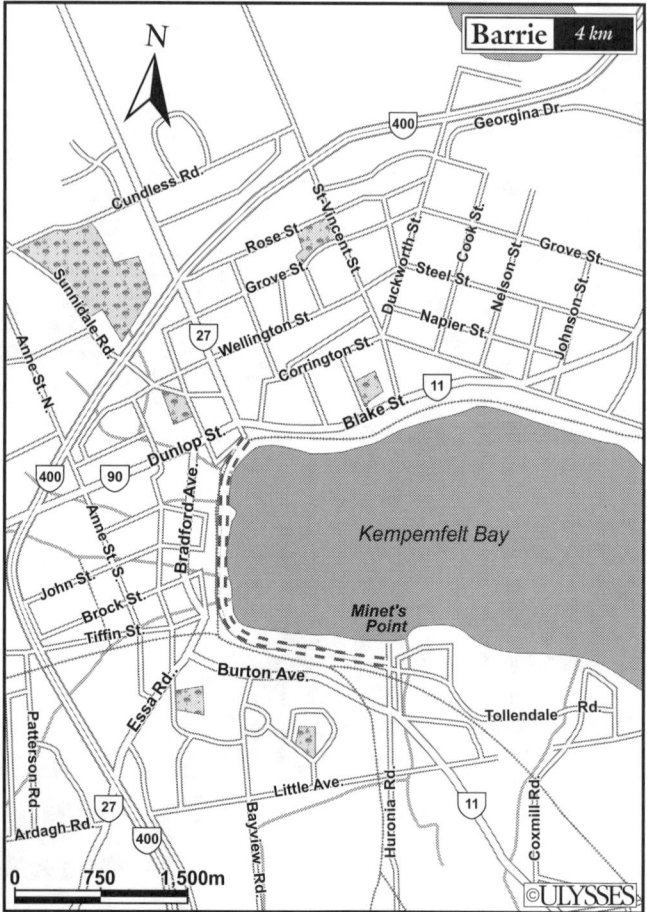

N

Barrie *4 km*

Georgina Dr.

400

Cundless Rd.

Sunnidale Rd.

Rose St.

St-Vincent St.

Grove St.

Cook St.

Grove St.

Duckworth St.

Steel St.

Nelson St.

Johnson St.

Anne St. N.

27

Wellington St.

Napier St.

Corrington St.

Blake St.

11

400

90

Dunlop St.

Bradford Ave.

Kempemfelt Bay

Anne St. S.

John St.

Brock St.

Tiffin St.

Minet's Point

Essa Rd.

Burton Ave.

Tollendale Rd.

Patterson Rd.

Huronia Rd.

Little Ave.

11

Coxmill Rd.

27

Ardagh Rd.

400

Bayview Rd.

0   750   1,500m

©ULYSSES

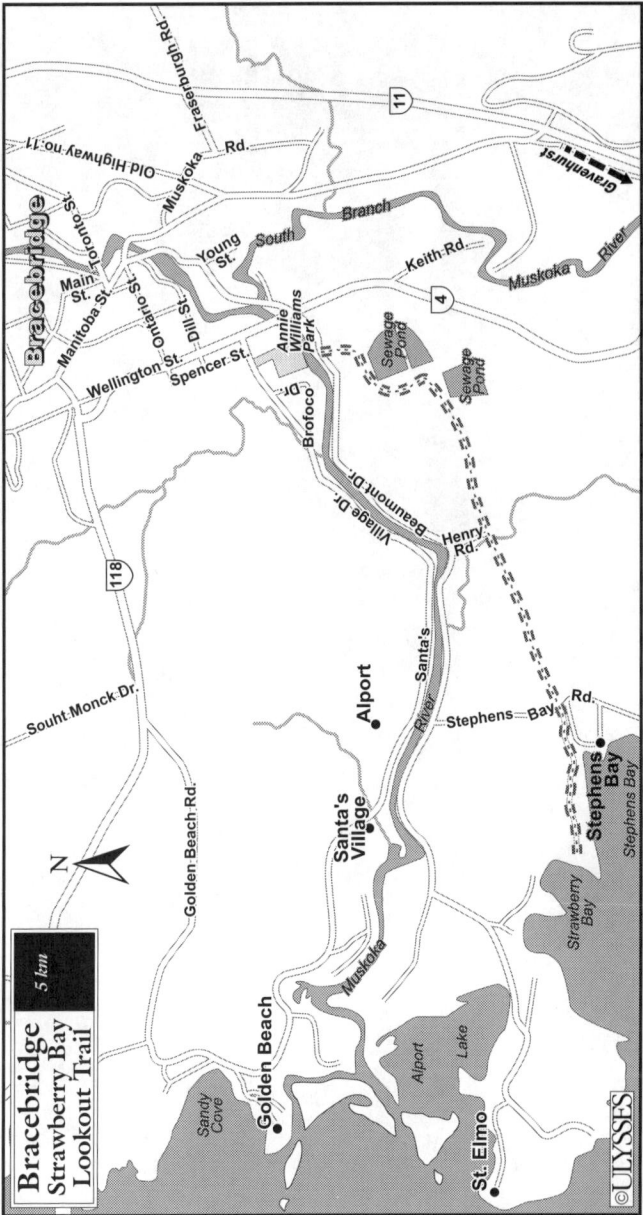

The Lakelands

Bracebridge
Strawberry Bay
Lookout Trail

5 km

N

Bracebridge

Old Highway no. 11
Muskoka Rd.
Fraserburgh Rd.
11
Gravenhurst

South Branch
Young St.
Keith Rd.
Muskoka River
4
Main St.
Manitoba St.
Toronto St.
Ontario St.
Dill St.
Wellington St.
Spencer St.
Annie Williams Park
Sewage Pond
Sewage Pond
Brofoco Dr.
118
Beaumont Dr.
Village Dr.
Henry Rd.
South Monck Dr.
Santa's River
Stephens Bay Rd.
Alport
Stephens Bay
Stephens Bay
Golden Beach Rd.
Santa's Village
Strawberry Bay
Muskoka
Alport Lake
Sandy Cove
Golden Beach
St. Elmo

© ULYSSES

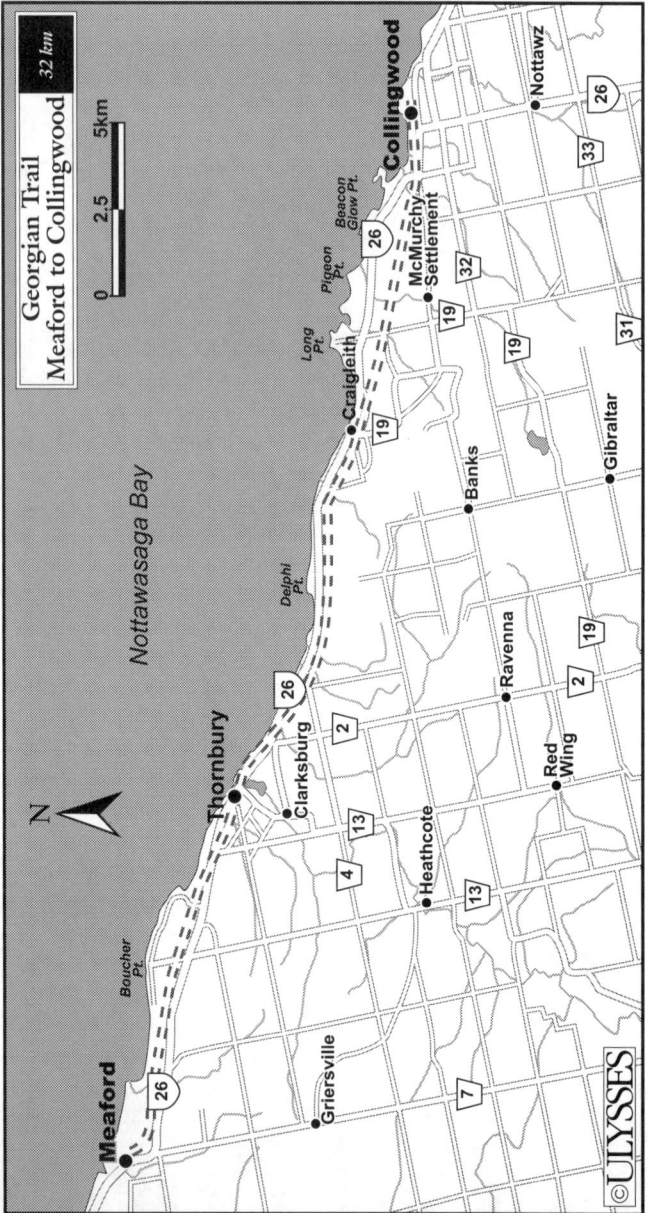

Georgian Trail
Meaford to Collingwood

32 km

0   2.5   5km

N

Nottawasaga Bay

Meaford
26

Boucher
Pt.

Thornbury
26

Clarksburg
2

4
13

Griersville
7

Heathcote
13

Delphi
Pt.

Long
Pt.

Craigleith
19

Pigeon
Pt.

Beacon
Glow Pt.
26

Collingwood

McMurchy
Settlement
19
32

19

33

26

Nottawz

31

Gibraltar

Banks

Ravenna
2
19

Red
Wing

© ULYSSES

Georgian Trail
Meaford

Susan St.

Thompson St.

Lombard St.

Collingwood St.

Nelson St.

Pearson St.

Sykes St.

Boucher St.

Margaret St.

Miller St.

Aikin St.

Grant Ave.

Bighead River

Centre St.

Union St.

Meaford Cr.

St. Vincent St.

Georgian Bay

Collingwood

12/13 Sideroad

©ULYSSES

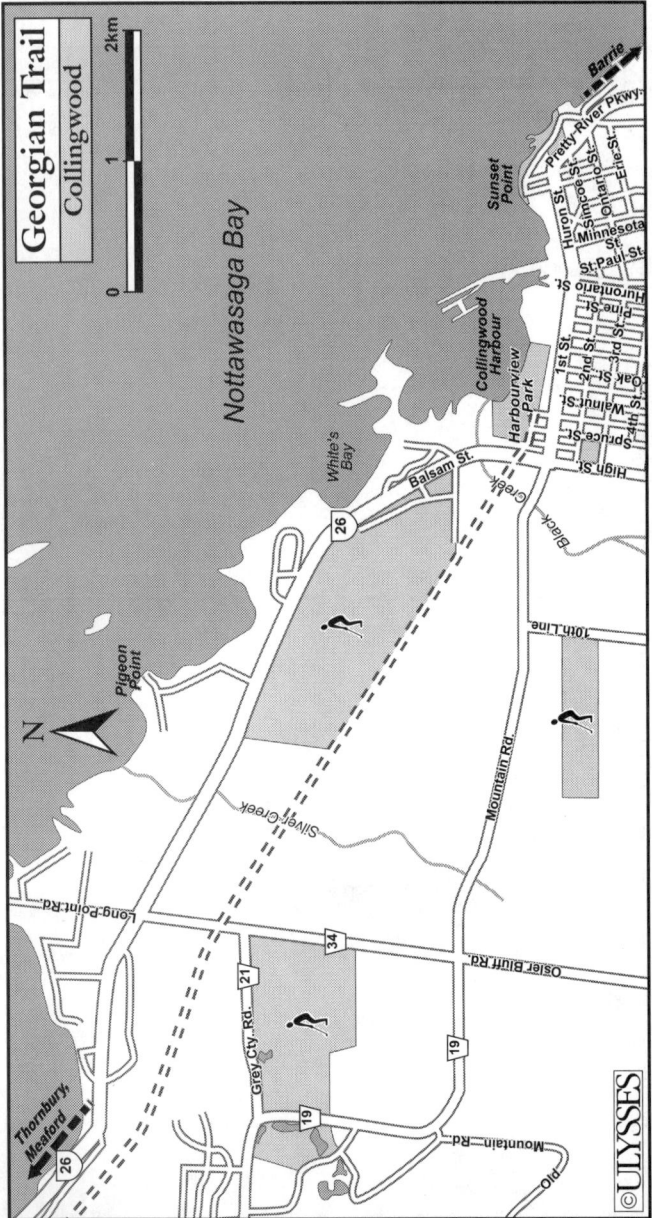

Georgian Trail
Collingwood

0   1   2km

Nottawasaga Bay

Barrie

Sunset
Point

Pretty River Pkwy

Huron St.
Simcoe St.
Ontario St.
Erie St.
Minnesota St.
St. Paul St.
Hurontario St.
Pine St.
1st St.
2nd St.
Oak St.
3rd St.
Walnut St.
4th St.
Spruce St.
High St.

Collingwood
Harbour

Harbourview
Park

White's
Bay

Balsam St.

Black Creek

26

10th Line

Mountain Rd.

Silver Creek

Pigeon
Point

N

Long Point Rd.

Osler Bluff Rd.

34

21

19

Grey Cty. Rd.

19

Mountain Rd.

Old

Thornbury,
Meaford

26

© ULYSSES

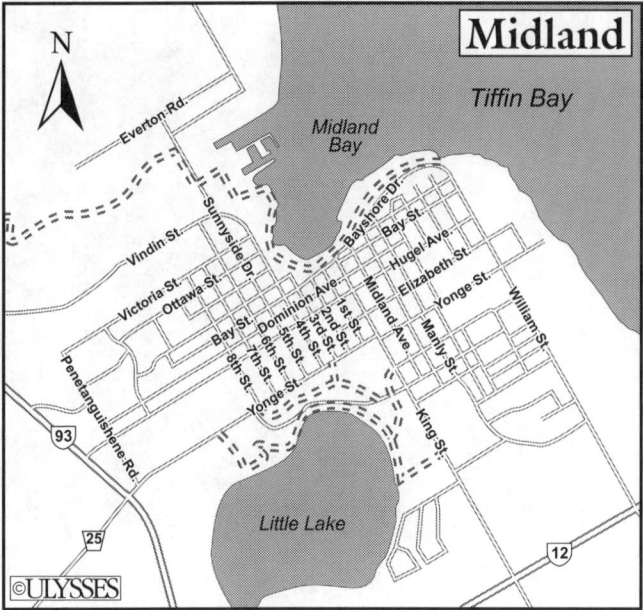

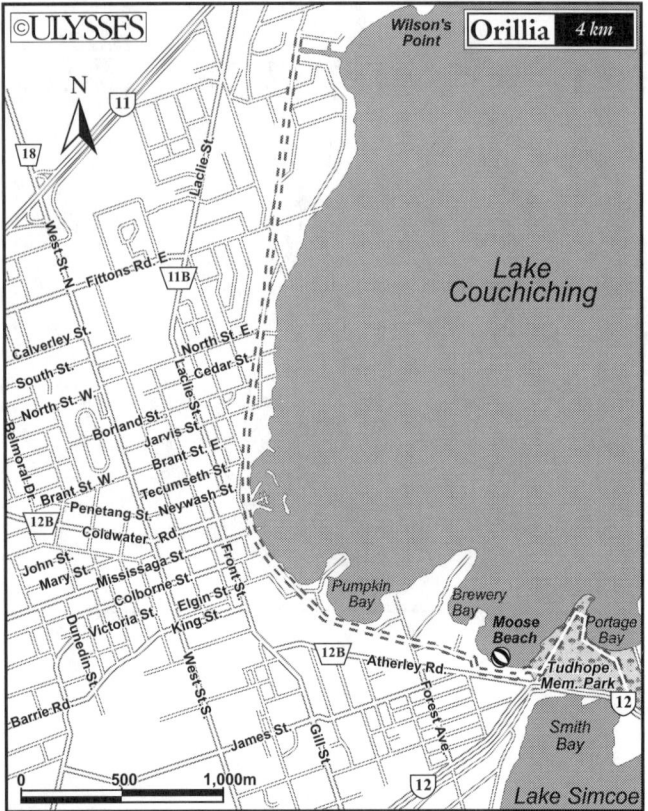

©ULYSSES

N

Orillia 4 km

Wilson's Point

Lake Couchiching

Lake Simcoe

West St. N.
Laclie St.
Fittons Rd. E.
11B
Calverley St.
South St.
North St. E.
North St. W.
Laclie St.
Cedar St.
Borland St.
Jarvis St.
Brant St. E.
Brant St. W.
Tecumseth St.
Penetang St.
Neywash St.
12B
Coldwater Rd.
John St.
Mary St.
Mississaga St.
Colborne St.
Victoria St.
Elgin St.
King St.
Front St.
Dunedin St.
Barrie Rd.
West St. S.
James St.
Gill St.
Pumpkin Bay
Brewery Bay
Moose Beach
Portage Bay
12B
Atherley Rd.
Forest Ave.
Tudhope Mem. Park
12
Smith Bay

0   500   1,000m

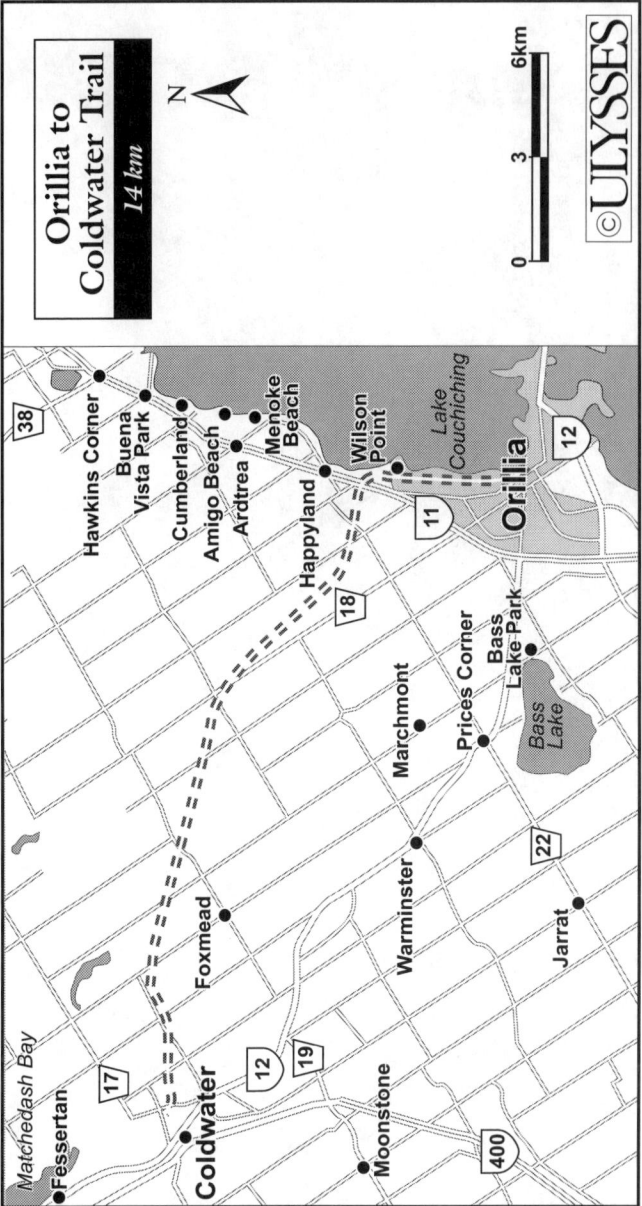

Orillia to
Coldwater Trail
14 km

N

© ULYSSES

0   3   6km

The Lakelands

Hawkins Corner

38

Buena
Vista Park

Cumberland

Amigo Beach

Ardtrea

Menoke
Beach

Happyland

Wilson
Point

*Lake
Couchiching*

11

18

Orillia

12

Prices Corner

Bass
Lake Park

Marchmont

*Bass
Lake*

22

Foxmead

Warminster

Jarrat

Matchedash Bay

Fessertan

17

Coldwater

12   19

Moonstone

400

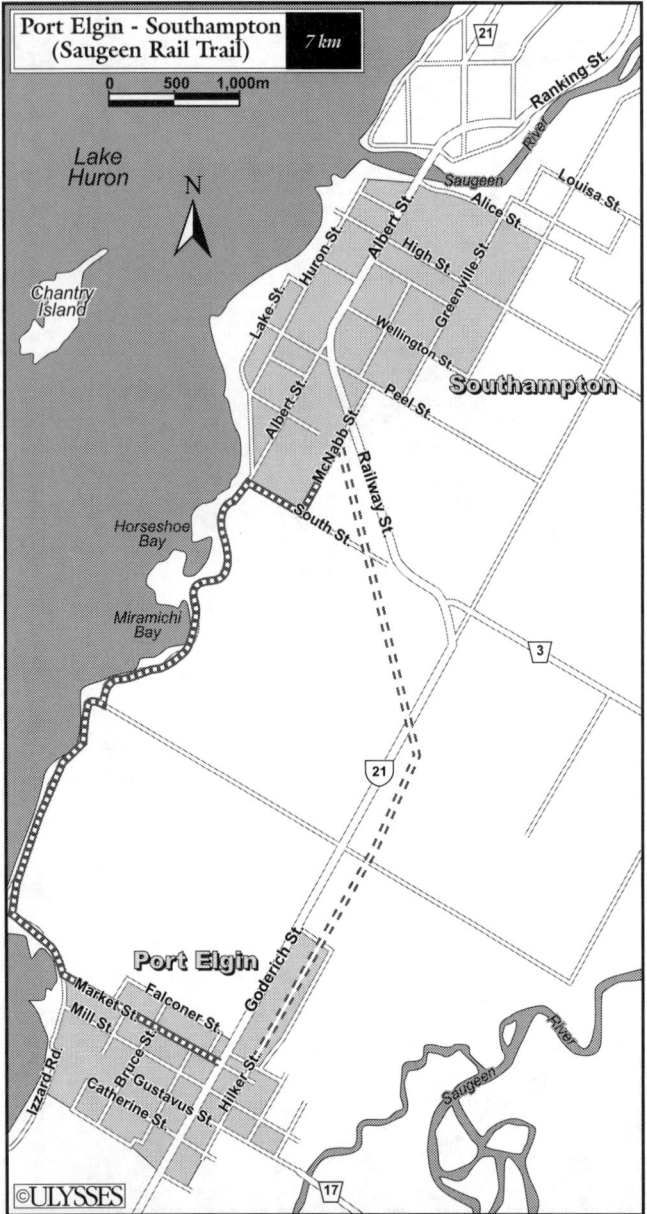

Port Elgin - Southampton
(Saugeen Rail Trail) 7 km

0   500   1,000m

Lake
Huron

Chantry
Island

N

Ranking St.

River

Saugeen

Alice St.

Louisa St.

Albert St.

High St.

Greenville St.

Lake St.

Huron St.

Wellington St.

Southampton

Peel St.

Albert St.

McNabb St.

Railway St.

Horseshoe
Bay

South St.

Miramichi
Bay

3

21

Goderich St.

Port Elgin

Market St.

Falconer St.

Mill St.

Bruce St.

Hilker St.

Gustavus St.

Izzard Rd.

Catherine St.

Saugeen

River

17

©ULYSSES

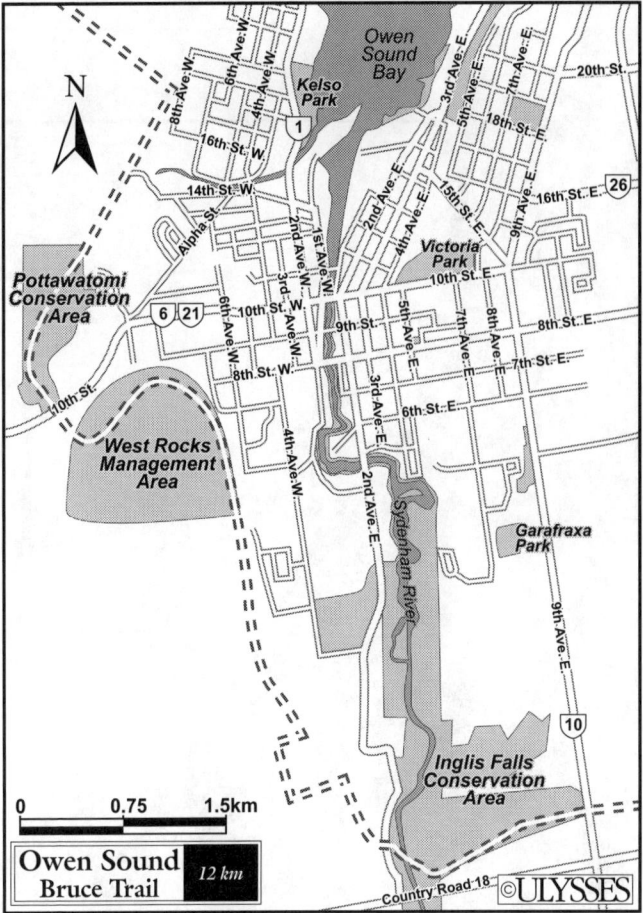

N

Owen Sound Bay

Kelso Park

8th Ave. W.
6th Ave. W.
4th Ave. W.

16th St. W.

14th St. W.

1

Alpha St.

2nd Ave. W.
1st Ave. W.

2nd Ave. E.

20th St.

3rd Ave. E.
5th Ave. E.
7th Ave. E.

18th St. E.

16th St. E.

26

15th St. E.

4th Ave. E.

9th Ave. E.

Victoria Park

10th St. E.

Pottawatomi Conservation Area

6 21

6th Ave. W.
10th Ave. W.

3rd Ave. W.

9th St.

5th Ave. E.

8th Ave. E.

8th St. E.

7th St. E.

10th St.

8th St. W.

3rd Ave. E.

6th St. E.

West Rocks Management Area

4th Ave. W.

2nd Ave. E.

Sydenham River

Garafraxa Park

9th Ave. E.

10

Inglis Falls Conservation Area

| 0 | 0.75 | 1.5km |

Owen Sound
Bruce Trail   12 km

Country Road 18

©ULYSSES

The Lakelands

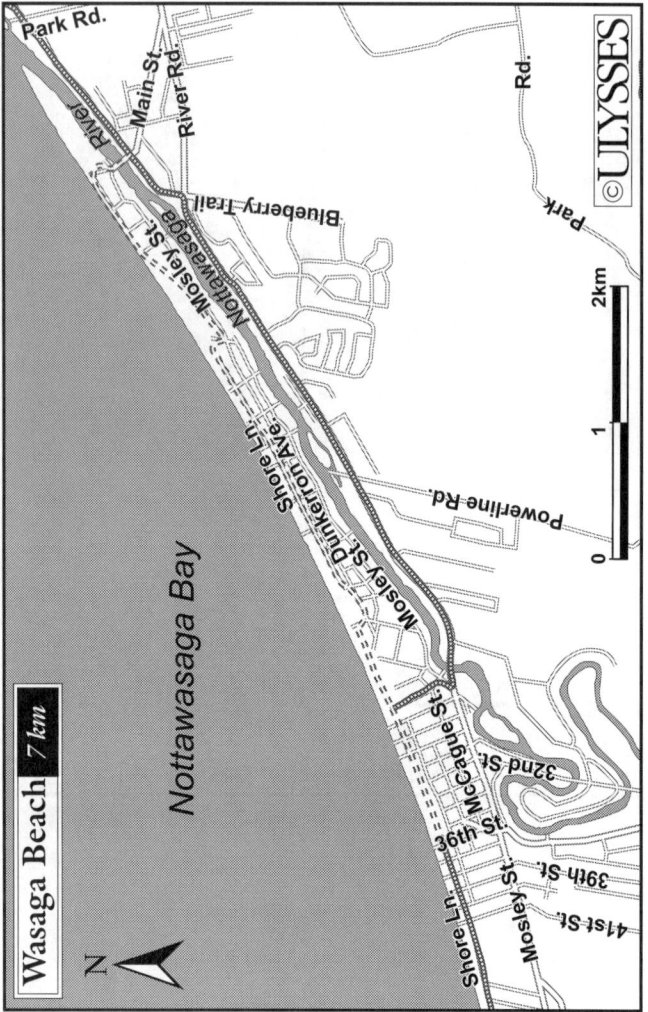

Wasaga Beach 7km

N

Nottawasaga Bay

Park Rd.

Main St.

River Rd.

River

Mosley St.

Nottawasaga

Blueberry Trail

Shore Ln.

Dunkerron Ave.

Mosley St.

Powerline Rd.

Park Rd.

McCague St.

32nd St.

36th St.

39th St.

41st St.

Mosley St.

Shore Ln.

© ULYSSES

0   1   2km

The Greater Toronto Area

Toronto's growth over the last 20 years has literally redefined the city.

It has blossomed into a metropolis with a decidedly cosmopolitan air.

Nowhere else in Canada are there as many different ethnic communities, a characteristic that distinguishes the city from the rest of Ontario and also with the Toronto of old. This cultural mosaic has created a dynamic microcosm, making Toronto the heart of culture in English-speaking Canada.

The Greater Toronto Area has something for everyone: excellent off-road cycling, a well-developed waterfront and world-class entertainment. When combined with its renowned inner-city cycling network, it is no wonder Toronto happens to be one of the most cycling-friendly cities in the world.

There is an extensive system of clearly indicated, well-used bicycle lanes in the city. The path network also happens to be well integrated with the subway system, allowing commuters to combine two environmentally friendly means of transportation. Cyclists can bring their bicycles into the subway but are restricted to the first and last cars. These lanes are not for the faint of heart, though, as the cars, buses and streetcars whiz by in all directions, separated from the cyclist by nothing but a white line painted on the asphalt.

A world away from these white lines, along the rivers that wind their way through the city, an entirely different type of cycling awaits. Forested riparian parks, which line the Humber and Don rivers, are home to some magical paths that transport cyclists, spiritually and physically, far from the exhaust fumes of the city.

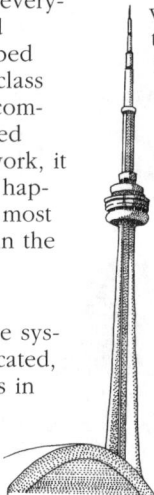

CN Tower

Yet another type of cycling opportunity is available in Toronto. Closed to cars, the Toronto Islands are a cyclist's heaven. Although busier than the riverside trails, the islands offer a view of the city skyline on one side, Lake Ontario on the other and people-watching opportunities galore everywhere in between!

Gooderham Building

The Greater Toronto Area

Bike Paths and Rail Trails

City/Area	Total Length (km)	Page
Toronto	223	105
Toronto West	-	106-107
Toronto East	-	108-109
Downtown Toronto	-	110
Toronto Islands	-	111
Bloor and Yorkville	-	112
Cabbagetown	-	113
The Annex	-	114
Rosedale, Forest Hill and North of Toronto	-	115
Eastern Toronto (The Beaches)	-	116
The Toronto Subway (TTC)	-	117

Provincial Parliament

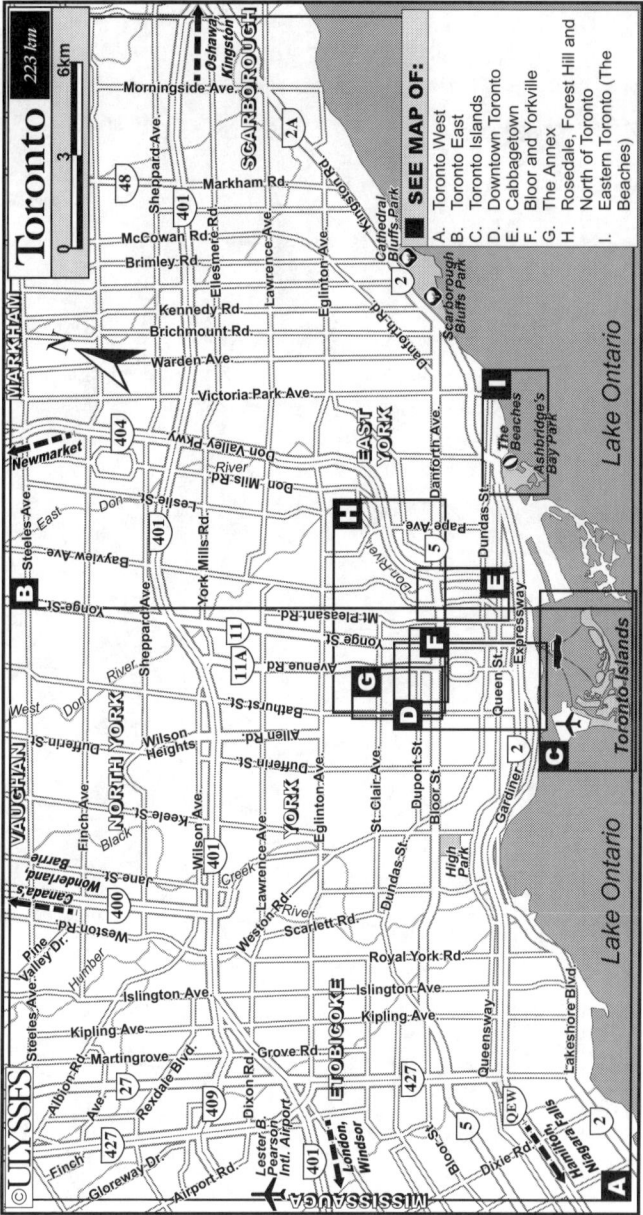

Toronto

0   3   6km

223 km

SEE MAP OF:

A. Toronto West
B. Toronto East
C. Toronto Islands
D. Downtown Toronto
E. Cabbagetown
F. Bloor and Yorkville
G. The Annex
H. Rosedale, Forest Hill and
   North of Toronto
I. Eastern Toronto (The
   Beaches)

MARKHAM

SCARBOROUGH

Oshawa
Kingston

Morningside Ave.

Sheppard Ave.

Markham Rd.

McCowan Rd.

Brimley Rd.

Kennedy Rd.

Birchmount Rd.

Warden Ave.

Victoria Park Ave.

Cathedral
Bluffs Park

Scarborough
Bluffs Park

Lake Ontario

The Beaches
Ashbridge's
Bay Park

Newmarket

Steeles Ave. East

Bayview Ave.

Leslie St.

York Mills Rd.

Don Mills Rd.

Don Valley Pkwy.

River

Danforth Ave.

Dundas St.

Pape Ave.

EAST YORK

NORTH YORK

Yonge St.

Sheppard Ave.

Finch Ave.

Wilson Heights

Bathurst St.

Avenue Rd.

Mt. Pleasant Rd.

Yonge St.

Queen St.

Expressway

Toronto Islands

VAUGHAN

Canada's
Wonderland
Barrie

Pine
Valley Dr.

Steeles Ave.

Dufferin St.

Keele St.

Jane St.

Black Creek

Wilson Ave.

Allen Rd.

Dufferin St.

Eglinton Ave.

St. Clair Ave.

Dupont St.

Bloor St.

Gardiner

YORK

Lawrence Ave.

Weston Rd.

Dundas St.

High Park

Humber River

Scarlett Rd.

Royal York Rd.

Islington Ave.

Kipling Ave.

Queensway

Lakeshore Blvd.

Lake Ontario

ETOBICOKE

Islington Ave.

Kipling Ave.

Martingrove

Albion Rd.

Rexdale Blvd.

Dixon Rd.

Grove Rd.

Finch

Gloreway Dr.

Airport Rd.

Lester B.
Pearson
Intl. Airport

London, Windsor

MISSISSAUGA

Bloor St.

Dixie Rd.

Hamilton
Niagara Falls

© ULYSSES

The Greater Toronto Area

Toronto West

0   2.5   5km

N

11
38
71
53
6
55
56
7
57
7

Bayview Ave.
Cummer Ave.
Willowdale Ave.
Yonge St.
Lawrence Ave. E.
Lawrence Ave.
Yonge St.
11
York Mills Rd.
Drewry Ave.
Finch Ave.
Avenue Rd.
River
Sheppard Ave.
Bathurst St.
Don
West
Dufferin St.
Allen Rd.
Wilson Heights
Dufferin St.
NORTH YORK
Downview Airport
Keele St.
Wilson Ave.
Macdonald-Cartier Freeway
Lawrence Ave. W.
YORK
Creek
Jane St.
Black
400
401
Weston Rd.
Weston Rd.
Fennar Dr.
River
St. Philip Rd.
Humber
Islington Ave.
The Westway
Kipling Ave.
Martingrove
Grove Rd.
Steeles
Albion Rd.
Ave.
27
Rexdale Blvd.
Dixon Rd.
409
Finch
427
Gloreway Dr.
Airport Rd.
Lester B. Pearson International Airport

The Greater Toronto Area

© ULYSSES

Lake Ontario

Toronto Islands

See Toronto Islands

See Downtown

MISSISSAUGA

ETOBICOKE

Bayview Ave.
Broadview Ave.
Don Valley Pkwy
404
Don River
Bayview Ave.
Mount Pleasant Cemetery
Pleasant Rd.
Mount Pleasant Rd.
Yonge St.
Yonge St.
Avenue Rd.
11A
Sherbourne St.
Jarvis St.
Gerrard St.
Parliament St.
Bay Ave.
University Ave.
St. George St.
Spadina Rd.
Bathurst St.
Commissioners Street
Expressway
Queen St.
Bloor St.
Vaughan Rd.
Davenport St.
Dupont St.
5
College St.
Dundas St.
Gardiner
2
Eglinton Ave.
St. Clair Ave. W.
Weston Rd.
Parkside Dr.
High Park
Jane St.
Dundas St.
Scarlett Rd.
Bloor St.
Royal York Rd.
Islington Ave.
Eglinton Ave.
Rathburn Rd.
Kipling Ave.
Queensway
Lakeshore Blvd.
Grove Rd.
Burnhamthorpe Rd.
427
Renforth Dr.
5
2
Bloor St.
Dixie Rd.
QEW
Eglinton Ave. W.

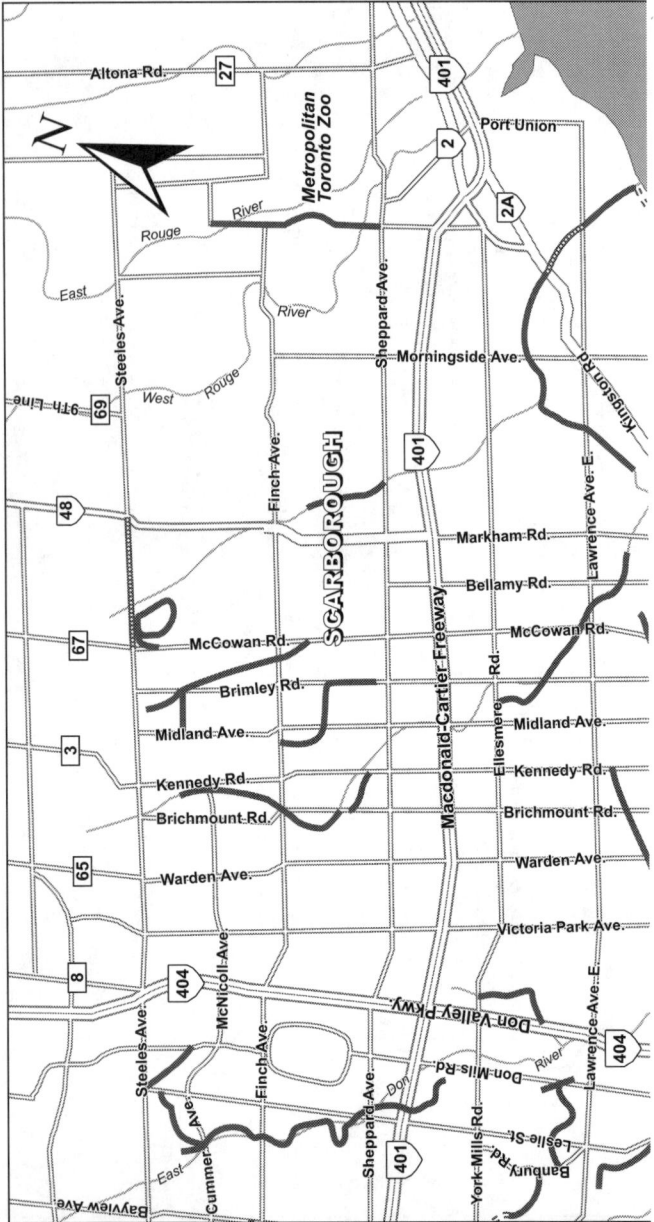

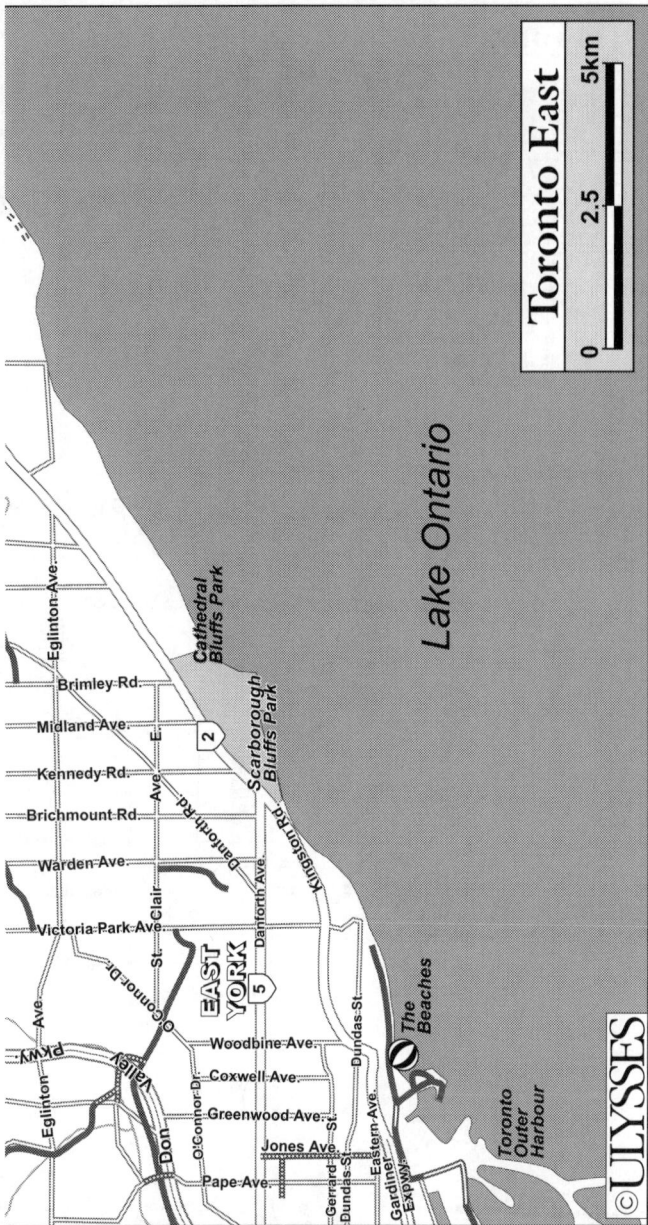

Toronto East

0   2.5   5km

Lake Ontario

Cathedral Bluffs Park

Scarborough Bluffs Park

Eglinton Ave.
Brimley Rd.
Midland Ave.
Kennedy Rd.
Brichmount Rd.
Warden Ave.
Victoria Park Ave.

Ave. E.

Danforth Rd.

(Kingston Rd.)

EAST YORK

St. Clair

Danforth Ave.

O'Connor Dr.

Eglinton Ave.

Valley PKWY.

Don

O'Connor Dr.

Woodbine Ave.
Coxwell Ave.
Greenwood Ave.
Jones Ave.
Pape Ave.

Gerrard St.
Dundas St.
Eastern Ave.

Dundas St.

The Beaches

Gardiner EXPWY.

Toronto Outer Harbour

© ULYSSES

The Greater Toronto Area

Downtown Toronto

©ULYSSES

N

Russell Hill Rd.
Poplar Plains Rd.
Davenport Rd.
Dupont St.
Yonge St.
Davenport
Belmont St.
Huron St.
Bedford Rd.
Avenue Rd.
Christie St.
Barton Ave.
Lowther Ave.
Brunswick Ave.
Spadina Ave.
Bathurst St.
Bloor St. W.
St. George St.
Bloor St. W.
Bay St.
Grace St.
Clinton St.
Hoskin Ave.
Queen's Park Circle
Harbord St.
Wellesley St.
Ulster St.
Manning Ave.
Grosvenor St.
College St.
Gerrard St. W
Bellevue Ave.
Beverly St.
Grace St.
Dundas St. W.
Dundas St. W.
Palmerston Blvd.
Bathurst St.
Huron St.
Bay St.
Queen St. W.
Spadina Ave.
Peter St.
Queen St. W.
University Ave.
Adelaide St. W.
Adelaide St. W.
King St. W.
King St. W.
Wellington St. W.
Wellington St. W.
Front St. W.

Lake Shore Blvd. W.
Gardiner Expressway
Harbour St.
Queens Quay W.

0   500   1,000m

Lake Ontario

Ferry to Toronto Island

Toronto Islands

0   500   1,000m

ATTRACTIONS

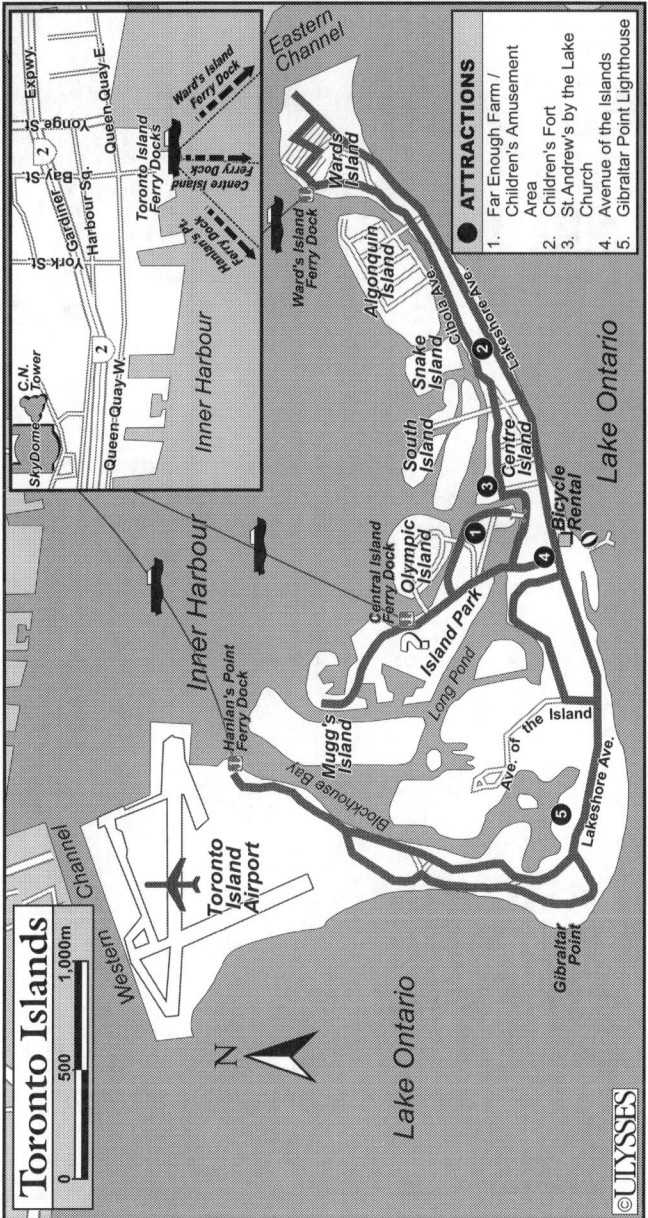

1. Far Enough Farm /
   Children's Amusement
   Area
2. Children's Fort
3. St.Andrew's by the Lake
   Church
4. Avenue of the Islands
5. Gibraltar Point Lighthouse

Eastern Channel

Ward's Island Ferry Dock

EXPWY.
Yonge St.
Queen Quay E.
Bay St.
Gardiner
Queen-Quay-W.
Harbour St.
York St.
C.N. Tower
Sky Dome

Toronto Island Ferry Docks

Centre Island Ferry Dock

Bathurst St. Ferry Dock

Inner Harbour

Ward's Island Ferry Dock

Algonquin Island

Snake Island

South Island

Centre Island

Cibola Ave.

Lakeshore Ave.

Lake Ontario

Central Island Ferry Dock

Olympic Island

Island Park

Long Pond

Inner Harbour

Hanlan's Point Ferry Dock

Mugg's Island

Blockhouse Bay

Ave. of the Island

Lakeshore Ave.

Western Channel

Toronto Island Airport

Lake Ontario

Gibraltar Point

N

© ULYSSES

The Greater Toronto Area

Bicycle Rental

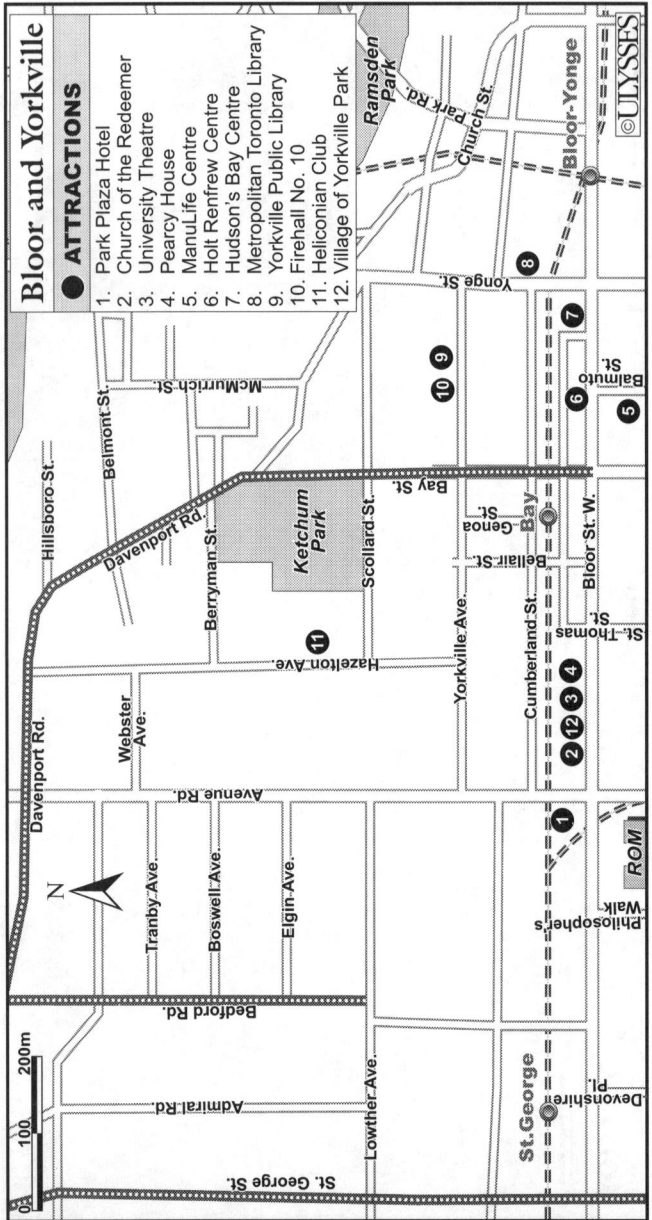

Bloor and Yorkville

● ATTRACTIONS

1. Park Plaza Hotel
2. Church of the Redeemer
3. University Theatre
4. Pearcy House
5. ManuLife Centre
6. Holt Renfrew Centre
7. Hudson's Bay Centre
8. Metropolitan Toronto Library
9. Yorkville Public Library
10. Firehall No. 10
11. Heliconian Club
12. Village of Yorkville Park

© ULYSSES

N

0 100 200m

Ramsden Park

Ketchum Park

ROM

Park Rd
Church St.
Bloor-Yonge
Yonge St.
Balmuto St.
McMurrich St.
Bay St.
Genoa St.
Bellair St.
Bloor St. W.
St. Thomas St.
Cumberland St.
Yorkville Ave.
Scollard St.
Berryman St.
Davenport Rd.
Hazelton Ave.
Webster Ave.
Avenue Rd.
Elgin Ave.
Boswell Ave.
Tranby Ave.
Belmont St.
Hillsboro St.
Davenport Rd.
Bedford Rd.
Philosopher's Walk
St. George
Devonshire Pl.
Lowther Ave.
Admiral Rd.
St. George St.

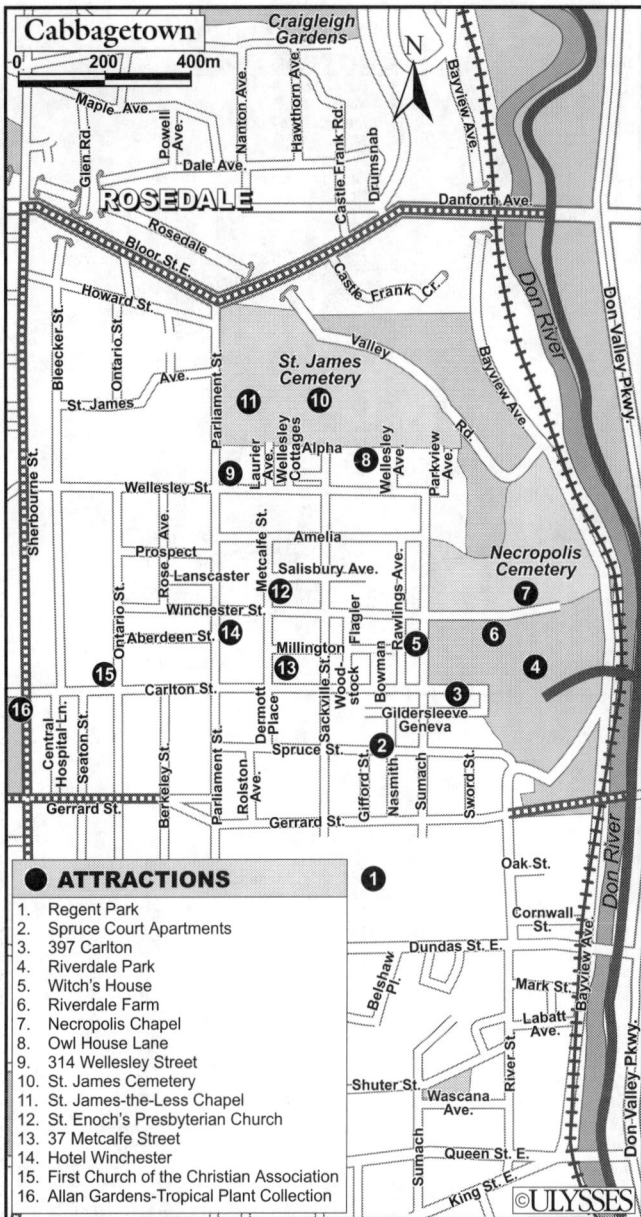

Cabbagetown

0   200   400m

Craigleigh Gardens

N

ROSEDALE

Maple Ave.
Glen Rd.
Powell Ave.
Nanton Ave.
Dale Ave.
Hawthorn Ave.
Castle Frank Rd.
Drumsnab

Rosedale
Danforth Ave.

Howard St.
Bloor St. E.
Castle Frank Cr.

Bleecker St.
Ontario St.
St. James
Ave.
Parliament St.
Valley
St. James Cemetery
11
10

Don River
Don Valley Pkwy.

Sherbourne St.
Wellesley St.
9
Laurier Ave.
Wellesley Cottages
Alpha
Wellesley Ave.
Parkview Ave.
8

Bayview Ave.
Rd.

Prospect
Rose Ave.
Amelia
Lanscaster
Metcalfe St.
Salisbury Ave.
12
Flagler
Rawlings Ave.
Necropolis Cemetery
7

Winchester St.
Aberdeen St.
14
Millington
13
Bowman
Wood-stock
Sackville St.
5
6
4

Ontario St.
15
Carlton St.
Dermott Place
Gildersleeve
Geneva
3
2

Central Hospital Ln.
Seaton St.
16
Berkeley St.
Parliament St.
Rolston Ave.
Gifford St.
Nasmith
Sumach
Spruce St.
Sword St.

Gerrard St.
Gerrard St.
Oak St.

1

Belshaw Pl.
Cornwall St.
Dundas St. E.

Mark St.
Labatt Ave.

River St.
Sumach
Bayview Ave.
Don River
Don Valley Pkwy.

Shuter St.
Wascana Ave.

Queen St. E.

King St. E.

©ULYSSES

● ATTRACTIONS

1. Regent Park
2. Spruce Court Apartments
3. 397 Carlton
4. Riverdale Park
5. Witch's House
6. Riverdale Farm
7. Necropolis Chapel
8. Owl House Lane
9. 314 Wellesley Street
10. St. James Cemetery
11. St. James-the-Less Chapel
12. St. Enoch's Presbyterian Church
13. 37 Metcalfe Street
14. Hotel Winchester
15. First Church of the Christian Association
16. Allan Gardens-Tropical Plant Collection

The Greater Toronto Area

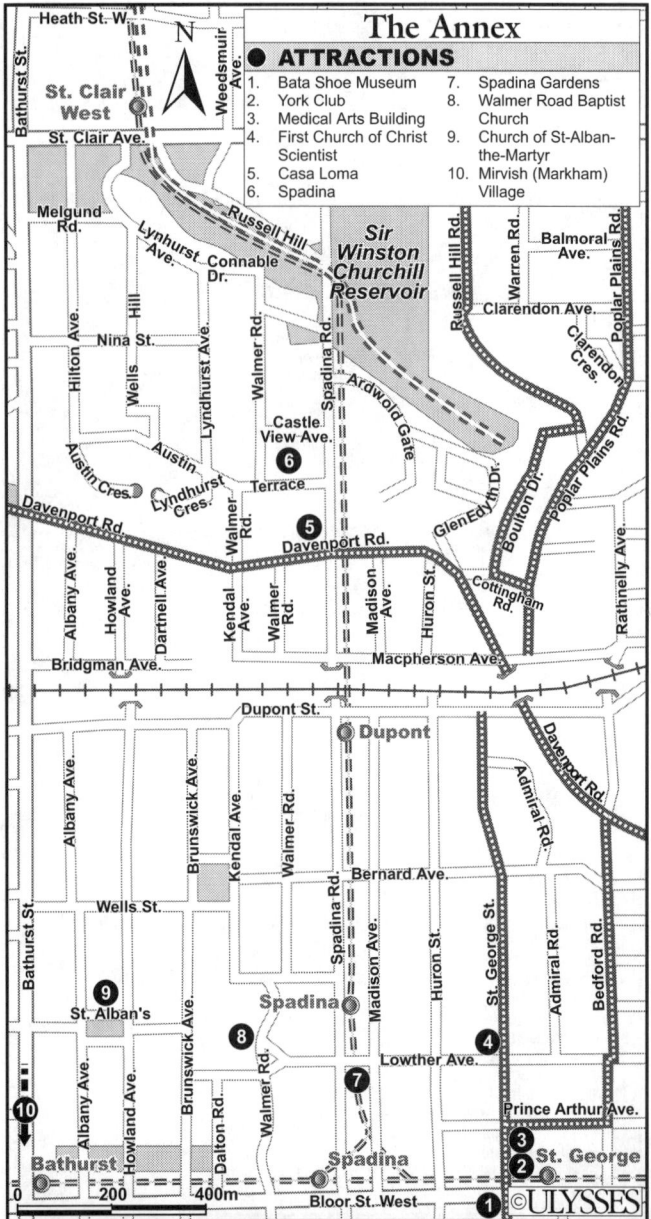

Heath St. W.

Bathurst St.

N

Weedsmuir

St. Clair West

St. Clair Ave.

The Annex

● ATTRACTIONS

1.	Bata Shoe Museum	7.	Spadina Gardens
2.	York Club	8.	Walmer Road Baptist
3.	Medical Arts Building		Church
4.	First Church of Christ	9.	Church of St-Alban-
	Scientist		the-Martyr
5.	Casa Loma	10.	Mirvish (Markham)
6.	Spadina		Village

Melgund Rd.

Lynhurst Ave.

Russell Hill

Connable Dr.

Sir Winston Churchill Reservoir

Russell Hill Rd.

Warren Rd.

Balmoral Ave.

Poplar Plains Rd.

Clarendon Ave.

Hilton Ave.

Nina St.

Wells

Lyndhurst Ave.

Walmer Rd.

Spadina Rd.

Ardwold Gate

Clarendon Cres.

Austin

Austin Cres.

Lyndhurst Cres.

Castle View Ave.

6

Terrace

GlenEdyth Dr.

Boulton Dr.

Poplar Plains Rd.

Rathnelly Ave.

Davenport Rd.

Walmer Rd.

5

Davenport Rd.

Cottingham Rd.

Albany Ave.

Howland Ave.

Dartnell Ave.

Kendal Ave.

Walmer Rd.

Madison Ave.

Huron St.

Macpherson Ave.

Bridgman Ave.

Dupont St.

Dupont

Davenport Rd.

Albany Ave.

Brunswick Ave.

Kendal Ave.

Walmer Rd.

Spadina Rd.

Bernard Ave.

Admiral Rd.

Wells St.

Bathurst St.

Madison Ave.

Huron St.

St. George St.

Admiral Rd.

Bedford Rd.

9

St. Alban's

Brunswick Ave.

Spadina

8

Walmer Rd.

Dalton Rd.

7

4

Lowther Ave.

Albany Ave.

Howland Ave.

Prince Arthur Ave.

10

3 **St. George**

Bathurst

Howland Ave.

Dalton Rd.

Spadina

Bloor St. West

2

1

©ULYSSES

0   200   400m

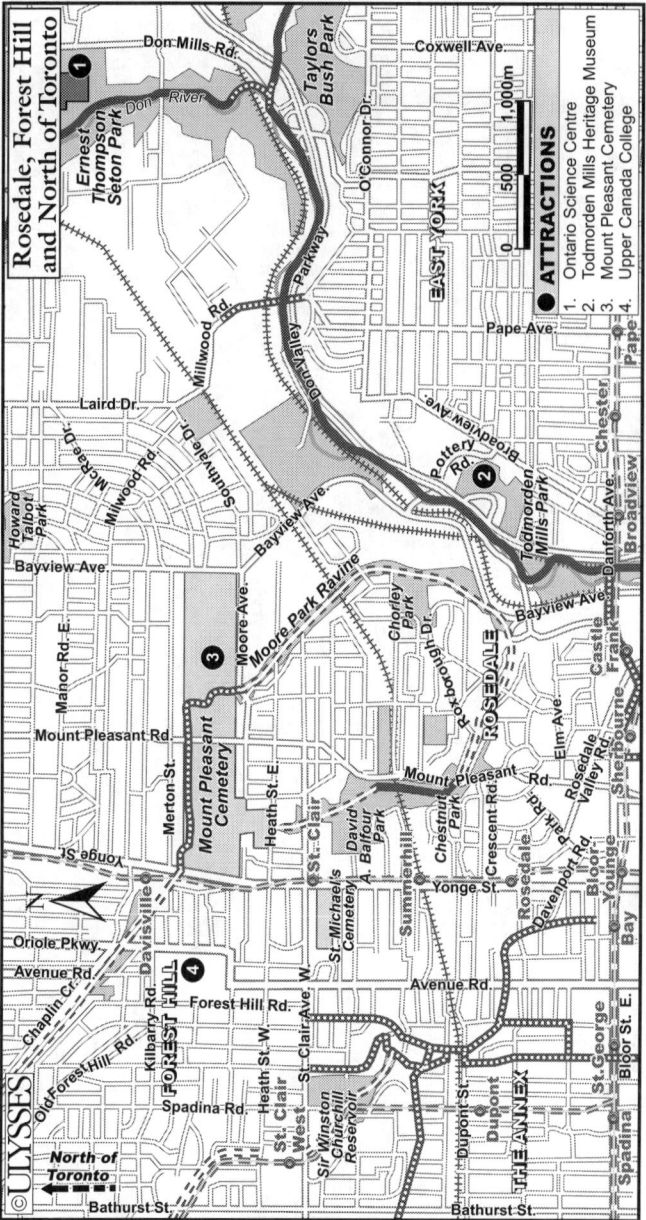

Rosedale, Forest Hill
and North of Toronto

ATTRACTIONS
1. Ontario Science Centre
2. Todmorden Mills Heritage Museum
3. Mount Pleasant Cemetery
4. Upper Canada College

0   500   1,000m

Don Mills Rd.
Coxwell Ave.
Taylors Bush Park
Don River
Ernest Thompson Seton Park
O'Connor Dr.
EAST YORK
Millwood Rd.
Don Valley Parkway
Laird Dr.
Pape Ave.
Southvale Dr.
McRae Dr.
Milwood Rd.
Broadview Ave.
Howard Talbot Park
Pottery Rd.
Bayview Ave.
Bayview Ave.
Todmorden Mills Park
Chester
Danforth Ave.
Manor Rd. E.
Moore Ave.
Moore Park Ravine
Chorley Park
Bayview Ave.
Pape
Broadview
Mount Pleasant Rd.
ROSEDALE
Merton St.
Mount Pleasant Cemetery
Heath St. E.
St. Clair
David A. Balfour Park
Mount Pleasant Rd.
Roxborough Dr.
Castle Frank
Elm Ave.
Rosedale Valley Rd.
Yonge St.
St. Michaels Cemetery
Summerhill Ave.
Chestnut Park
Crescent Rd.
Sherbourne
Oriole Pkwy.
Davisville
Avenue Rd.
FOREST HILL
Forest Hill Rd.
Avenue Rd.
Yonge St.
Rosedale Valley Rd.
Davenport Rd.
Bay
Bloor
Yonge
Chaplin Cr.
Old Forest Hill Rd.
Kilbarry Rd.
Heath St. W.
St. Clair Ave.
St. Clair
Bloor St. E.
St. George
Spadina Rd.
St. Clair West
Winston Churchill Reservoir
Dupont St.
THE ANNEX
St. George
Spadina
Bay
North of Toronto
Bathurst St.
Bathurst St.

ULYSSES

The Greater Toronto Area

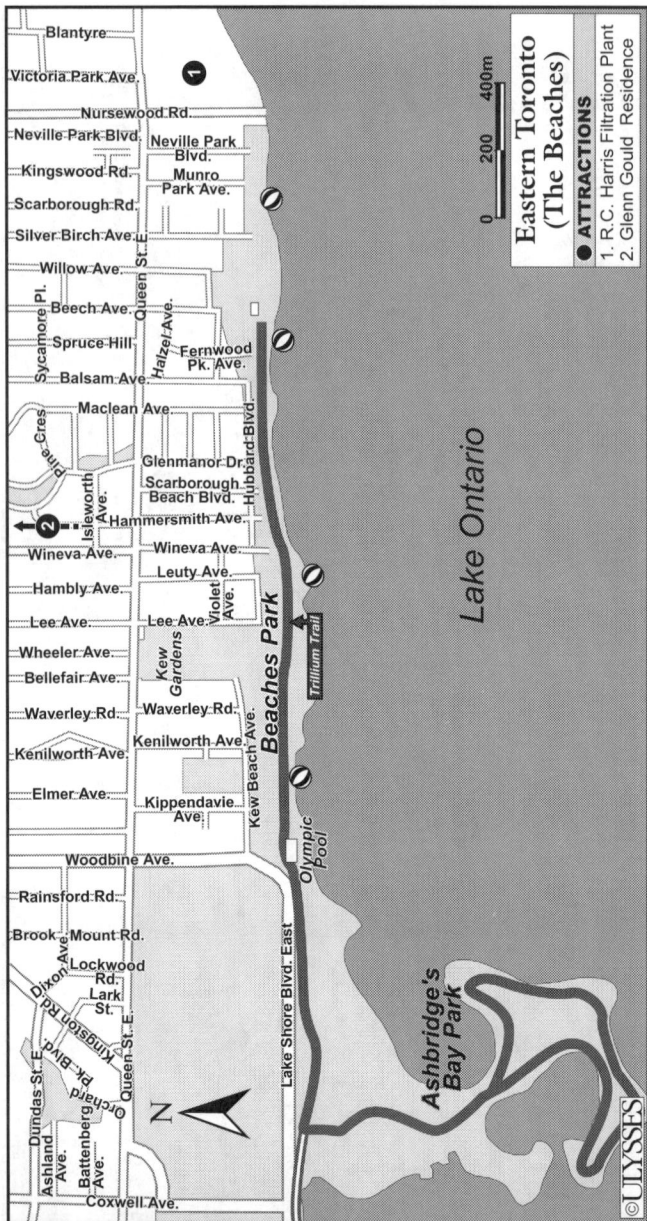

Eastern Toronto
(The Beaches)

● **ATTRACTIONS**
1. R.C. Harris Filtration Plant
2. Glenn Gould Residence

0   200   400m

Lake Ontario

Blantyre
Victoria Park Ave.
Nursewood Rd.
Neville Park Blvd.
Neville Park Blvd.
Kingswood Rd.
Munro Park Ave.
Scarborough Rd.
Silver Birch Ave. E.
Willow Ave.
Beech Ave.
Spruce Hill
Fernwood Pk. Ave.
Balsam Ave.
Maclean Ave.
Glenmanor Dr.
Scarborough Beach Blvd.
Hammersmith Ave.
Wineva Ave.
Wineva Ave.
Leuty Ave.
Hambly Ave.
Lee Ave.
Lee Ave.
Wheeler Ave.
Bellefair Ave.
Waverley Rd.
Waverley Rd.
Kenilworth Ave.
Kenilworth Ave.
Elmer Ave.
Kippendavie Ave.
Woodbine Ave.
Rainsford Rd.
Brook Mount Rd.
Lockwood Rd.
Lark St.

Queen St. E.
Hazel Ave.
Hubbard Blvd.
Sycamore Pl.
Pine Cres.
Isleworth Ave.
Violet Ave.
Kew Gardens
Kew Beach Ave.
Beaches Park
Trillium Trail
Olympic Pool

Dixon Ave.
Kingston Rd.
Orchard Pk. Blvd.
Dundas St. E.
Ashland Ave.
Battenberg Ave.
Queen St. E.
Coxwell Ave.

Lake Shore Blvd. East

Ashbridge's Bay Park

N

© ULYSSES

The Toronto Subway (TTC)

The Greater Toronto Area

Lake Ontario

Toronto Islands

SCARBOROUGH CENTRE
MIDLAND
McCOWAN
ELLESMERE
LAWRENCE EAST
KENNEDY
WARDEN
MAIN ST.
VICTORIA PARK
WOODBINE
COXWELL
GREENWOOD
DONLANDS
PAPE
CHESTER
BROADVIEW
CASTLE FRANK

FINCH
NORTH YORK
SHEPPARD
YORK MILLS
LAWRENCE
EGLINTON
DAVISVILLE
ST. CLAIR
SUMMERHILL
ROSEDALE
SHERBOURNE
BLOOR-YONGE
WELLESLEY
COLLEGE
DUNDAS
QUEEN
KING
BAY
UNION

DOWNSVIEW
WILSON
YORKDALE
LAWRENCE WEST
GLENCAIRN
EGLINTON WEST
ST. CLAIR WEST
DUPONT
BATHURST
CHRISTIE
OSSINGTON
DUFFERIN
LANSDOWNE
DUNDAS WEST
KEELE
HIGH PARK
RUNNYMEDE
JANE
OLD MILL
ROYAL YORK
ISLINGTON
KIPLING

SPADINA
ST. GEORGE
MUSEUM
QUEEN'S PARK
ST. PATRICK
OSGOODE
ST. ANDREW

Legend

Bloor-Danforth Line
Yonge-University-Spadina Line
Scarborough Rapid Transit

TTC: Toronto Transit Commission

© ULYSSES

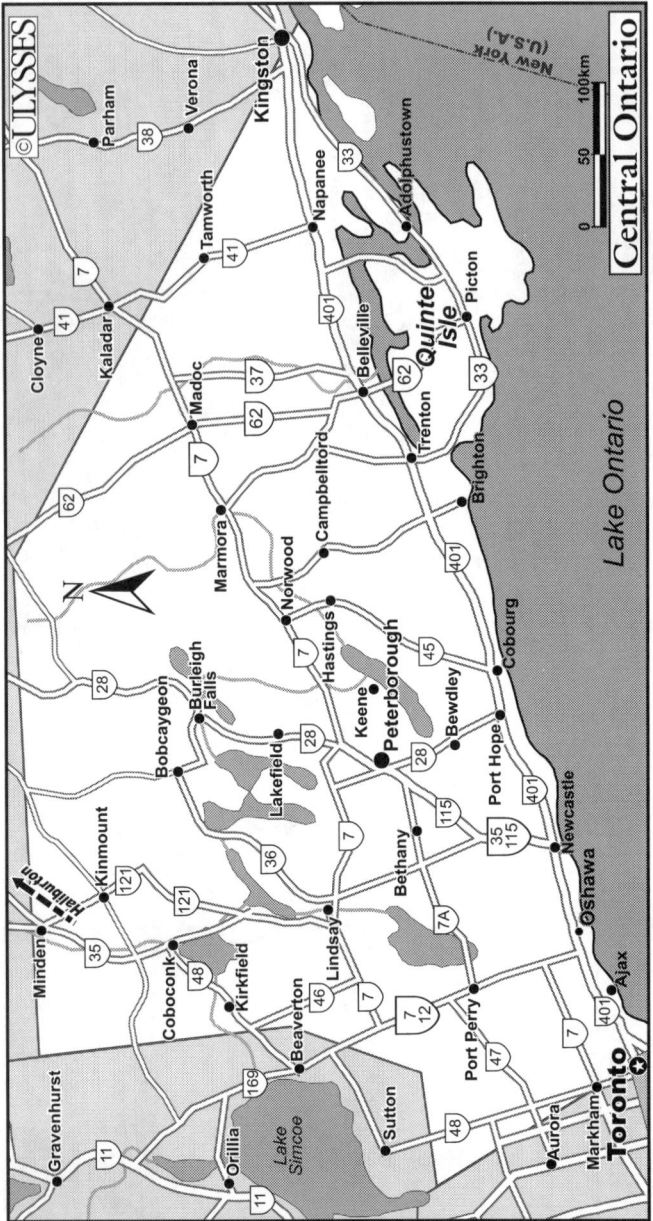

Central Ontario

Central Ontario
is the province's heartland.

Beginning along the north shore of busy Lake Ontario, it follows the Trent-Severn waterway to the Kawartha Lakes, including the highlands of Victoria and the unique liftlocks of the city of Peterborough.

As one continues north, more than 600 beautiful little lakes are scattered throughout the hills, cliffs and forests. The resort town and cycling trails of Haliburton are also found in this area.

The still relatively unpop-ulated stretch from Kingston to Toronto has some wonderful rural scenery, with charming little

hamlets tucked away in the countryside and some spec-tacular views of Lake Ontario.

Following the American War of Independence, a surge of loyalists crossed the border to settle in this vast territory still under the British crown. Many of them established themselves around the Bay of Quinte, founding a string of villages that grew rapidly thanks to their proximity to the St. Lawrence Seaway and the rich agricultural land in the region, especially on Quinte's Isle.

The back country was set-tled in the 19th century by new arrivals lured here by the lovely countryside surrounding the Kawartha Lakes, which quickly became a popular vacation spot.

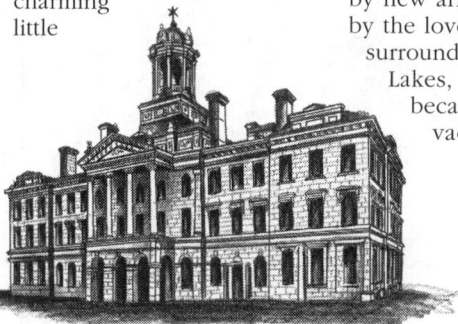

Cobourg City Hall

Central Ontario

Bike Paths and Rail Trails

City/Area	Total Length (km)	Page
Peterborough (Rotary Greenway Trail)	10	120
Peterborough (Jackson Creek Kiwanis Trail)	5	121
Caledon Trailway	34	122
Port Hope to Cobourg Area Trail	70.5	123
Port Hope to Cobourg Area Trail (Port Hope)	-	124
Port Hope to Cobourg Area Trail (Cobourg)	-	124
Victoria Rail Trail	85	125
Haliburton Rail Trail	36	126

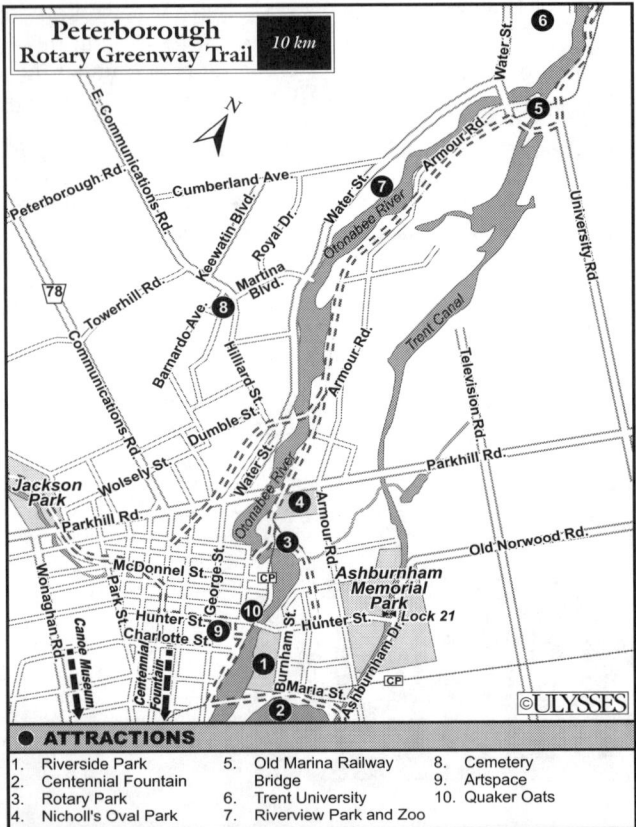

Peterborough Rotary Greenway Trail — 10 km

● ATTRACTIONS

1. Riverside Park
2. Centennial Fountain
3. Rotary Park
4. Nicholl's Oval Park
5. Old Marina Railway Bridge
6. Trent University
7. Riverview Park and Zoo
8. Cemetery
9. Artspace
10. Quaker Oats

©ULYSSES

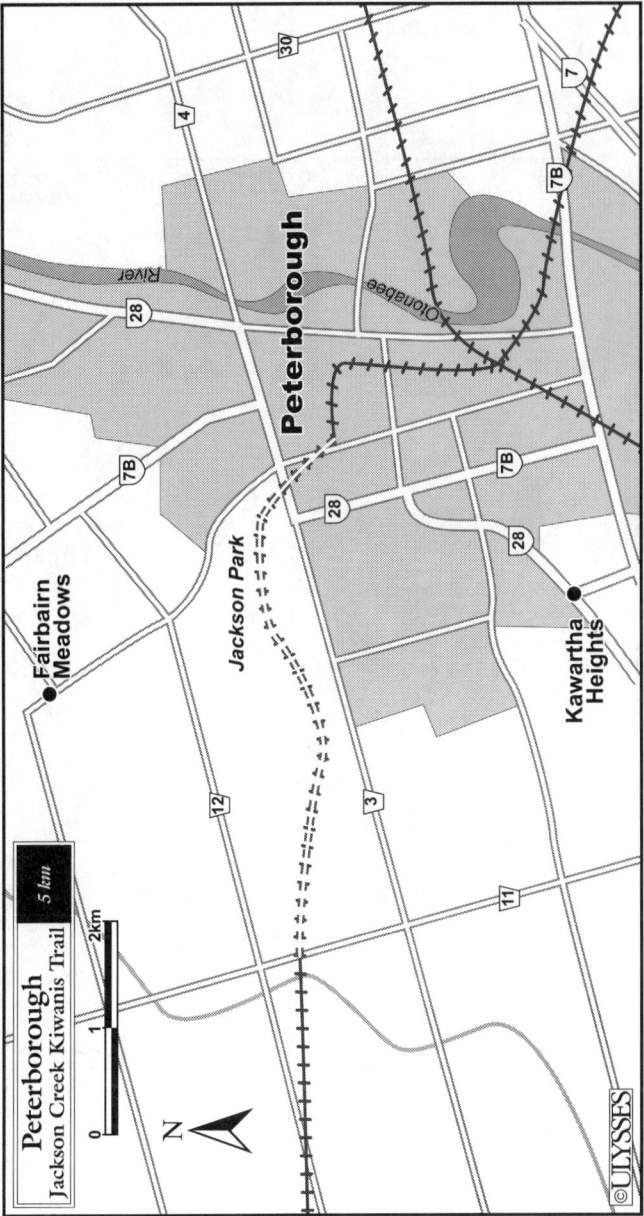

Peterborough
Jackson Creek Kiwanis Trail

0   1   2km
5 km

N

Peterborough

Otonabee River

Jackson Park

Fairbairn
Meadows

Kawartha
Heights

30
4
7
7B
28
7B
28
7B
28
12
3
11

Central Ontario

© ULYSSES

Caledon Trailway 34 km

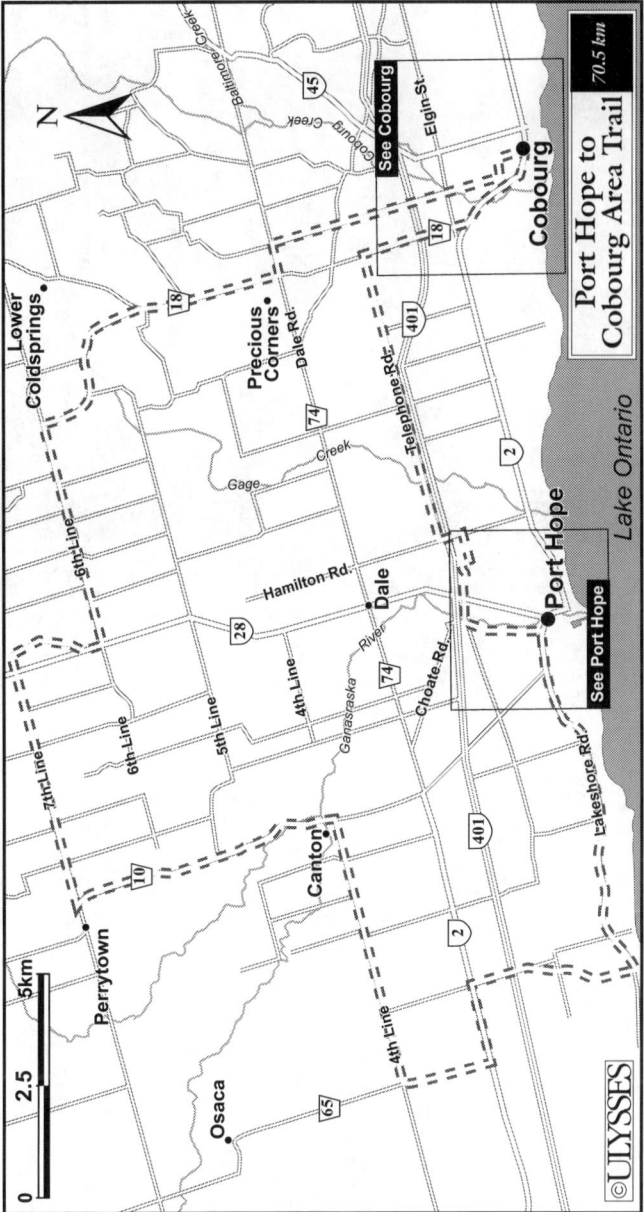

Port Hope to
Cobourg Area Trail

70.5 km

Central Ontario

© ULYSSES

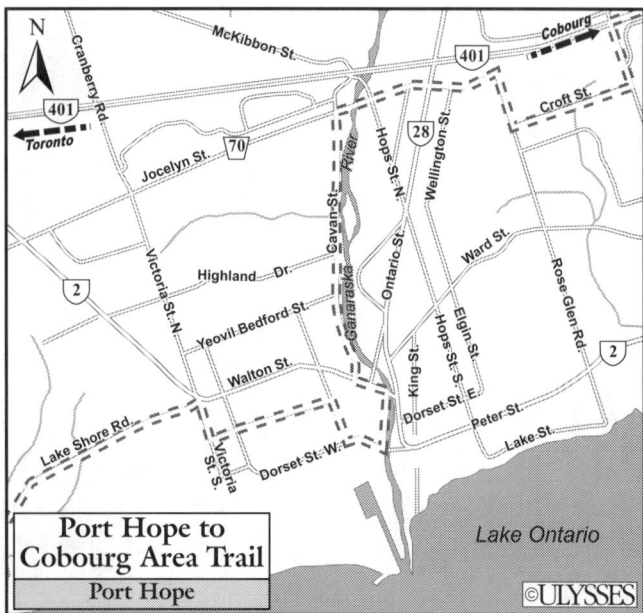

N

McKibbon St.

Cranberry Rd.

401

401
Toronto

Cobourg

401

Croft St.

Jocelyn St.

70

Hops St. N.

Wellington St.

28

Victoria St. N.

Highland   Dr.

Cavan St.

Ganaraska River

Ontario St.

Ward St.

Rose Glen Rd.

2

Yeovil Bedford St.

King St.

Elgin St.

Hops St. S. E.

2

Walton St.

Dorset St.

Peter St.

Lake St.

Lake Shore Rd.

Victoria St. S.

Dorset St. W.

Lake Ontario

Port Hope to Cobourg Area Trail

Port Hope

©ULYSSES

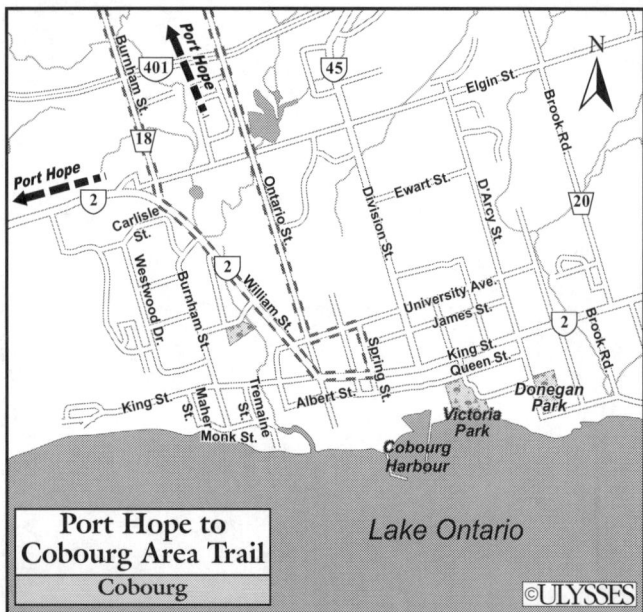

Burnham St.

401

Port Hope

45

Elgin St.

Brook Rd.

N

18

Port Hope

2

Ontario St.

Ewart St.

Division St.

D'Arcy St.

20

Carlisle St.

Westwood Dr.

Burnham St.

2

William St.

University Ave.

James St.

2

Brook Rd.

King St.

Queen St.

Donegan Park

King St.

Maher

Tremaine

Albert St.

Spring St.

Victoria Park

Monk St.

Cobourg Harbour

Port Hope to Cobourg Area Trail

Cobourg

Lake Ontario

©ULYSSES

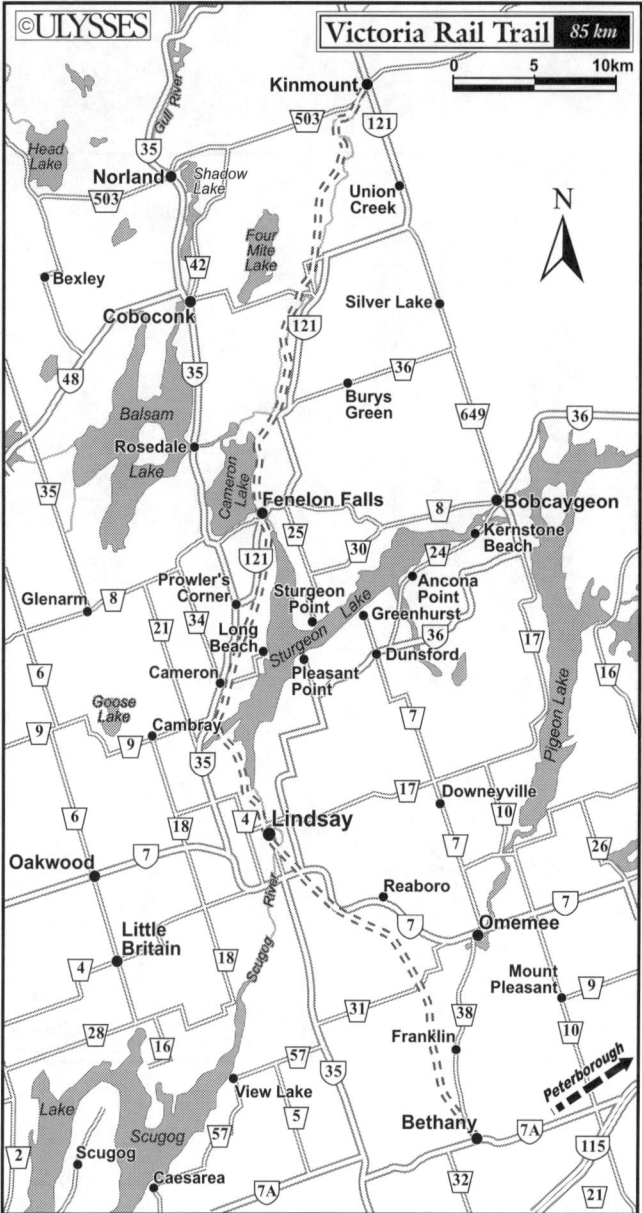

© ULYSSES

Victoria Rail Trail 85 km

0   5   10km

N

Kinmount

503   121

35

Norland   Shadow Lake

Head Lake

503

Gull River

Union Creek

42

Four Mile Lake

Bexley

Coboconk

121

Silver Lake

35

36

649

36

48

Burys Green

Balsam

Rosedale Lake

Cameron Lake

35

Fenelon Falls

Bobcaygeon

25   30   8   24   Kernstone Beach

Glenarm   8

Prowler's Corner

121

Sturgeon Point

Ancona Point

Greenhurst

21   34

Long Beach

Sturgeon Lake

36   17

16

6

Cameron   Pleasant Point

Dunsford

Goose Lake

9   Cambray

7

9   35

17   Downeyville

10

6

18   Lindsay   7   26

Oakwood   7   4   7

Reaboro

Little Britain   7   Omemee

4   18   Scugog River

Mount Pleasant   9

28   16   31   38   10

57   Franklin

35   Peterborough

View Lake   5

2   Scugog   Scugog Lake   57   Bethany   7A

Caesarea   7A   32   115

21

Central Ontario

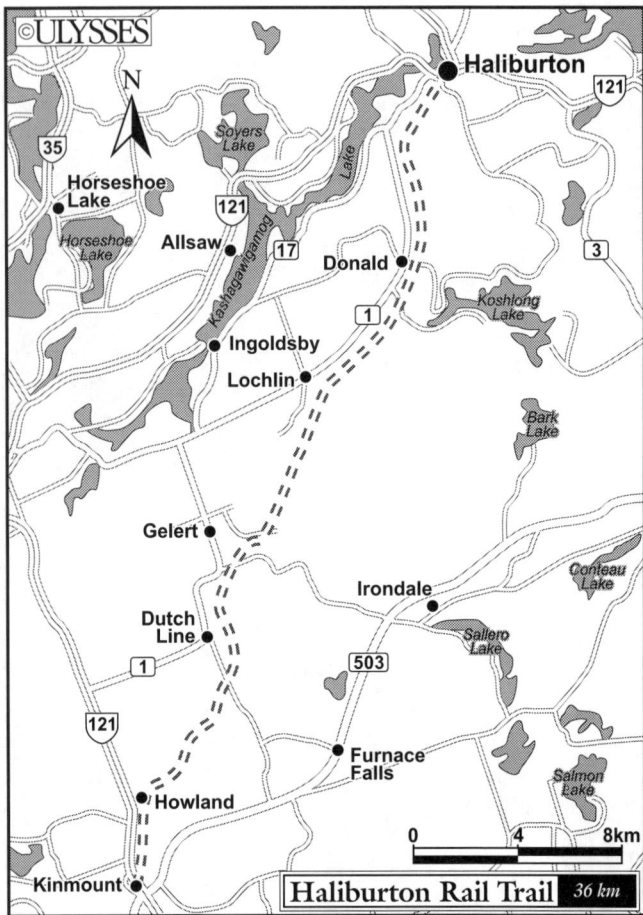

©ULYSSES

N

35

Horseshoe
Lake

Horseshoe
Lake

Soyers
Lake

121

Allsaw

17

Kashagawigamog Lake

Ingoldsby

Lochlin

Haliburton

121

3

Donald

Koshlong
Lake

1

Bark
Lake

Gelert

Irondale

Conteau
Lake

Dutch
Line

1

Sallero
Lake

121

503

Furnace
Falls

Salmon
Lake

Howland

0   4   8km

Kinmount

Haliburton Rail Trail 36 km

Eastern Ontario

Eastern Ontario is rich in natural wonders.

Kingston City Hall

In the south, enjoy the allure of the St. Lawrence River, the cool clean waters of Lake Ontario and the area's unique attraction, the Thousand Islands.

Travelling north along the meandering Rideau River, take in the rolling hills and the spectacular scenery of the Ottawa Valley, home to Canada's capital, Ottawa. Savour the pageantry, the history and the impressive natural sights found along the Ottawa River and the Ontario-Quebec border.

Eastern Ontario, a rich plain between the St. Lawrence River and the

Canadian Shield, has always been a favourable place for human habitation. Natives were drawn here by the fertile land and abundant supply of fresh water; French colonists, by the region's strategic location along the lucrative fur route. Later, Loyalists arriving from the newly independent United States chose to establish their new villages in these vast spaces. This hospitable region has been welcoming new inhabitants ever since, and some villages have since developed into lovely cities, like Kingston, while others, having preserved their old-fashioned character, have become popular vacation spots.

Vast, rolling fields greet visitors who explore this magnificent region. Splendid old houses that seem to have been there since the

Johnston District Courthouse

Eastern Ontario

earliest days of colonization, pop up around every other bend in the road. The region's first hamlets, now cities like Brockville, remain virtually unchanged and are still graced with lovely Victorian buildings. In some places, where the human presence is less obvious, the landscape consists largely of a forest of hardwoods and conifers strewn with lakes and rivers.

Villa Bellevue

Eastern Ontario

Bike Paths and Rail Trails

City/Area	Total Length (km)	Page
Hasting Heritage Trail	156	130
Brockville	6	131
St. Lawrence Recreational Trail	40	132
Upper Canada Migratory Sanctuary	15	133
Finch Area	1.5	134
Trenton	1.5	135
Quinte Island	122	136
Kingston	-	137

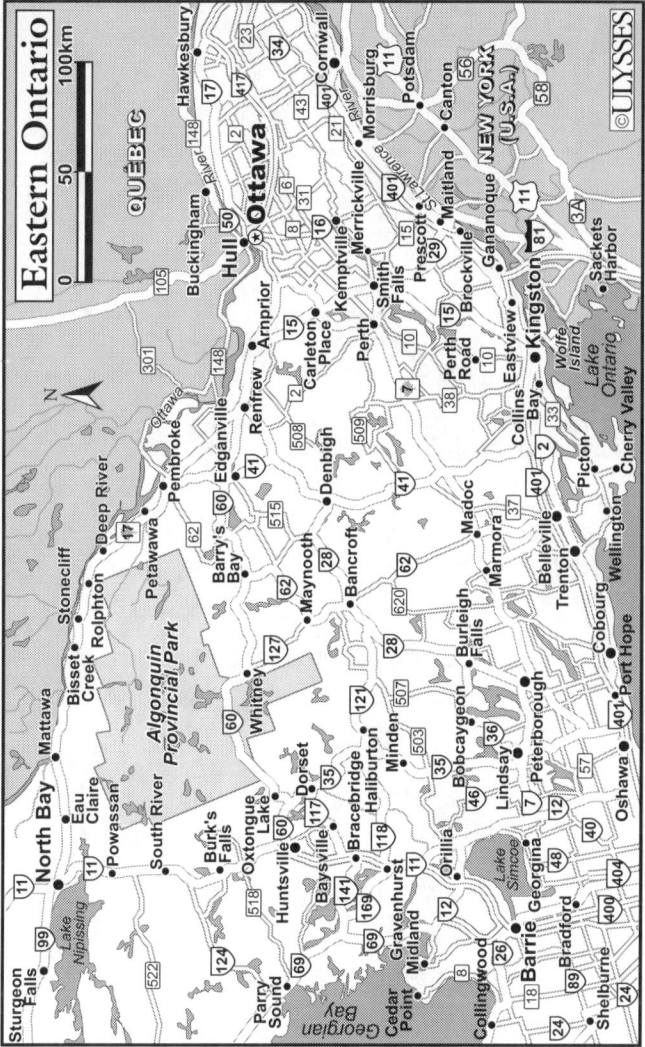

Eastern Ontario

Eastern Ontario

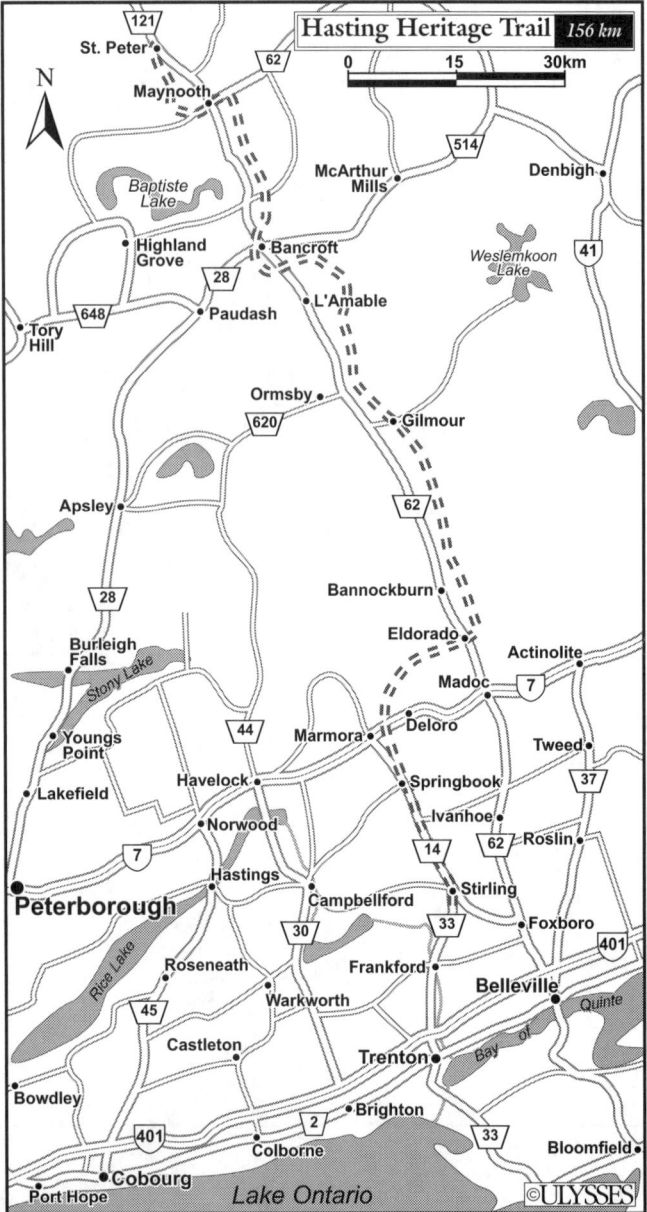

Hasting Heritage Trail *156 km*

0   15   30km

121
St. Peter
62
Maynooth
N
514
McArthur Mills
Denbigh
Baptiste Lake
Highland Grove
28
Bancroft
Weslemkoon Lake
41
L'Amable
648
Paudash
Tory Hill
Ormsby
620
Gilmour
Apsley
62
28
Bannockburn
Eldorado
Actinolite
Burleigh Falls
Madoc
7
Stony Lake
44
Marmora
Deloro
Tweed
Youngs Point
Havelock
Springbook
37
Lakefield
Norwood
Ivanhoe
62
Roslin
7
14
Hastings
Stirling
Peterborough
Campbellford
Foxboro
30
33
401
Roseneath
Frankford
Belleville
45
Warkworth
Quinte
Castleton
Trenton
Bay of
Bowdley
Brighton
401
2
33
Colborne
Bloomfield
Cobourg
Port Hope
Lake Ontario
©ULYSSES

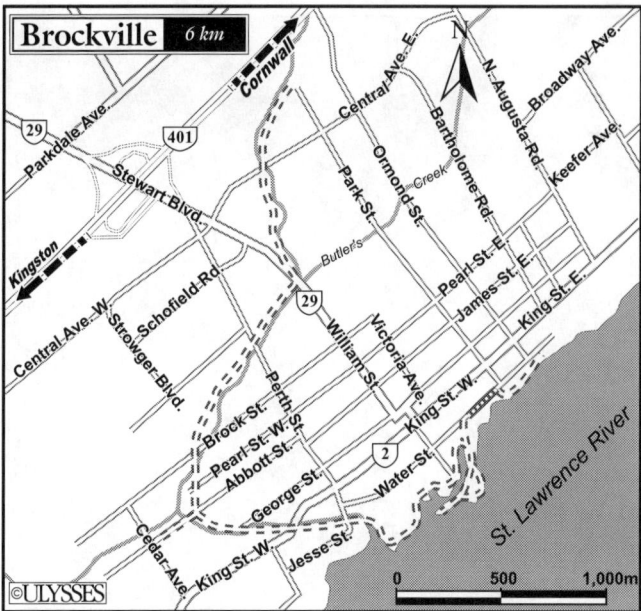

Homewood

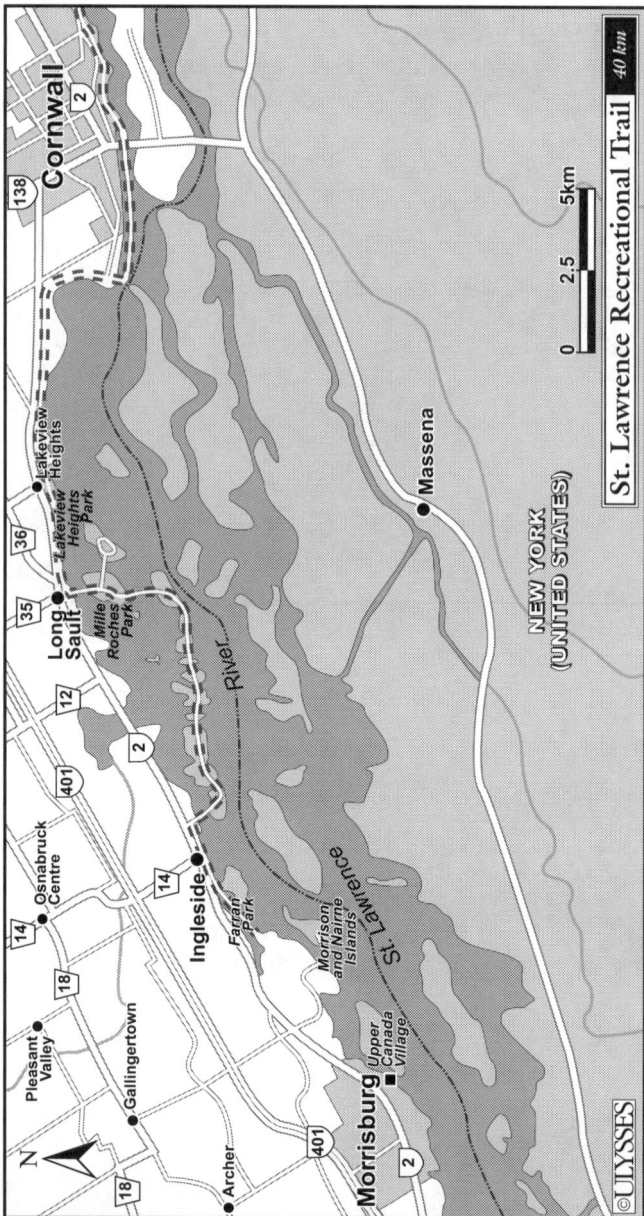

St. Lawrence Recreational Trail

40 km

5km

0   2.5   5km

Cornwall

2

138

Lakeview Heights

Lakeview Heights Park

36

35

Long Sault

Mille Roches Park

12

2

River

St. Lawrence

Massena

NEW YORK (UNITED STATES)

401

Osnabruck Centre

14

14

Ingleside

Farran Park

Morrison and Nairne Islands

18

Pleasant Valley

Gallingertown

Morrisburg

Upper Canada Village

401

Archer

2

18

N

© ULYSSES

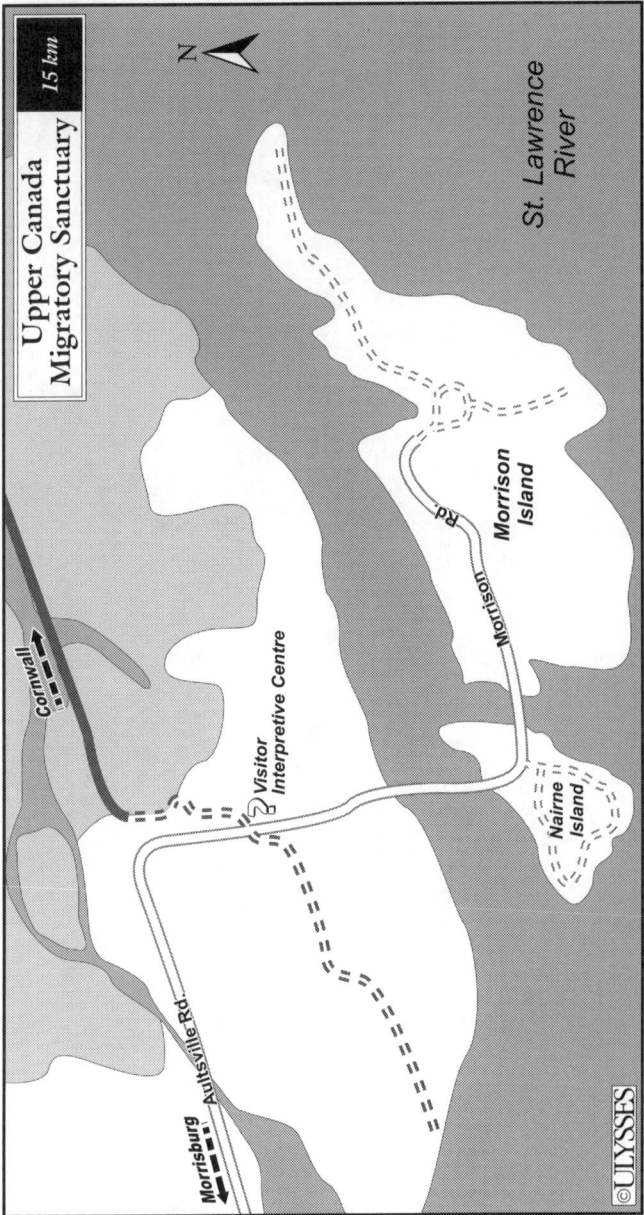

Upper Canada
Migratory Sanctuary

15 km

N

St. Lawrence
River

Morrison Island

Morrison Rd.

Nairne Island

Cornwall

Visitor
Interpretive Centre

Aultsville Rd.

Morrisburg

© ULYSSES

Eastern Ontario

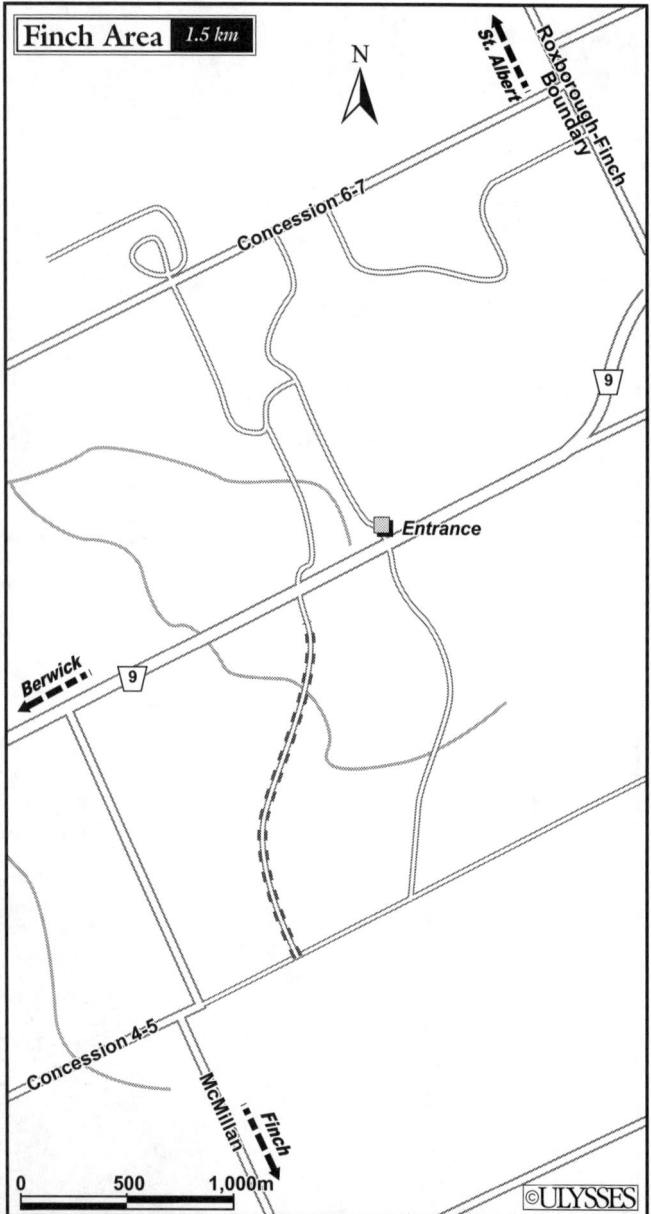

Finch Area 1.5 km

N

St. Albert

Roxborough-Finch Boundary

Concession 6-7

9

Entrance

Berwick

9

Concession 4-5

McMillan

Finch

0   500   1,000m

©ULYSSES

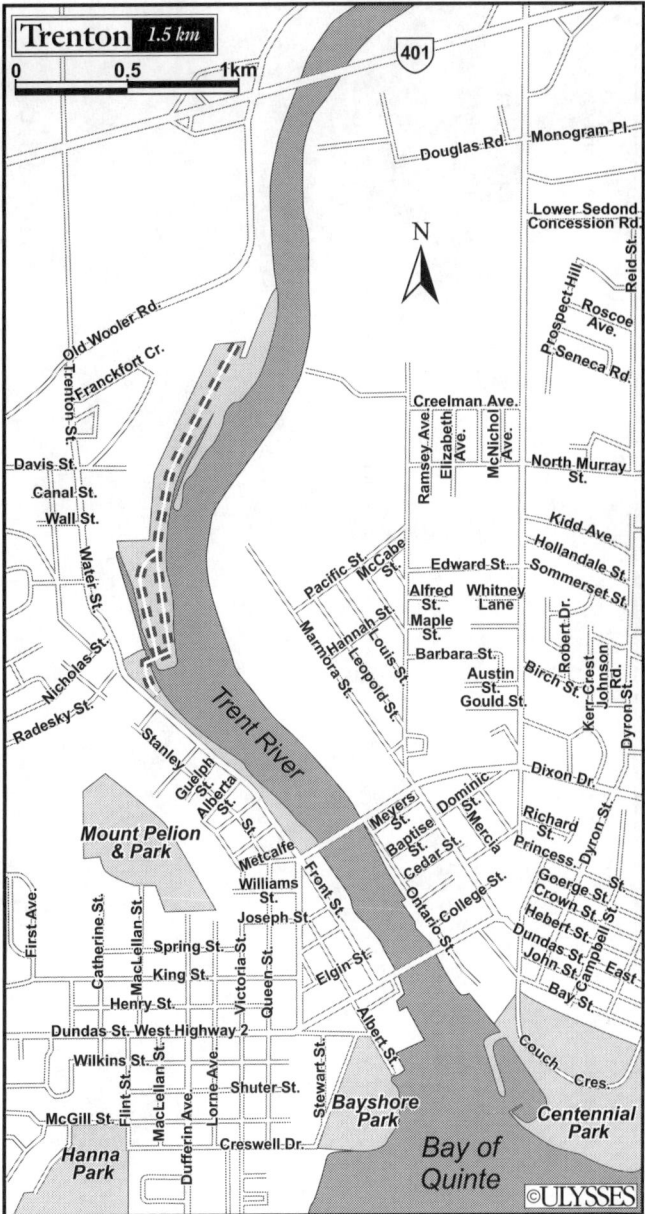

Trenton *1.5 km*

0   0.5   1km

401

Douglas Rd.   Monogram Pl.

Lower Sedond
Concession Rd.

Reid St.

Roscoe
Ave.

Prospect Hill

P. Seneca Rd.

N

Old Wooler Rd.

Franckfort Cr.

Trenton St.

Creelman Ave.

Ramsey Ave.
Elizabeth Ave.
McNichol Ave.

North Murray
St.

Davis St.

Canal St.

Wall St.

Water St.

Kidd Ave.

Hollandale St.

Sommerset St.

Pacific St.   McCabe St.

Edward St.

Alfred St.

Whitney Lane

Maple St.

Barbara St.

Austin St.

Gould St.

Robert Dr.

Birch St.

Kerr Crest

Johnson Rd.

Dyron St.

Nicholas St.

Hannah St.

Louis St.

Leopold St.

Marmora St.

Radesky St.

Trent River

Dixon Dr.

Stanley St.

Guelph St.

Alberta St.

Meyers St.

Baptise St.

Dominic St.

Mercia St.

Cedar St.

Richard St.

Princess St.

Dyron St.

Mount Pelion
& Park

Metcalfe

Williams St.

Joseph St.

Front St.

Ontario St.

College St.

Goerge St.

Crown St.

Hebert St.

Dundas St. East

John St.

Campbell St.

Bay St.

First Ave.

Catherine St.

MacLellan St.

Spring St.

King St.

Henry St.

Victoria St.

Queen St.

Elgin St.

Dundas St. West Highway 2

Wilkins St.

Flint St.

MacLellan St.

Lorne Ave.

Shuter St.

Stewart St.

Albert St.

Couch Cres.

McGill St.

Dufferin St.

Creswell Dr.

Bayshore
Park

Centennial
Park

Hanna
Park

Bay of
Quinte

©ULYSSES

Eastern Ontario

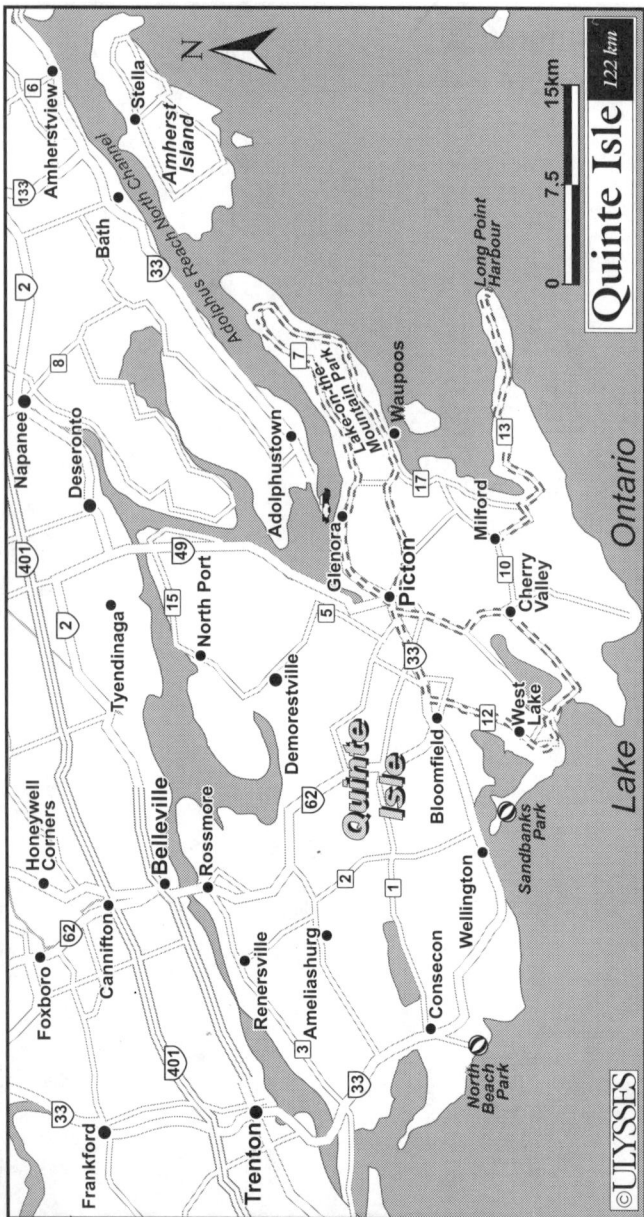

Quinte Isle

122 km

0 7.5 15km

Kingston

Tugwood Park

Belle Park Fairways

Railway St.

Duff St.

Fifth Ave.

Fraser St.

Fourth Ave.

Third Ave.

Joseph St.

Dunkirk Ave.

Russell St.

Fergus St.

First Ave.

Thomas St.

Stephen St.

Katings-Megaffin Park

Concession St.

Cataraqui St.

Kingston Memorial

18

Adelaide St.

James St.

Rideau Park

York St.

Pine St.

Charles St.

Victoria St.

Quebec St.

2

Riverview Park

Frontenac St.

Elm St.

Patrick

Nelson St.

Alfred St.

Division St.

York St.

Raglan Road

Mc Burney Park

Victoria Park

Colborne St.

Queen St.

Montreal St.

Bagot St.

1 **2**

Lasalle Causeway

Victoria St.

Princess St.

Artillery Park

2

Wellington

Albert St.

Brock St.

Johnson St.

Clergy St.

Ontario St.

Kingston Harbour

Earl St.

University Ave.

William St.

7

Bagot St.

Clarence St.

King East

4

Frontenac St.

Clergy St. W.

14

Union St.

12

Earl St.

6

19

3

Gore St.

5

Collingwood St.

Queen's University

13

Lower Union St.

Barrie St.

Stuart St.

8

City Park

9

15 **16** **17**

King St. West

Breakwater

11

10

Ontario and West St. Park

Macdonald Park

Lake Ontario

©ULYSSES

N

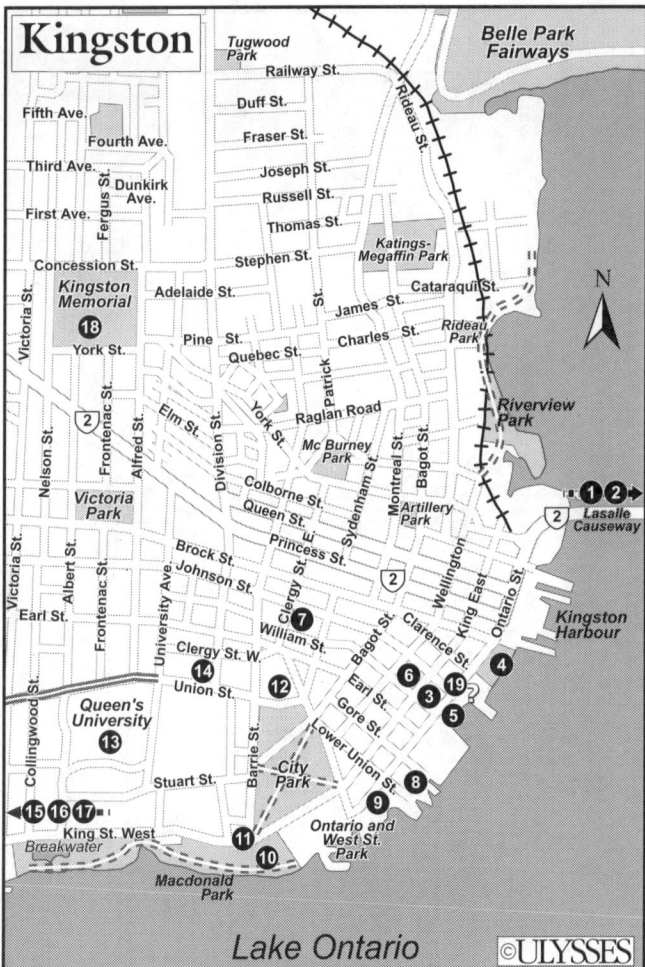

Eastern Ontario

● ATTRACTIONS

1. Royal Military College and the National Defense College
2. Fort Henry
3. Kingston City Hall
4. Confederation Park
5. Prince George Hotel
6. St. George's Cathedral
7. St. Mary's Roman Catholic Cathedral
8. Marine Museum of the Great Lakes
9. Pump House Steam Museum
10. Murney
11. Tower Museum
12. Frontenac County Court House
13. Queen's University
14. Miller Museum of Geology and Mineralogy
15. Villa Bellevue
16. Kingston Archeological Centre
17. Correctional Service of Canada Museum
18. International Hockey Hall of Fame and Museum
19. Kingston Haunted Walk

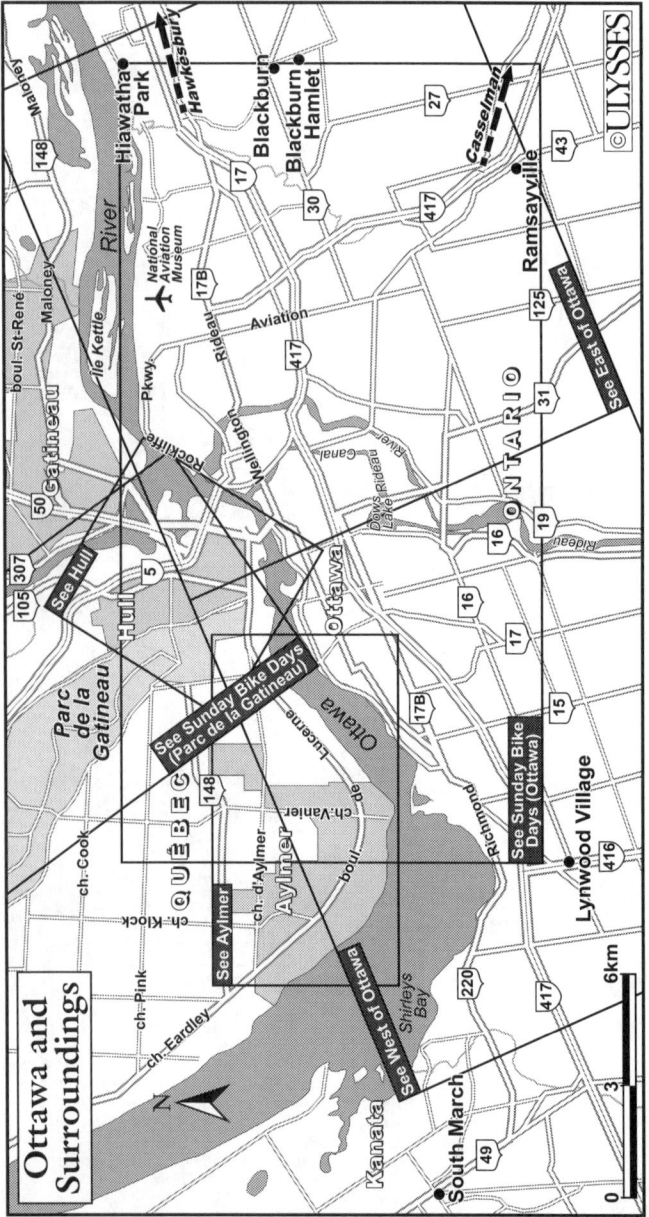

Ottawa and Surroundings

© ULYSSES

Ottawa and Surroundings

Since the earliest days of the city, the creation of green spaces was a priority for city leaders, who, over the years, proceeded to lay out vast, beautiful parks and gardens.

Whether you are looking for an urban park such as Major's Hill or Rockliffe, or untouched natural spaces like Gatineau Park, the Ottawa-Hull region has a bit of everything to please nature lovers and outdoor enthusiasts. All of these natural attractions are located either in or near the city. Hiking, cycling and cross-country skiing are among the sports that are easily practised in the National Capital Region.

The Ottawa region is crisscrossed by no less than 150km of pathways that are very pleasant for meandering on foot or by bicycle. Whether you opt for an outing along the Rideau Canal, on the Rockliffe promenade or along the Ottawa River, you will benefit from pleasant landscapes, peace and quiet and, above all, from trails that are very well laid-out for cycling. On Sunday mornings from late May to early September, cyclists are in seventh heaven, as these routes are closed to automobile traffic.

Ottawa and Surroundings

Bike Paths and Rail Trails

City/Area	Total Length (km)	Page
Ottawa (West of Ottawa)	-	140-141
Ottawa (East of Ottawa)	-	142-143
Along the two Rideaus	-	144-145
Upper Town	-	146
Downtown	-	147
Near 24 Sussex Drive	-	148
Aylmer	23.4	149
Hull	64.8	150-151
Sunday Bike Days (Ottawa)	25	152
Sunday Bike Days (Parc de la Gatineau)	40	153

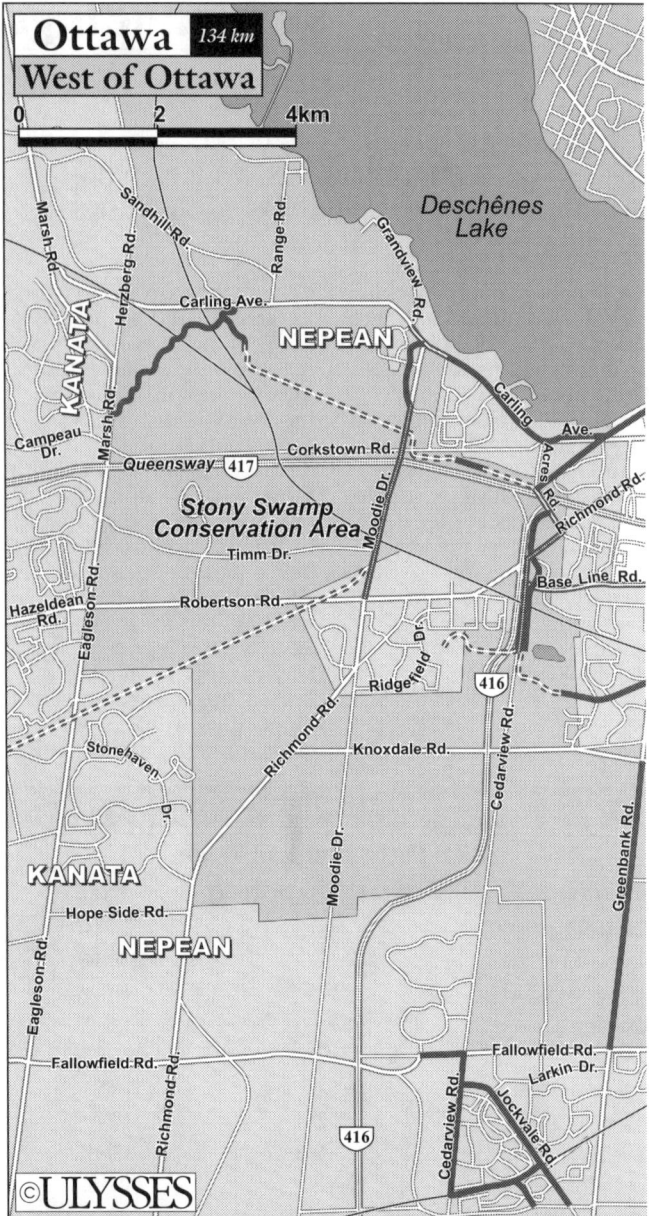

Ottawa 134 km
West of Ottawa

0   2   4km

Marsh-Rd.

Sandhill-Rd.

Herzberg Rd.

Range-Rd.

Grandview-Rd.

Deschênes Lake

Carling Ave.

NEPEAN

KANATA

Marsh-Rd.

Campeau Dr.

Queensway 417

Corkstown-Rd.

Carling Ave.

Acres-Rd.

Richmond Rd.

Stony Swamp Conservation Area

Moodie Dr.

Timm-Dr.

Hazeldean Rd.

Eagleson-Rd.

Robertson-Rd.

Base Line Rd.

Ridgefield Dr.

416

Stonehaven Dr.

Richmond-Rd.

Knoxdale-Rd.

Cedarview Rd.

Greenbank Rd.

KANATA

Eagleson-Rd.

Hope Side Rd.

NEPEAN

Moodie Dr.

Fallowfield-Rd.

Richmond-Rd.

416

Cedarview Rd.

Fallowfield-Rd.

Larkin Dr.

Jockvale-Rd.

©ULYSSES

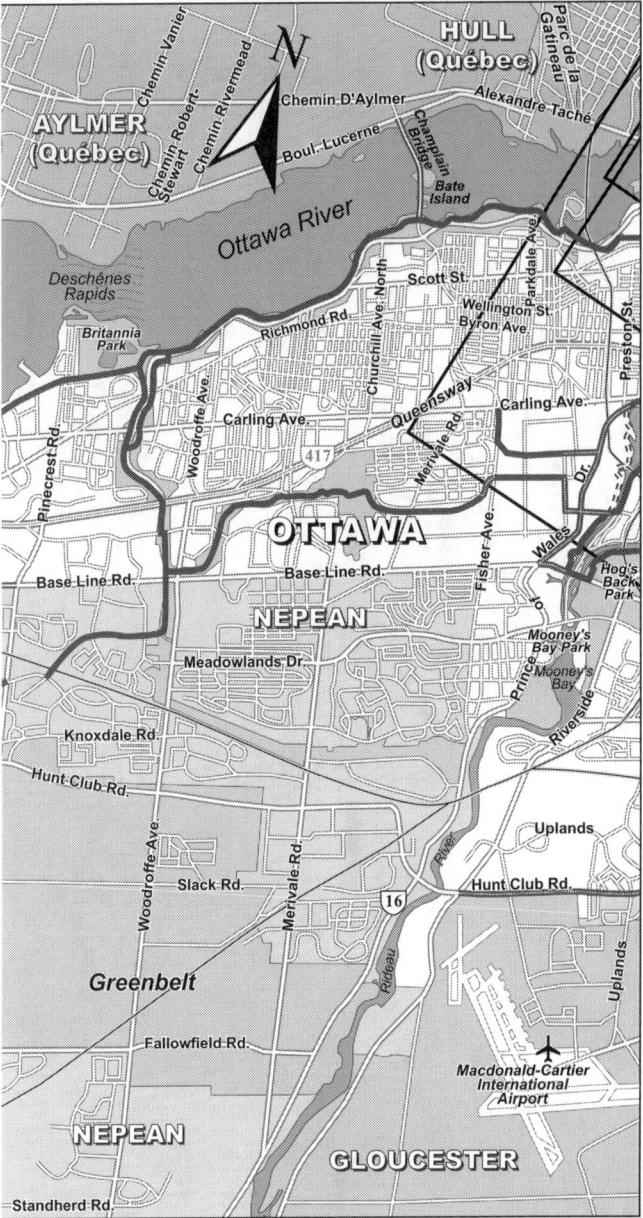

N

HULL
(Québec)

Parc de la Gatineau

Chemin D'Aylmer

Alexandre Taché

AYLMER
(Québec)

Chemin-Vanier

Chemin-Robert-Stewart

Chemin-Rivermead

Boul.-Lucerne

Champlain Bridge

Bate Island

Ottawa River

Deschênes Rapids

Britannia Park

Richmond Rd.

Scott St.

Wellington St.

Byron Ave.

Parkdale Ave.

Preston St.

Pinecrest Rd.

Woodroffe Ave.

Carling Ave.

Churchill-Ave.-North

Queensway

Merivale Rd.

Carling Ave.

417

OTTAWA

Base Line Rd.

Base Line Rd.

NEPEAN

Fisher Ave.

Wales

Dr.

Hog's Back Park

Meadowlands Dr.

Mooney's Bay Park

Prince

Mooney's Bay

Knoxdale Rd.

Riverside

Hunt-Club-Rd.

Woodroffe Ave.

Merivale Rd.

Slack-Rd.

16

Uplands

Rideau

Hunt Club Rd.

Uplands

Greenbelt

Fallowfield Rd.

Macdonald-Cartier International Airport

NEPEAN

GLOUCESTER

Standherd Rd.

Ottawa and Surroundings

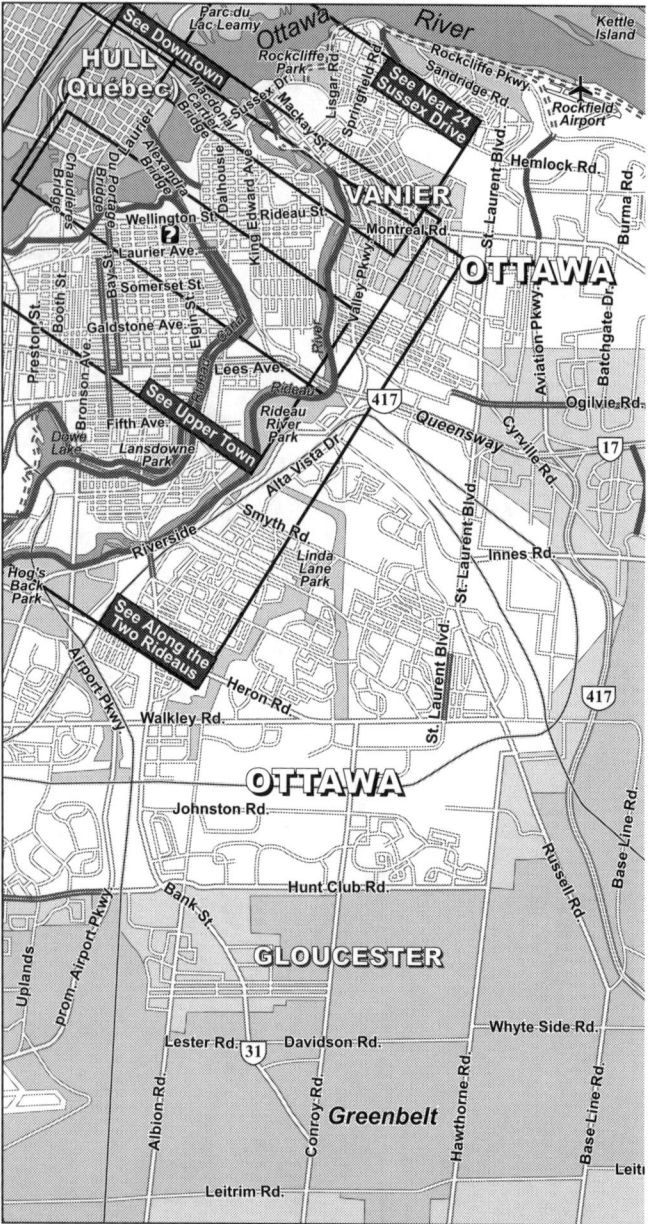

Parc du Lac Leamy

Ottawa River

Kettle Island

See Downtown

HULL (Québec)

Rockcliffe Park

Rockcliffe Rd.

Sandridge Rd.

Rockfield Airport

Springfield Rd.

Lisgar Rd.

Mackay St.

See Near 24 Sussex Drive

Hemlock Rd.

Burma Rd.

Macdonald Cartier Bridge

Sussex Dr.

Dalhousie

St-Laurent Blvd.

Portage Bridge

Alexandra Bridge

Chaudière Bridges

Wellington St.

King Edward Ave.

Rideau St.

VANIER

Montreal Rd.

OTTAWA

Laurier Ave.

Somerset St.

Bronson Ave.

Booth St.

Preston St.

Gladstone Ave.

Eglin St.

Vanier Pkwy.

Aviation Pkwy.

Batchgate Dr.

Lees Ave.

Rideau River Park

417

Queensway

Ogilvie Rd.

Cyrville Rd.

17

See Upper Town

Fifth Ave.

Dowe Lake

Lansdowne Park

Alta Vista Dr.

Riverside

Smyth Rd.

Linda Lane Park

St-Laurent Blvd.

Innes Rd.

Hog's Back Park

See Along the Two Rideaus

417

Airport Pkwy.

Heron Rd.

Walkley Rd.

OTTAWA

Johnston Rd.

St. Laurent Blvd.

Russell Rd.

Base Line Rd.

Hunt Club Rd.

Bank St.

GLOUCESTER

Uplands

prom. Airport Pkwy.

Albion Rd.

Lester Rd.

31

Davidson Rd.

Conroy Rd.

Greenbelt

Hawthorne Rd.

Whyte Side Rd.

Base Line Rd.

Leitrim Rd.

Leitr

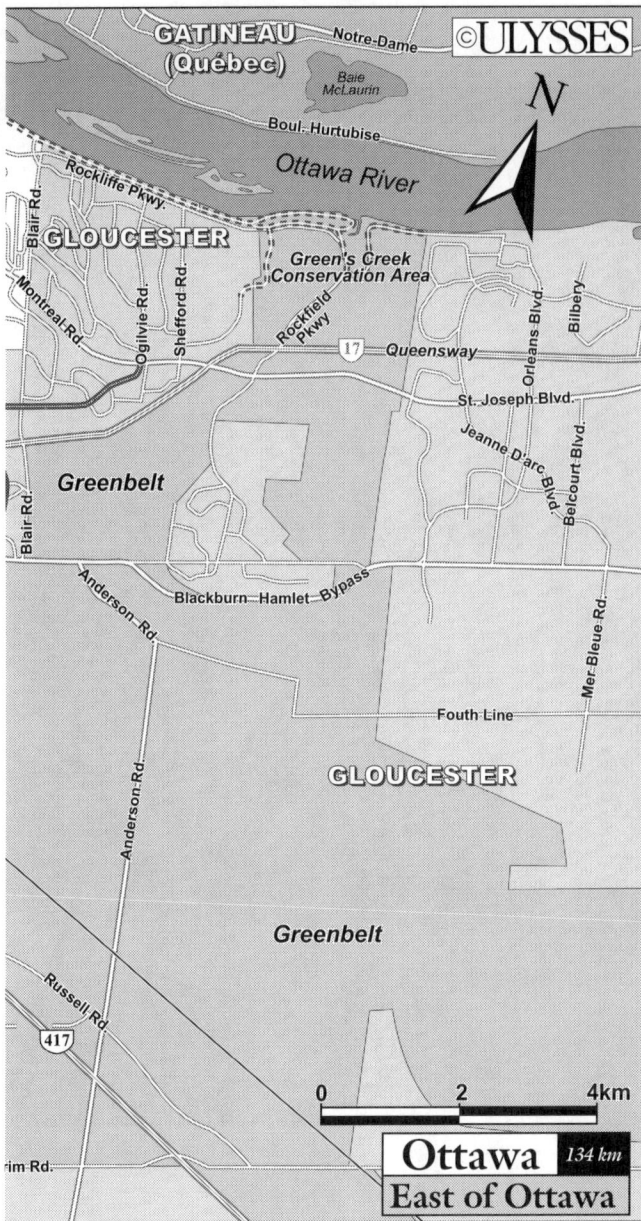

GATINEAU
(Québec)
Notre-Dame
©ULYSSES

Baie
McLaurin

Boul. Hurtubise

Ottawa River

N

Rockcliffe Pkwy.

Blair Rd.

GLOUCESTER

Green's Creek
Conservation Area

Montreal Rd.

Ogilvie Rd.

Shefford Rd.

Rockfield Pkwy

17 Queensway

Orleans Blvd.

Bilbery

St. Joseph Blvd.

Jeanne D'arc Blvd.

Belcourt Blvd.

Greenbelt

Blair Rd.

Anderson Rd.

Blackburn Hamlet Bypass

Mer Bleue Rd.

Fouth Line

GLOUCESTER

Anderson Rd.

Greenbelt

Russell Rd.

417

0   2   4km

rim Rd.

Ottawa   134 km
East of Ottawa

Ottawa and Surroundings

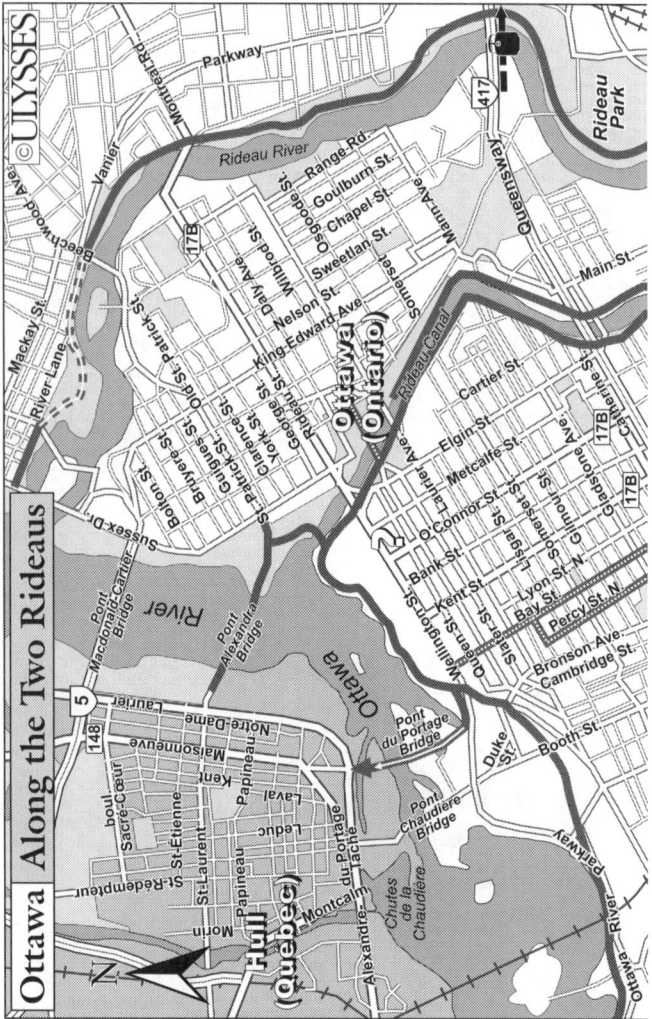

Ottawa Along the Two Rideaus
©ULYSSES

Parkway
Rideau River
Range Rd.
Goulburn St.
Chapel St.
Sweetlan St.
Nelson St.
King-Edward-Ave.
Cartier St.
Elgin St.
Metcalfe St.
O'Connor St.
Bank St.
Kent St.
Bay St.
Percy St. N.
Bronson Ave.
Cambridge St.
Main St.
Rideau Park
Rideau Canal
Ottawa (Ontario)
Beechwood Ave.
Mackay St.
Vanier
Montreal Rd.
River Lane
St-Patrick-St.
Sussex Dr.
Bolton St.
Bruyère St.
Clarence St.
York St.
George St.
Pont Macdonald-Cartier Bridge
Pont Alexandra Bridge
River
Ottawa
Pont du Portage Bridge
Pont Chaudière Bridge
Duke St.
Booth St.
Parkway
Ottawa River
Laurier
Notre-Dame
Maisonneuve
boul. Sacré-Cœur
St-Etienne
Kent
Papineau
Laval
Leduc
Morin
St-Laurent
St-Rédempteur
Papineau
Montcalm
Alexandre
du Portage
Taché
Chutes de la Chaudière
Hull (Québec)

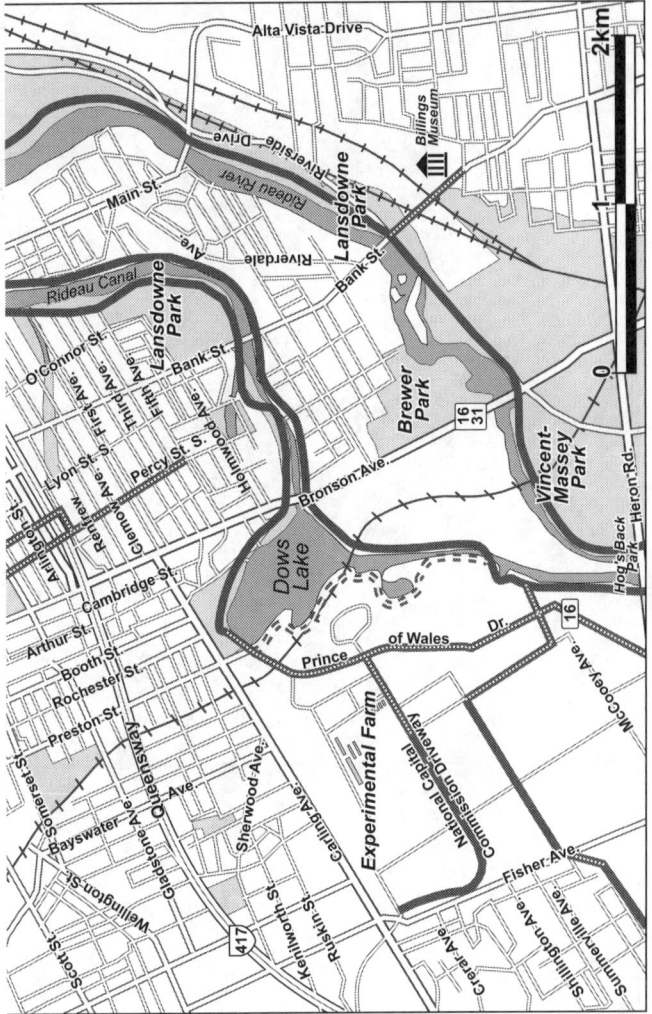

2km

Alta Vista Drive

Billings Museum

Riverside Drive

Rideau River

Main St.

Riverdale Ave.

Landsdowne Park

Rideau Canal

Bank St.

O'Connor St.

Landsdowne Park

Bank St.

Brewer Park

Vincent-Massey Park

Lyon St. S.
Renfrew Ave. S.
Clemow Ave.
Percy St. S.

First Ave.
Third Ave.
Fifth Ave.
Holmwood Ave.

Bronson Ave.

16
31

Hog's Back Park

Heron Rd.

Arlington

Dows Lake

Cambridge St.

Arthur St.

Booth St.

Rochester St.

Preston St.

Prince   of Wales   Dr.

16

McCooey Ave.

Somerset St.

Bayswater Ave.

Gladstone Ave.

Queensway

Sherwood Ave.

Experimental Farm

National Capital Commission Driveway

Fisher Ave.

Wellington St.

Scott St.

417

Kenilworth St.

Ruskin St.

Carling Ave.

Crerar Ave.

Shillington Ave.

Summerville Ave.

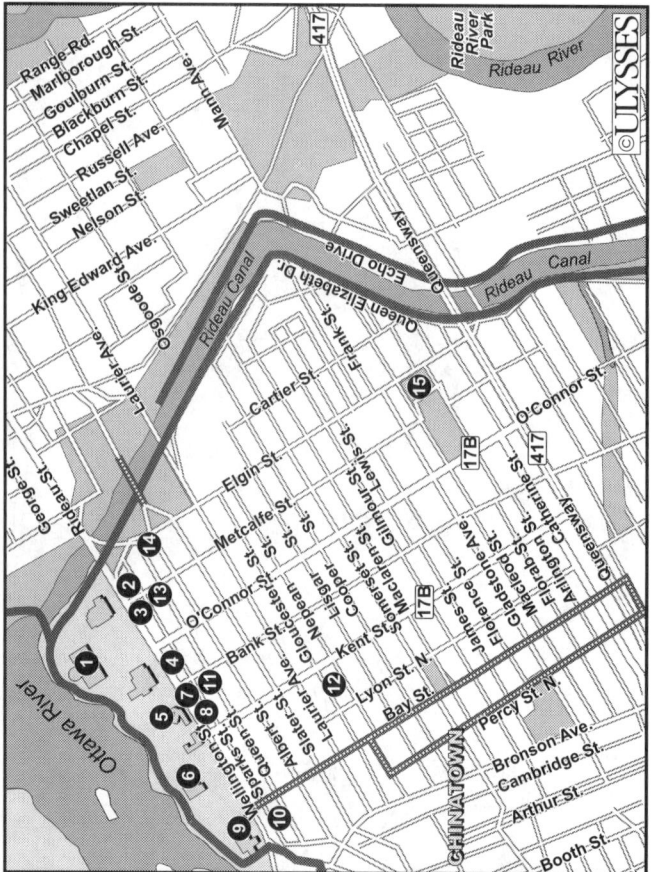

Ottawa
Upper Town

N

0   250   500m

● **ATTRACTIONS**

1. Parliament
   Buildings
2. Langevin
   Block
3. Infocentre
4. Bank of
   Montreal
5. Confederation
   Building

6. Supreme Court of
   Canada
7. Bank of Canada
8. Memorial Building
9. National Library and
   Archives of Canada
10. Christ Church
    Cathedral

© ULYSSES

Range Rd.
Marlborough St.
Goulburn St.
Blackburn St.
Chapel St.
Russell Ave.
Sweetlan. St.
Nelson St.
King Edward Ave.
Osgoode St.
Laurier Ave.
Mann Ave.
417
Rideau River Park
Rideau River
Rideau Canal
Echo Drive
Queensway
Rideau Canal
Queen Elizabeth Dr.
Frank St.
Cartier St.
O'Connor St.
17B
Gladstone St.
MacLeod St.
Florabe St.
Catherine
Arlington
Queensway
Elgin St.
George St.
Rideau St.
Metcalfe St.
O'Connor St.
Gilmour St.
Lewis St.
Somerset St.
MacLaren St.
Florence Ave.
James St.
Cooper St.
Lisgar
Nepean St.
Gloucester St.
Bank St.
Kent St.
Lyon St. N.
Bay St.
Percy St. N.
Bronson Ave.
Cambridge St.
Arthur St.
Booth St.
CHINATOWN
17B
12
15
14
2
3
13
1
4
7
5
8
11
6
9
10
Ottawa River
Wellington St.
Sparks St.
Albert St.
Queen St.
Slater St.
Laurier Ave.

© ULYSSES

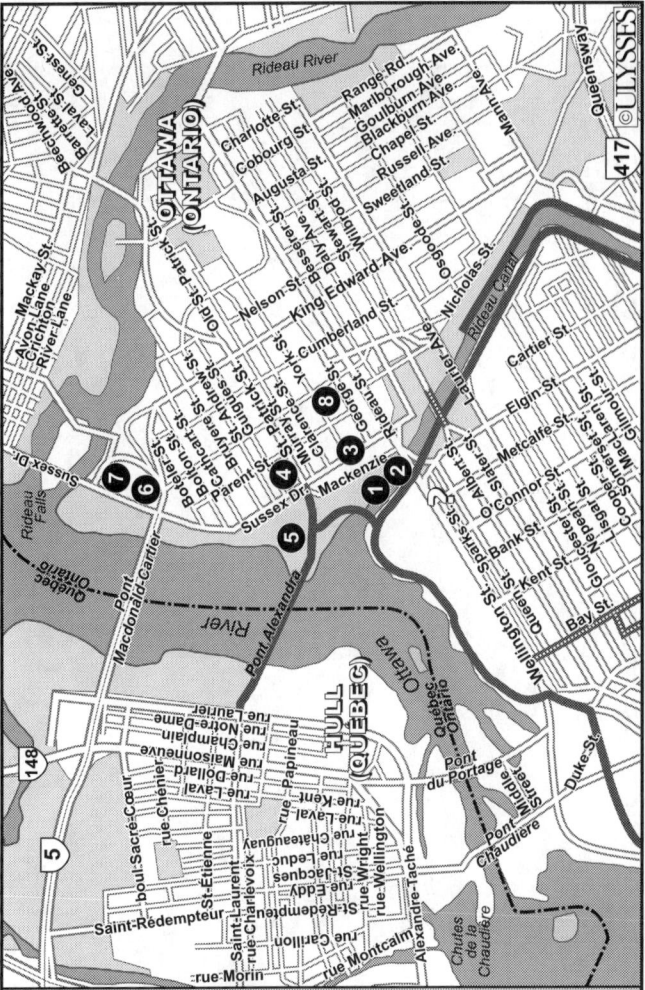

Ottawa Downtown

N

0   400   800m

● ATTRACTIONS

1. Château Laurier
2. Canadian Museum of Contemporary Photography
3. Connaught Building
4. Notre-Dame Basilica
5. National Gallery of Canada
6. Canadian War Museum
7. Royal Canadian Mint
8. Byward Market

Ottawa and Surroundings

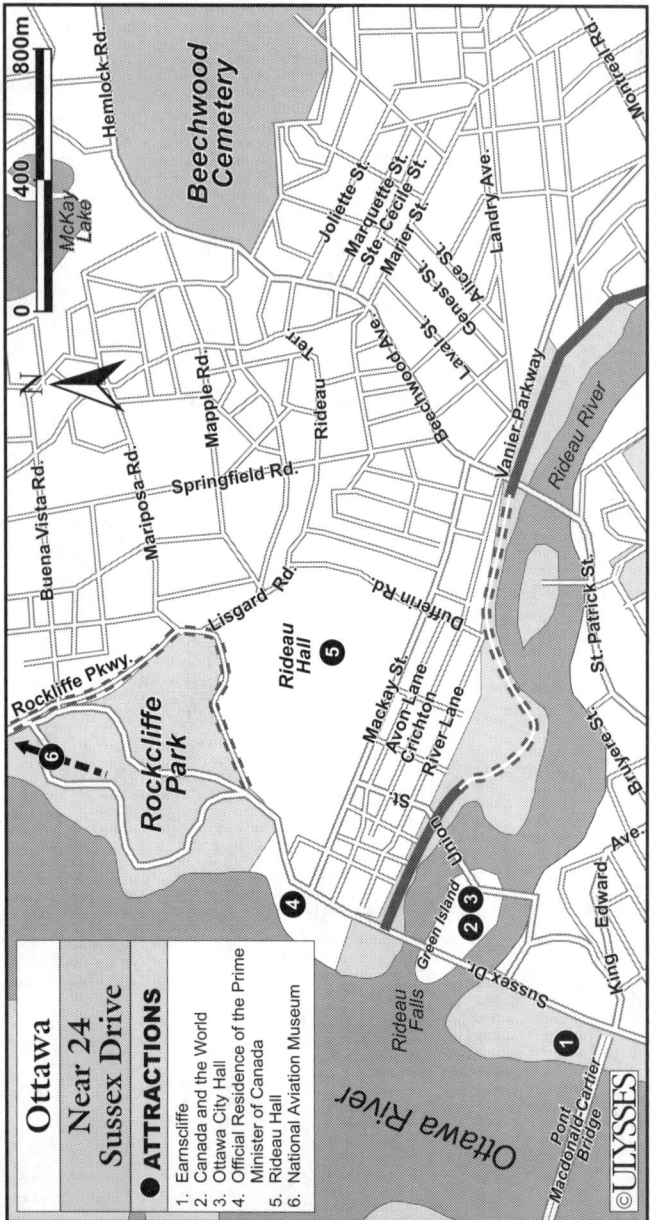

Ottawa
Near 24 Sussex Drive

● **ATTRACTIONS**

1. Earnscliffe
2. Canada and the World
3. Ottawa City Hall
4. Official Residence of the Prime Minister of Canada
5. Rideau Hall
6. National Aviation Museum

Beechwood Cemetery

McKay Lake

Henlock Rd.

Joliette St.
Marquette St.
Ste-Cécile St.
Marier St.
Genest St.
Alice St.
Landry Ave.
Laval St.

Beechwood Ave.
Vanier Parkway

Rideau River

Springfield Rd.

Mapple Rd.
Terr.
Rideau
Rideau

Buena-Vista Rd.
Mariposa Rd.
Rockcliffe Pkwy.

Lisgard Rd.
Dufferin Rd.

Rideau Hall

⑤

Rockcliffe Park

⑥

⑤

④

Mackay St.
Avon Lane
Crichton
River Lane
St.
Union

Green Island

② ③

② ③

King
Edward Ave.

Sussex Dr.

Rideau Falls

Bruyère St.
St-Patrick St.

Ottawa River

①

Pont Macdonald-Cartier Bridge

0   400   800m

N

© ULYSSES

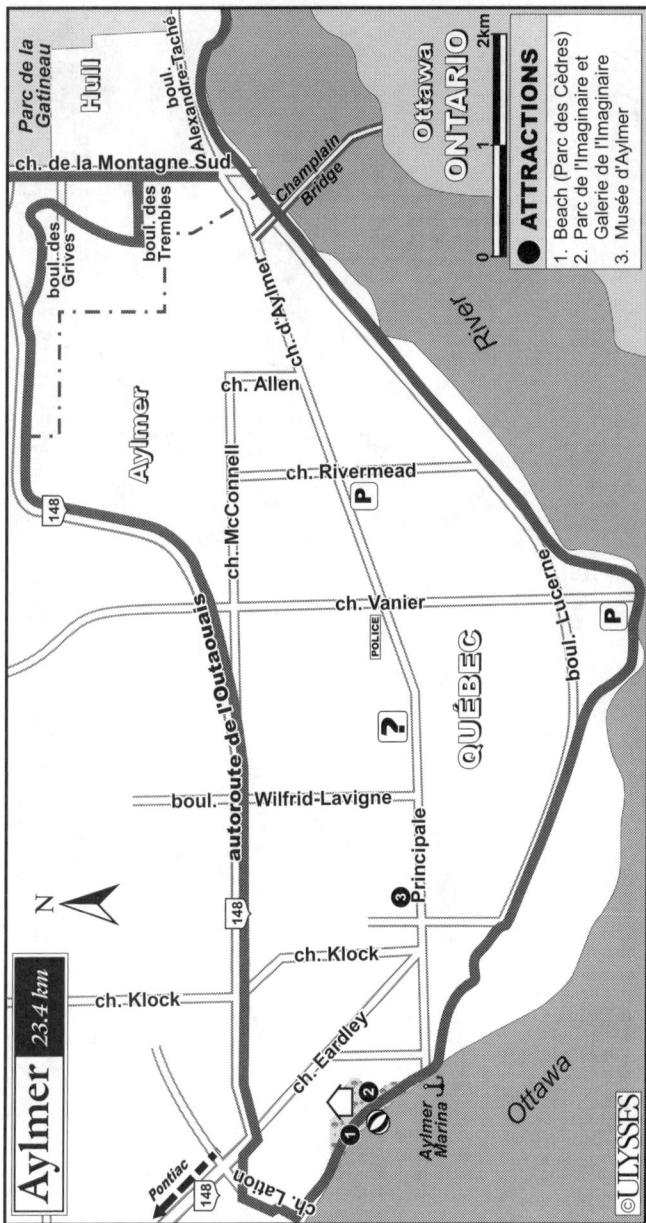

Aylmer 23.4 km

N

ATTRACTIONS

1. Beach (Parc des Cèdres)
2. Parc de l'Imaginaire et Galerie de l'Imaginaire
3. Musée d'Aylmer

Parc de la Gatineau

Hull

boul. des Grives

boul. des Trembles

ch. de la Montagne Sud

boul. Alexandre-Taché

Champlain Bridge

ch. d'Aylmer

ch. Allen

ch. Rivermead

ch. Vanier

POLICE

boul. Wilfrid-Lavigne

ch. McConnell

Principale

ch. Klock

ch. Klock

ch. Eardley

autoroute de l'Outaouais

148

148

QUÉBEC

ONTARIO

Ottawa River

boul. Lucerne

Aylmer Marina

Pontiac

ch. Lattion

148

Ottawa

© ULYSSES

Ottawa and Surroundings

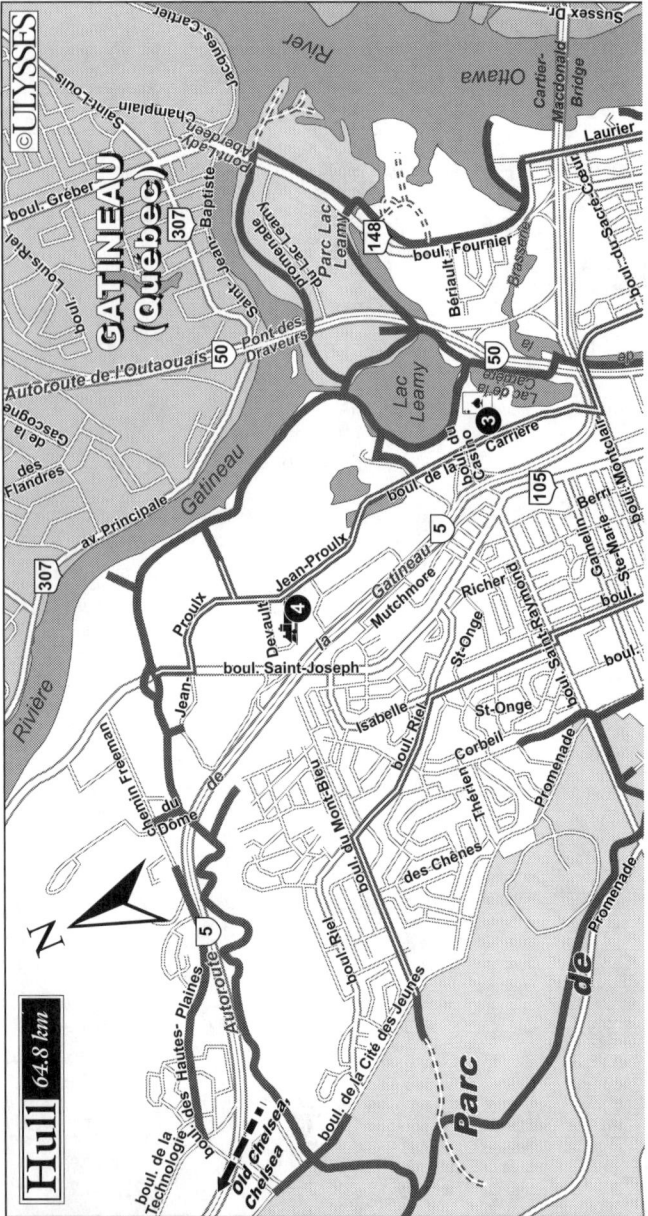

Hull 64.8 km

GATINEAU (Québec)

Parc de

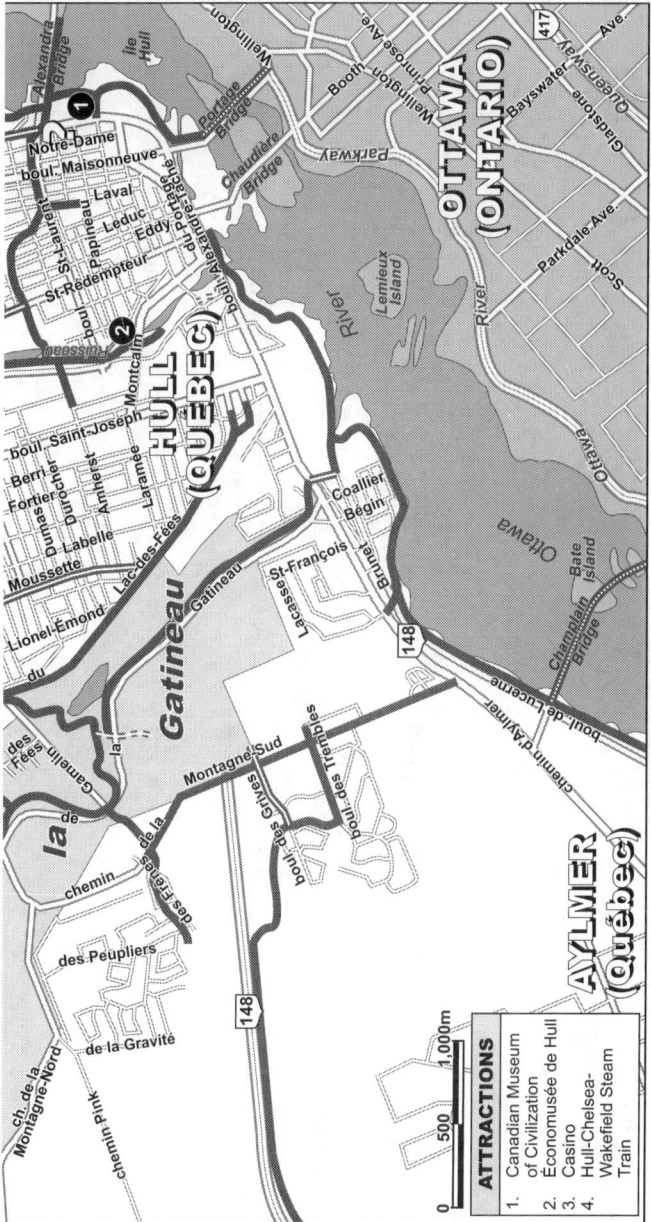

OTTAWA (ONTARIO)

HULL (QUÉBEC)

AYLMER (Québec)

Ottawa River

Gatineau

Île Hull

Notre-Dame
boul. Maisonneuve
Laval
Leduc
St-Laurent
Papineau
St-Rédempteur
boul. Alexandre-Taché
Eddy
du Portage

Wellington
Pont du Portage
Chaudière Bridge
Alexandra Bridge

boul. Saint-Joseph
Berri
Fortier
Durocher
Dumas
Amherst
Laramée
Montcalm
Labelle
Lac-des-Fées
Moussette
Lionel-Émond
Gatineau
Gamelin
du
des Fées
de la
de la
chemin
des Peupliers
de la Gravité
ch. de la Montagne-Nord
chemin-Pink

Coallier
Bégin
St-François
Lacasse
Brunet
148
Montagne-Sud
boul. des Grives
boul. des Trembles
148

chemin d'Aylmer
boul. de Lucerne

Lemieux Island
Bate Island
Champlain Bridge

Wellington
Booth
Primrose Ave.
Parkway
Scott
Parkdale Ave.
Bayswater
Gladstone Ave.
Queensway
417
Ave.

ATTRACTIONS

1. Canadian Museum of Civilization
2. Économusée de Hull
3. Casino
4. Hull-Chelsea-Wakefield Steam Train

0   500   1,000m

Ottawa and Surroundings

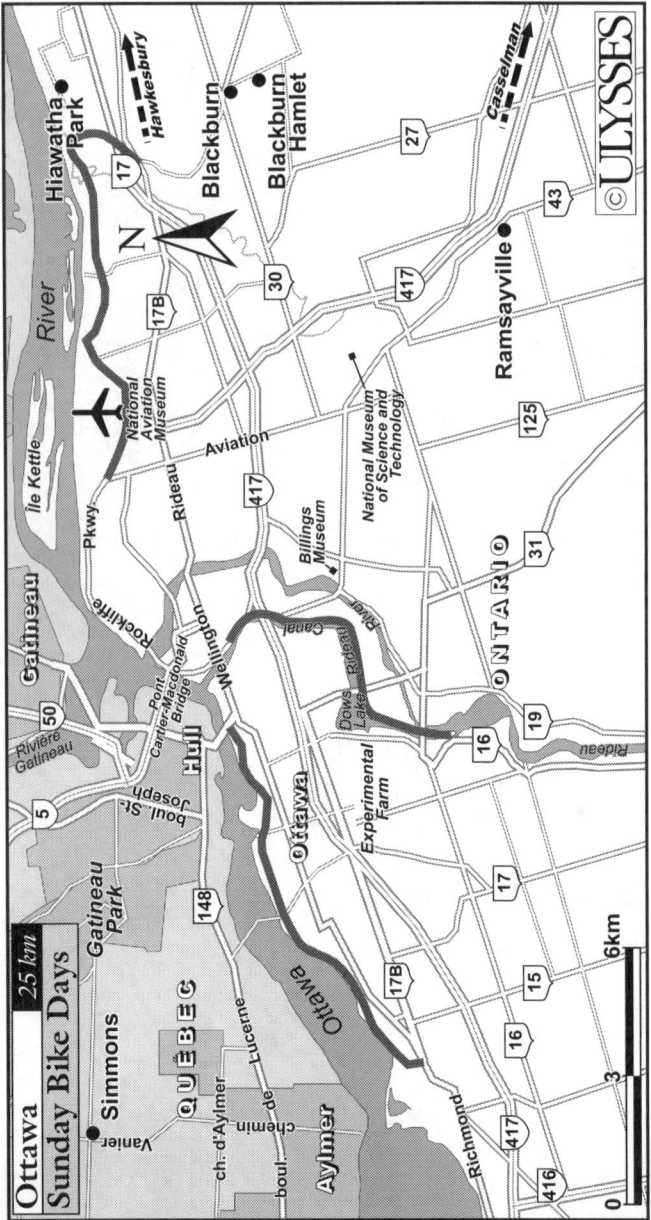

Ottawa
Sunday Bike Days

25 km

© ULYSSES

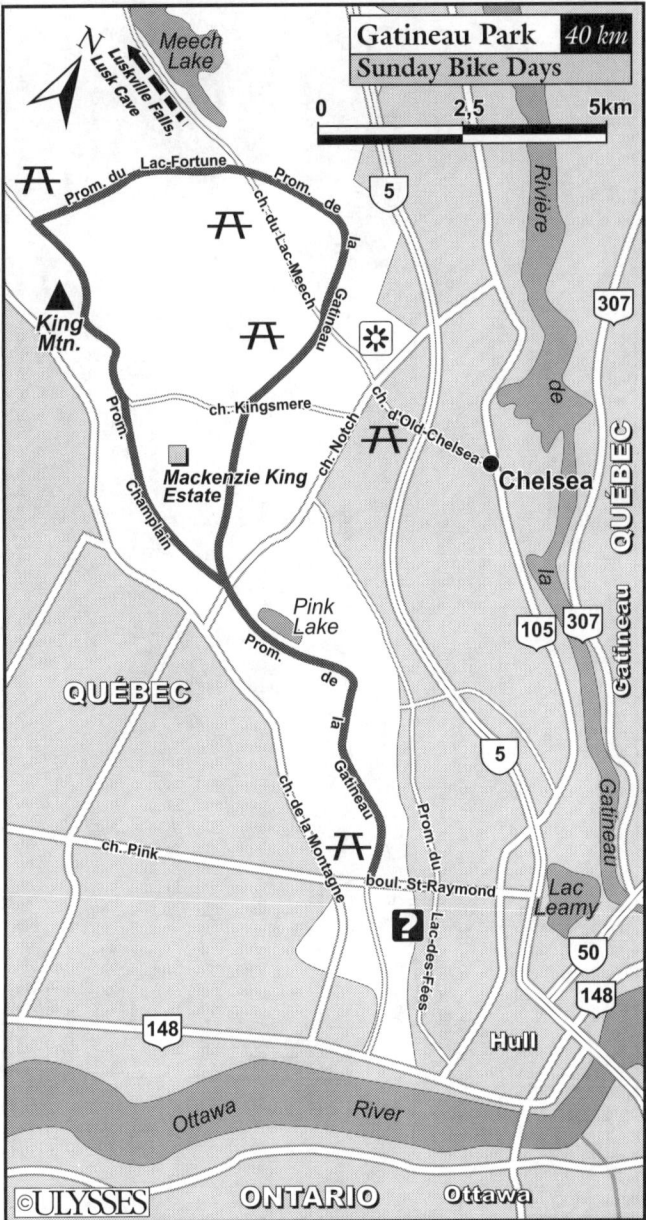

Gatineau Park *40 km*
Sunday Bike Days

0   2,5   5km

N

Meech Lake

Luskville Falls,
Lusk Cave

Prom. du   Lac-Fortune

ch. du Lac-Meech

Prom. de la Gatineau

▲ *King Mtn.*

Prom.

Champlain

ch. Kingsmere

☐ *Mackenzie King Estate*

ch. Notch

ch. d'Old-Chelsea

● **Chelsea**

Pink Lake

Prom. de la Gatineau

QUÉBEC

QUÉBEC

ch. Pink

ch. de la Montagne

boul. St-Raymond

Prom. du Lac-des-Fées

?

Lac Leamy

5

307

105 **307**

5

50

148

148

Hull

Ottawa   River

ONTARIO   *Ottawa*

©ULYSSES

Rivière   de   la   Gatineau   QUÉBEC

Ottawa and Surroundings

© ULYSSES

Northern Ontario

QUÉBEC

UNITED STATES

Lake Superior

Lake Huron

Lake Michigan

Lake Nipigon

Georgian Bay

Manitoulin Island

Réserve faunique de La Vérendrye

Algonquin Provincial Park

S. de Champlain Prov. Park

Killarney Prov. Park

Quetico Prov. Park

Lake Superior Provincial Park

Pukaskwa National Park

Chapleau Crown Game Preserve

Neys P.P.

Sleeping Giant P.P.

Ouimet Canyon

Kakabeka Falls

Lovicourt
Amos
La Sarre
Rouyn-Noranda
Cobalt
Iroquois Falls
Cochrane
Smooth Rock Falls
Kapuskasing
Moonbeam
Opasatika
Mattice
Hearst
Fraserdale
Kirkland Lake
Elk Lake
Matachewan
Timmins
Foleyet
Chapleau
Temagami
Sturgeon Falls
North Bay
Mattawa
Sudbury
Copper Cliff
Massey
Gore Bay
Sault St. Mary
Tobermory
Alpena
Petoskey
Gros Cap
Wawa
White River
Marathon
Terrace bay
Rossport
Manitouwadge
Hornepayne
Caramat
Jellicoe
Nipigon
Red Rock
Pine Portage
Thunder Bay
Gulf Bay
Upsala
Ignace
Raith
Atikokan
Marquette
Escanaba
Menominee
Wausau
Menomonie
Ashland
Owen Sound
Wasaga Beach
Barrie
Midland
Parry Sound
Huntsville
Bancroft
Peterborough

11
11
11
11
17
17
17
17
61
69
75
101
129
28

0   200   400km

N

Northern Ontario

Northern Ontario extends from the nearly inaccessible, century-old Algonquin Park over a land of unspoiled character and rugged beauty, crossing hundreds of lakes, wetlands and rivers to the lands north of Lake Superior.

North of the 46th parallel lies a vast, untamed stretch of territory dominated by forests, lakes and rivers. It was by exploring these rivers that Europeans first penetrated deep into this wilderness and discovered two virtual inland seas, lakes Huron and Superior. They also encountered Aboriginal peoples who lived by hunting and fishing, and soon developed an interest in a luxury product in great demand in the Old World: fur. In the 17th century, the Europeans decided to set up trading posts so that they could do business with the northern Aboriginals, who were masters in the art of hunting. It wasn't until the 19th century, however, that these first settlements, which were scattered all over the territory, began to grow into small towns.

Northeastern Ontario was colonized relatively late. Although the beginning of the 20th century saw a wave of immigrants (mostly from Québec), the villages remain small and are few and far between. The colonists settled on arid, infertile land hoping to earn a living from the rich mineral deposits of gold and silver that had been discovered in the area. The forest industry also provided a source of employment. Villages began springing up here and there, but the number of people willing to take on such a harsh existence has remained small. Today, mining and the pulp and paper industry are the principal activities in this vast territory.

Northwestern Ontario is the province's final frontier, stretching west from the shores of Lake Superior, the largest freshwater lake in the world, to Manitoba, and north to Hudson Bay.

Northern Ontario

Bike Paths and Rail Trails

City/Area	Total Length (km)	Page
North Bay	28	157
Thunder Bay	32	158-159
Sault Ste. Marie	-	160
Mattawa	-	161
Algonquin Park (J.R. Booth Rail Trail)	10	162
Algonquin Park (Minnesing Bike Trail)	27	163
Seguin Trail	55	164
Manitoulin Island	-	165

Caribou

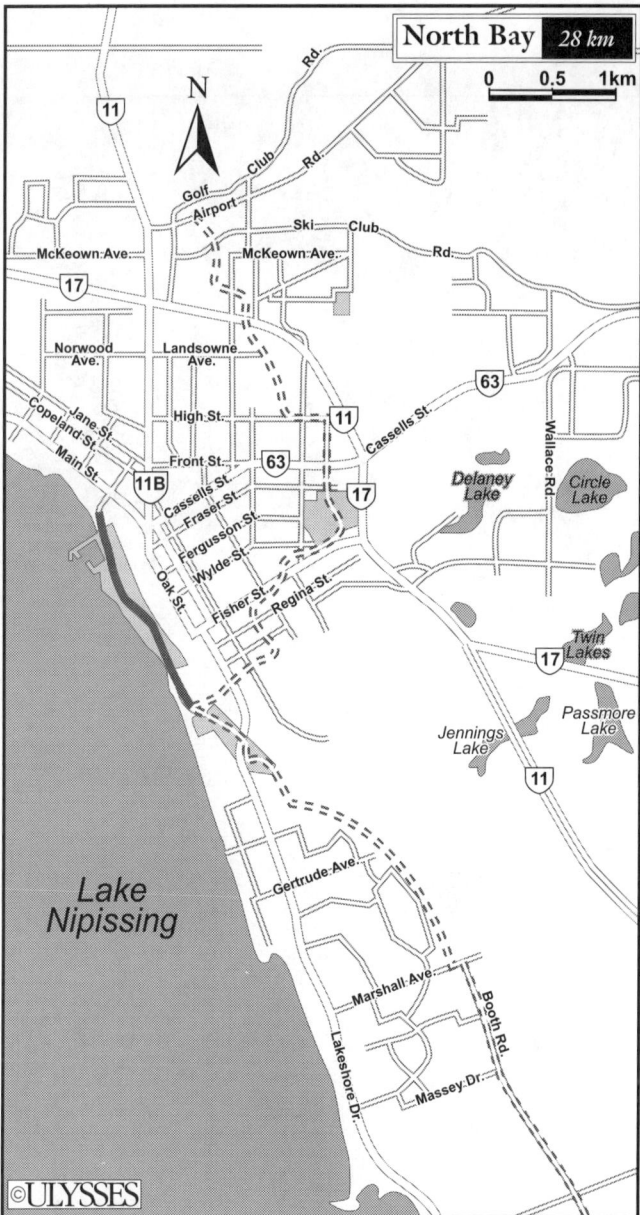

Northern Onatrio

North Bay *28 km*

0   0.5   1km

11

N

Golf Club Rd.

Rd.

Airport

Ski Club Rd.

McKeown Ave.

McKeown Ave.

Rd.

17

63

Norwood Ave.

Landsowne Ave.

High St.

11

Cassells St.

Wallace Rd.

Circle Lake

Jane St.

Front St.

63

Delaney Lake

Copeland St.

Main St.

11B

Cassells St.

Fraser St.

17

Fergusson St.

Oak St.

Wylde St.

Fisher St.

Regina St.

Twin Lakes

17

Passmore Lake

Jennings Lake

11

Gertrude Ave.

Lake Nipissing

Marshall Ave.

Booth Rd.

Lakeshore Dr.

Massey Dr.

©ULYSSES

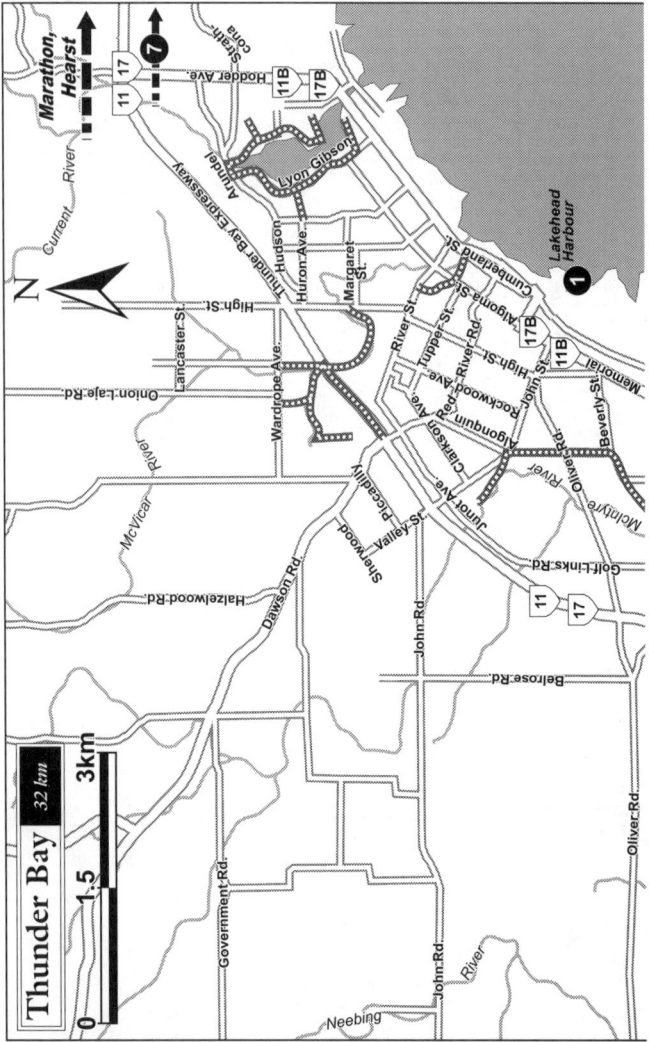

Thunder Bay 32 km

Northern Onatrio

Lake Superior

ATTRACTIONS

1. MV Welcome
2. Old Fort William
3. Thunder Bay Museum
4. Thunder Bay Art Gallery
5. Chippewa Park
6. Mount McKay Lookout
7. Thunder Bay Amethyst Mine Panorama

Dryden, Fort Frances, Manitoba

McKellar River

108th Ave.

100th Ave.

Mission River

Pacific Ave.

Simpson St.

Fort William

Main St.

May St.

10th Ave.

Balmoral St.

11th Ave.

Harbour Expwy.

Cameron St.

Syndicate Ave.

Walsh St.

Christina St.

Francis St.

Kingsway

Waterloo St.

William St.

River

View Dr.

Victoria Ave.

Isabella St.

Edward St.

Central Ave.

Expressway

James St.

Redwood Ave.

Churchill Dr.

River

Thunder Bay

James St.

Mary St.

Frederica St.

Montdale Ave.

Neebing Ave.

Montreal Ave.

Kaministiquia

City Rd.

Mission St.

City Rd.

61B

61

Neebing

Arthur St.

Rosslyn Rd.

Victor Rd.

Riverdale Rd.

Broadway Ave.

17

11

© ULYSSES

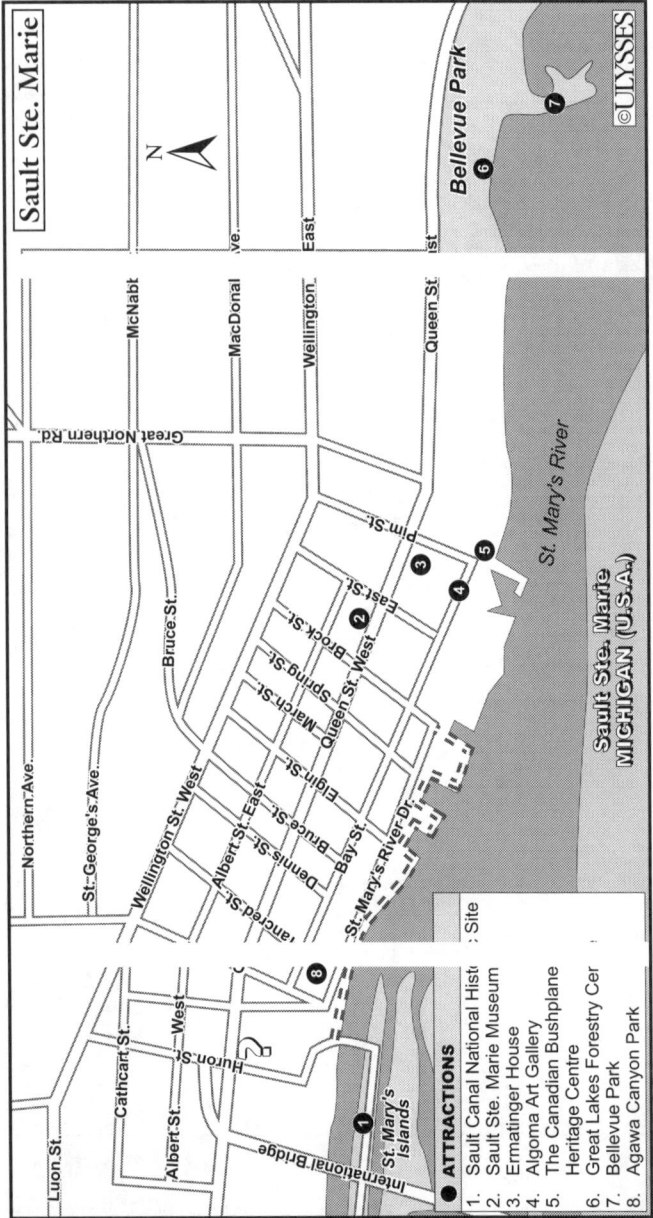

Sault Ste. Marie

N

Bellevue Park

Great Northern Rd.

McNabt

MacDonal

Wellington

Queen St.

St. Mary's River

Pim St.

East St.

Brock St.

Spring St.

Queen St. West

March St.

Elgin St.

Bruce St.

Bay St.

St. Mary's River Dr.

Albert St. East

Dennis St.

Bruce St.

Queen St. West

Wellington St. West

Bruce St.

St. George's Ave.

Northern Ave.

Huron St.

Cathcart St.

Albert St. West

Luon St.

International Bridge

St. Mary's Islands

Sault Ste. Marie
MICHIGAN (U.S.A.)

© ULYSSES

ATTRACTIONS

: Site

1. Sault Canal National Hist
2. Sault Ste. Marie Museum
3. Ermatinger House
4. Algoma Art Gallery
5. The Canadian Bushplane
   Heritage Centre
6. Great Lakes Forestry Cer
7. Bellevue Park
8. Agawa Canyon Park

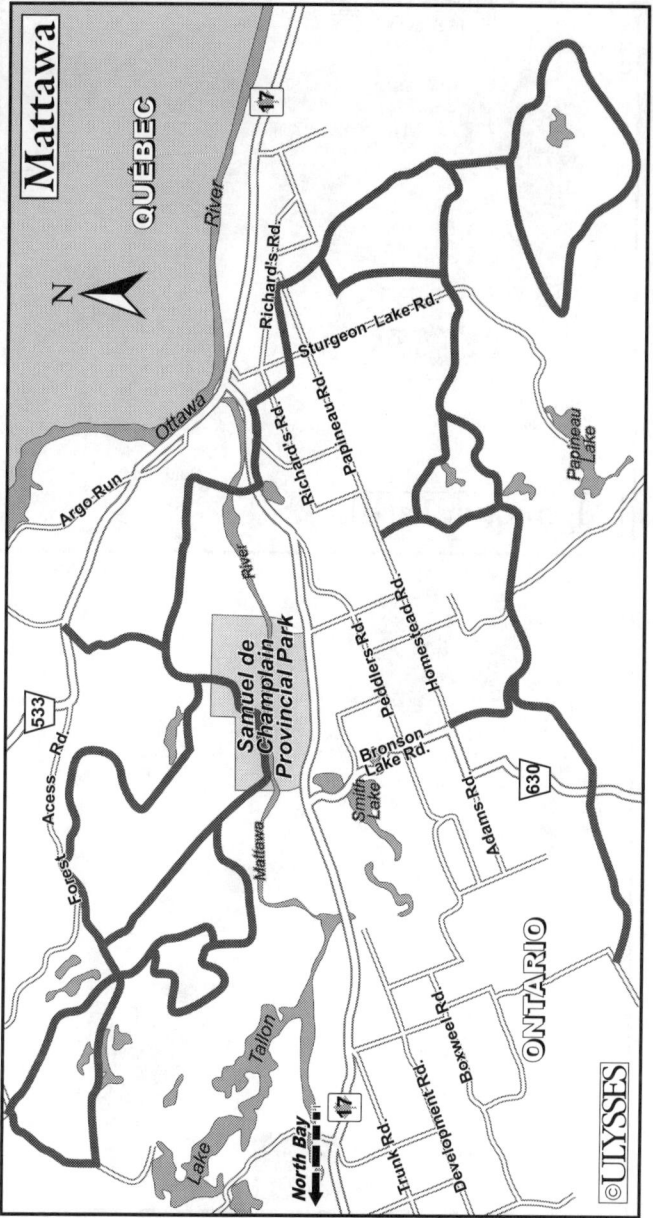

Northern Onatrio

Mattawa

QUÉBEC

N

17

Richard's Rd.

Sturgeon-Lake-Rd.

Ottawa

River

Argo Run

Papineau-Rd.

Richard's-Rd.

Papineau
Lake

533

Forest-Acess-Rd.

Samuel de
Champlain
Provincial Park

River

Mattawa

Peddler's-Rd.

Homestead-Rd.

Bronson-
Lake-Rd.

Smith
Lake

Adams-Rd.

630

Lake

Tallon

North Bay

17

Trunk-Rd.

Development-Rd.

Boxweel-Rd.

ONTARIO

©ULYSSES

Algonquin Park

Algonquin Park
J.R. Booth Rail Trail

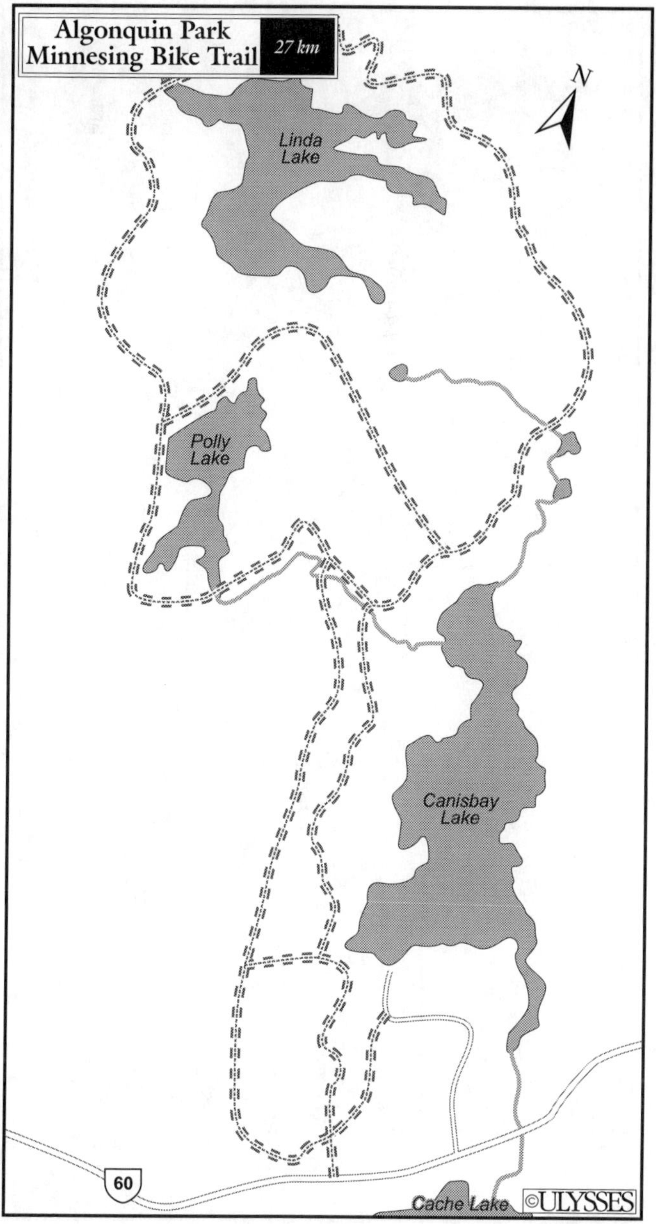

Algonquin Park
Minnesing Bike Trail   *27 km*

N

Linda
Lake

Polly
Lake

Canisbay
Lake

60

Cache Lake   ©ULYSSES

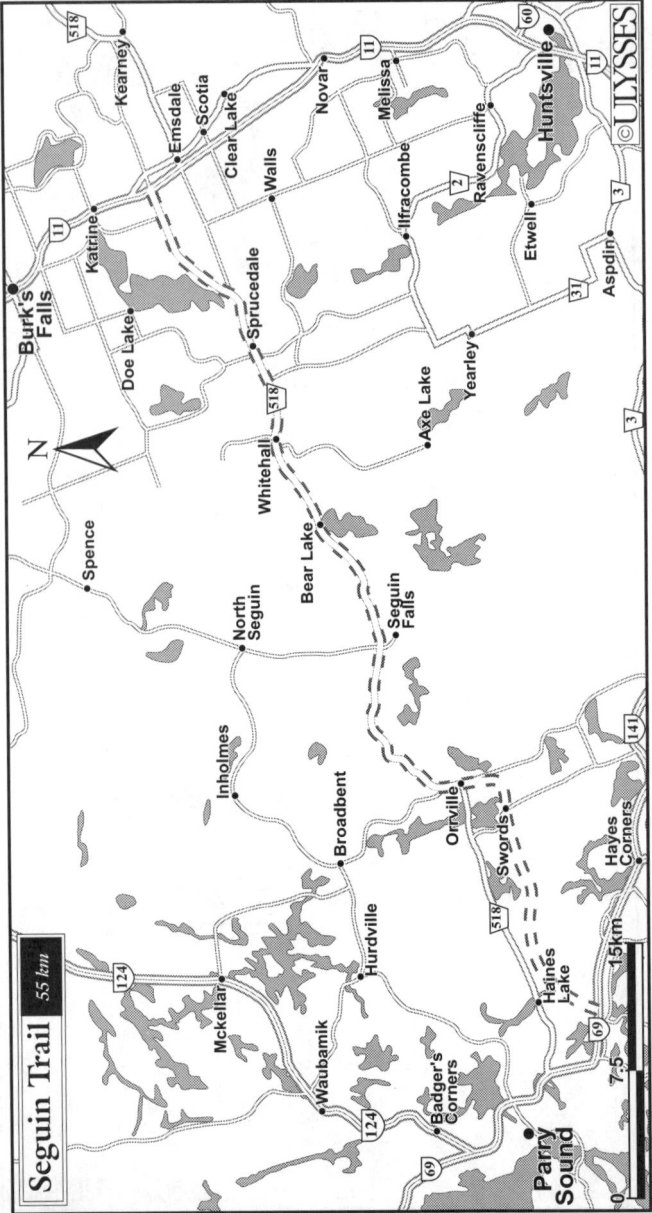

Seguin Trail 55 km

N

© ULYSSES

0   7.5   15 km

518 Kearney
Emsdale
Scotia
Clear Lake
Walls
Novar
11
Melissa
Ilfracombe
2 Ravenscliffe
Huntsville
60
11
Etwell
3
Aspdin
31
Katrine
11
Burk's Falls
Sprucedale
Doe Lake
Whitehall
518
Axe Lake
Yearley
3
Spence
North Seguin
Bear Lake
Seguin Falls
141
Inholmes
Broadbent
Orrville
Swords
Hayes Corners
124
Hurdville
518
McKellar
Waubamik
Badger's Corners
Haines Lake
69
124
69
Parry Sound

Northern Ontario

© ULYSSES

Manitoulin Island

North Channel

Lake Huron

N

Georgian Bay

Owen Channel

South Bay

Tobermory

South Baymouth

Blue Jay R.

Manitou R.

Michael Bay

Tehkummah

542

Manitowaning

6

Turtle L.

Manitowaning Bay

Wikwemikong

Smith Bay

Fraser Bay

McGregor Bay

Espanola

Whitefish Falls

Birch Island

6

Great La Cloche Island

Little Current

Sucker Creek

Sheguiandah Bay

Sheguiandah

Bass L.

Long Lake

Sucker Lake

Windfall Lake

Rock Lake

Providence Bay

551

Martin R.

Mindemoya

Mindemoya Lake

551

Spring Bay

542

Mud L.

Kagawong Lake

Wosley Lake

Tobacco Lake

540

Ice L.

Gore Bay

Gore Bay

540

Julia Bay

Barrie Island

Bayfield Sound

Helen Bay

Elizabeth Bay

Evansville

Silver Water

Silver L.

540

Maple L.

Loon L.

Lily Falls L.

Meldrum Bay

Meldrum Bay

Vidal Bay

Mississagi Strait

Cockburn Island

West Bay

West Bay

540

Perch L.

Pike L.

Kagawong

Magawong Village

Mudge Bay

Sheshegwanning

0   10   20km

Waterfront Trail 475 km

N

200km
100
0

Lake Ontario

Georgian Bay

NEW YORK (U.S.A.)

Potsdam
Ogdensburgh
Prescott
Brockville
Crosby
Maberly
Sharboth
Lake
Parham
Cloyne
Kaladar
Gananoque
Kingston
Bath
Napanee
Adolphustown
Picton
Belleville
Campbellford
Trenton
Brighton
Wicklow
Port Hope
Oshawa
Ajax
Toronto
Mississauga
Oakville
Hamilton
St. Catharines
Niagara Falls
Fort Erie
Welland
Cayuga
Brantford
Cambridge
Kitchener/Waterloo
Guelph
Fergus
Orangeville
Shelburne
Brampton
Schomberg
Alliston
Angus
Cookstown
Barrie
Sutton
Lindsay
Beaverton
Lakefield
Kirkfield
Coboconk
Minden
Kinmount
Tory Hill
Bobcaygeon
Burleigh Falls
Norwood
Hastings
Peterborough
Marmora
Madoc
Cobourg
Creemore
Collingwood
Meaford
Midland
Wasaga Beach
Orillia
Lake Simcoe

Brockville to Bath
Wicklow to Bath
Ajax to Wicklow
Oakville to Ajax
St. Catharines to Oakville

St. Lawrence River

Watertown
Alder Creek
Rome
Utica
Sangerfield
Syracuse
Oswego
Rochester
Geneva
Avon
Batavia
Buffalo

© ULYSSES

The Waterfront Trail

What could be more appealing than cycling with the wind at your back, the sunshine on your face and the sound of the waves lapping against the shores of Lake Ontario?

The Waterfront Trail stretches from Trenton, alongside Quinte Isle, to Niagara-on-the-Lake, spanning a total of 350km. Along the way, it runs through 28 towns and villages (notably Brighton, Port Hope, Oakville and Niagara-on-the-Lake), more than 100 parks, historic sites, museums, and other natural and cultural attractions—not to mention some breathtaking panoramas. There are as many reasons to drag you away from the trail as there are to keep you on it!

Once little more than post-industrial waste-lands, these shores have been invested with new life. The Waterfront Trail was inaugurated in 1995 and designed to regenerate the lakeshore and preserve its natural resources. Its current 350km length represents half of its projected length of 700km, which will span the entire north shore of Lake Ontario. While the Waterfront Trail is more or less complete between Burlington and Quinte West, major gaps still exist in the Niagara Peninsula, the Toronto area and Hope Township. Plans are to extend the trail east from Trenton to Kingston.

But you needn't be a long-distance cyclist to enjoy it. Do as much—or as little—of it as you can manage. There is no shortage of access points, many with parking available.

The trail is surfaced with a variety of materials, from asphalt to stone dust to gravel. Cyclists share the trails with walkers, in-line skaters and joggers. It is marked with signs bearing the Waterfront Trail logo: a stylized bird, leaf and fish (representing the sky, the land and the water) in blue and green.

With its terrestrial and aquatic attractions, the Waterfront Trail offers the best of both worlds: two wheels spinning on solid ground, often through natural areas, with the sights, sounds and smells of a lake that has drawn people to its shores for centuries.

Waterfront Regeneration Trust
207 Queen's Quay W.
P.O. Box 129
Toronto, ON M5J 1A7
☎(416) 943-8080, ext. 228
www.waterfronttrail.org

The Waterfront Trail

Bike Paths and Rail Trails

City/Area	Total Length (km)	Page
Waterfront Trail	475	166
Waterfront Trail (St. Catharines to Oakville)	-	169
Waterfront Trail (Oakville to Ajax)	-	170
Waterfront Trail (Ajax to Wicklow)	-	171
Waterfront Trail (Wicklow to Bath)	-	172
Waterfront Trail (Bath to Brockville)	-	173

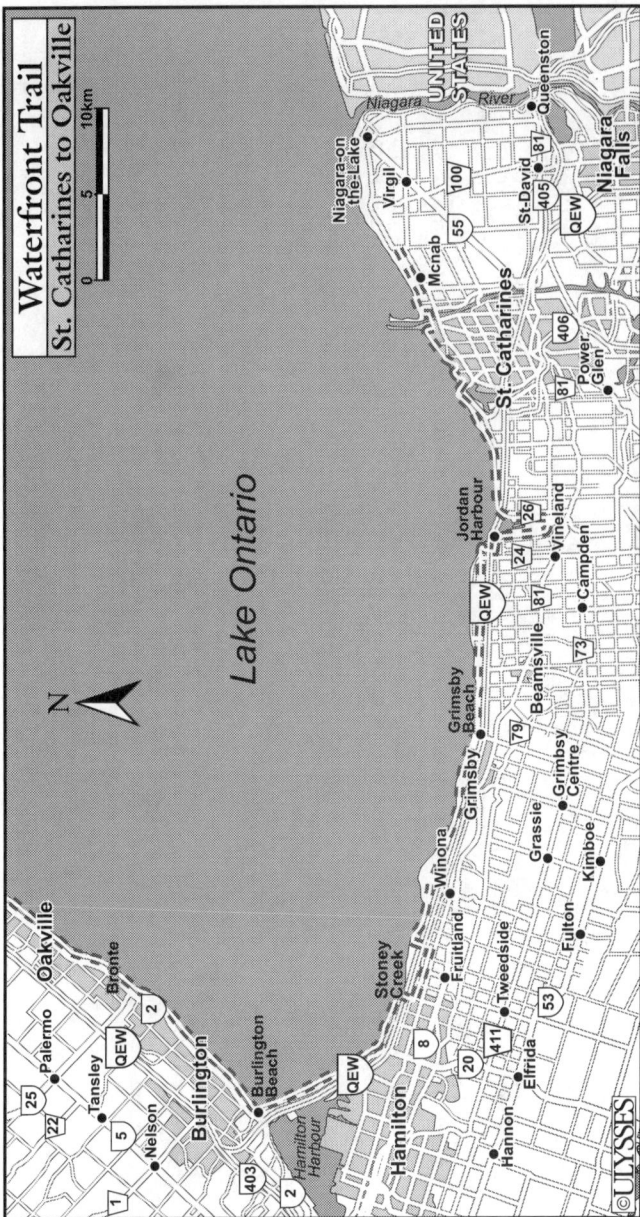

Waterfront Trail
St. Catharines to Oakville

0   5   10km

Lake Ontario

N

UNITED STATES

Niagara River

Queenston

Niagara-on-the-Lake

Virgil

Mcnab

100

55

St-David

81

405

Niagara Falls

QEW

406

St. Catharines

81

Power Glen

Jordan Harbour

26

24

Vineland

Campden

QEW

81

Beamsville

73

Grimsby Beach

79

Grimsby

Grassie

Grimsby Centre

Kimboe

Winona

Fulton

Fruitland

Stoney Creek

Tweedside

53

8

20

411

Effrida

Hannon

Hamilton

QEW

Hamilton Harbour

403

2

Burlington

Burlington Beach

Nelson

5

QEW

Tansley

Bronte

Oakville

Palermo

25

22

1

The Waterfront Trail

© ULYSSES

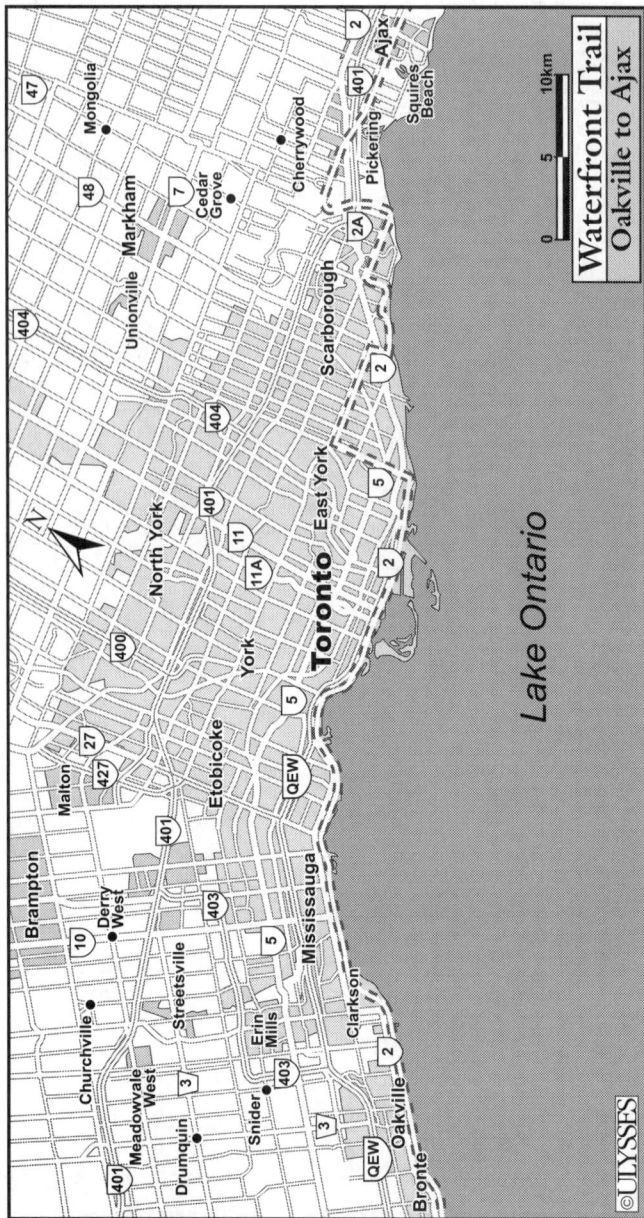

Waterfront Trail
Oakville to Ajax

Lake Ontario

© ULYSSES

Waterfront Trail
Ajax to Wicklow

The Waterfront Trail

Manchester

7
2

Ashburn

Columbus

Brooklin

Audley

12

Whitby

7

401

Ajax

Port Whitby

Oshawa

Courtice

2

Taunton

Hampton

Salem

Maple Grove

Enniskillen

Tyrone

Burketon Station

35

115

Leskard

115
35

Bowansville

West Side Beach

Newcastle

Starkville

Kendal

Elizabethville

Newtonville

Osaca

Perrytown

28

Garden Hill

Welcome

2

106

401

Port Britain

Port Hope

Davidson's Corners

Precious Corners

Plainville

Gores Landing

Rice Lake

Harwood

Fenella

Centreton

45

Baltimore

Brookside

Cobourg

2

401

Wicklow

Lake Ontario

N

© ULYSSES

0   5   10km

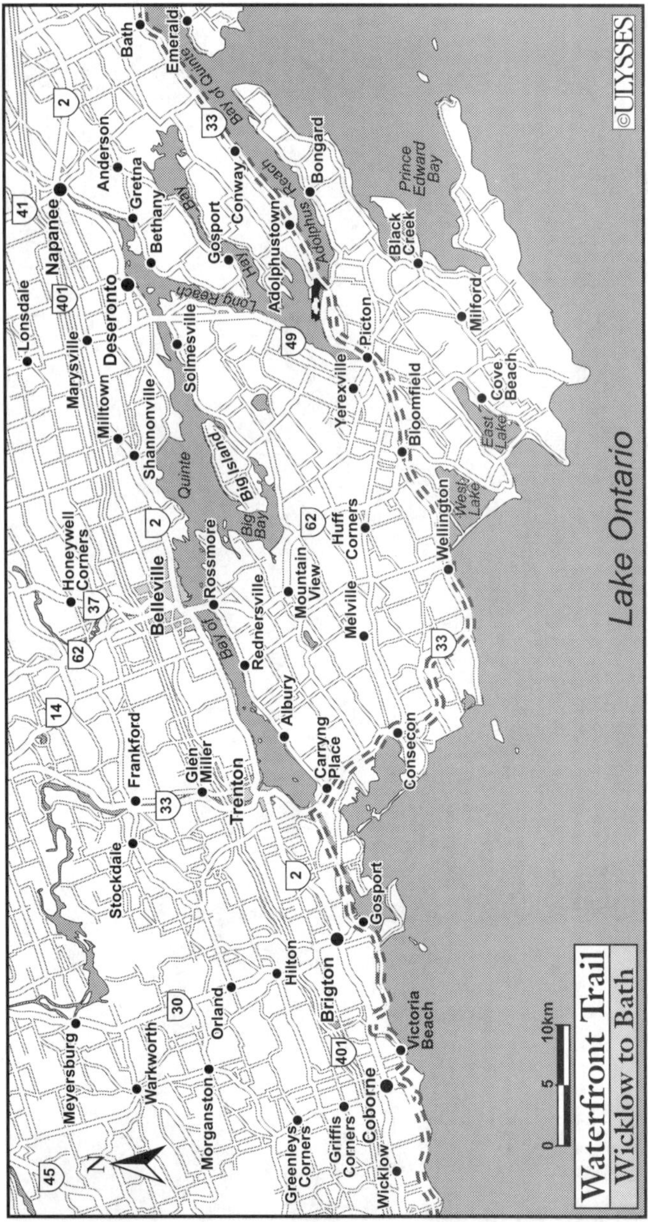

Waterfront Trail
Wicklow to Bath
©ULYSSES
0
5
10km
N
Lake Ontario
Prince Edward Bay
Bay of Quinte
Quinte
Big Island
Big Bay
Hay Bay
Long Reach
Adolphus Reach
East Lake
West Lake
Bath
Emerald
Napanee
Anderson
Gretna
Bethany
Lonsdale
Marysville
Deseronto
Milltown
Shannonville
Solmesville
Gosport
Conway
Adolphustown
Bongard
Black Creek
Milford
Picton
Yerexville
Bloomfield
Cove Beach
Wellington
Huff Corners
Honeywell Corners
Belleville
Rossmore
Mountain View
Rednersville
Melville
Albury
Carryng Place
Consecon
Frankford
Glen Miller
Trenton
Stockdale
Gosport
Brigton
Hilton
Orland
Meyersburg
Warkworth
Morganston
Greenleys Corners
Griffis Corners
Coborne
Victoria Beach
Wicklow
2
41
401
33
49
62
37
14
30
45

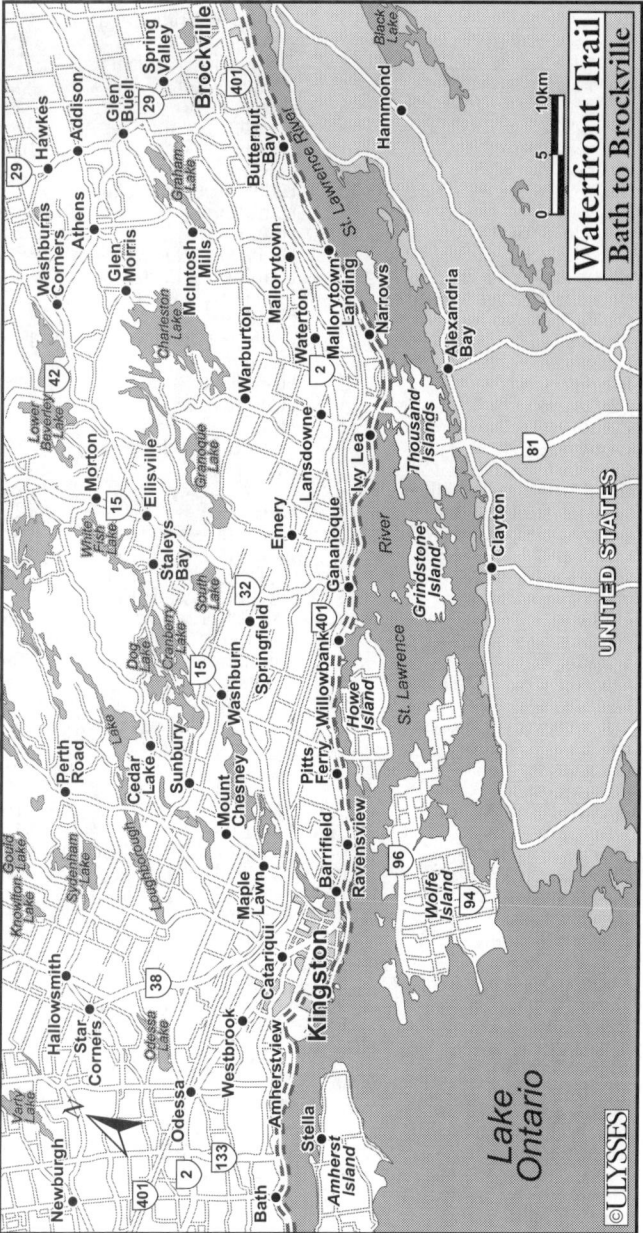

Waterfront Trail
Bath to Brockville

0   5   10km

The Waterfront Trail

© ULYSSES

UNITED STATES

Lake
Ontario

St. Lawrence River

St. Lawrence River

Brockville
Spring Valley
Addison
Hawkes
Glen Buell
29
401
Black Lake
Hammond
Washburns Corners
Athens
Glen Morris
McIntosh Mills
Mallorytown
Butternut Bay
Graham Lake
29
42
Warburton
Mallorytown Landing
Narrows
Waterton
2
Alexandria Bay
Lower Beverley Lake
Morton
Ellisville
Charleston Lake
Lansdowne
Ivy Lea
Thousand Islands
15
Staleys Bay
Granque Lake
Emery
81
White Fish Lake
Smith Lake
Gananoque
Clayton
Dog Lake
Cranberry Lake
32
Springfield
Grindstone Island
River
Perth Road
Cedar Lake
Washburn
15
Willowbank
401
Howe Island
Knowlton Lake
Gould Lake
Sunbury
Mount Chesney
Pitts Ferry
St. Lawrence
Sydenham Lake
Loughborough Lake
Maple Lawn
Barriefield
Ravensview
96
Wolfe Island
94
Hallowsmith
38
Cataraqui
Kingston
Star Corners
Westbrook
Amherstview
Varty Lake
Newburgh
2
Odessa
33
Odessa Lake
Bath
Stella
Amherst Island
401

Index

Index

Order Form

Ulysses Green Escapes

☐ Cycling in France $22.95 CAN
                    $16.95 US
☐ Cycling in . . . . . $22.95 CAN
   Ontario $16.95 US

☐ Hiking in the . . $22.95 CAN
   Northeastern U.S.A. $16.95 US
☐ Hiking in . . . . . $22.95 CAN
   Québec $16.95 US
☐ Hiking in . . . . . $22.95 CAN
   Ontario $16.95 US

Title	Qty	Price	Total
Name:		Subtotal	
		Shipping	$4 CAN $3 US
Address:		Subtotal	
	GST in Canada 7%		
		Total	

Tel: Fax:

E-mail:

Payment: ☐ Cheque ☐ Visa ☐ MasterCard

Card number_____

Expiry date_____

Signature_____

ULYSSES TRAVEL GUIDES

4176 Saint-Denis,
Montréal, Québec,
H2W 2M5
☎(514) 843-9447
Fax: (514) 843-9448

305 Madison Avenue,
Suite 1166,
New York, NY 10165

Toll-free: 1-877-542-7247
Info@ulysses.ca
www.ulyssesguides.com